MAITHILI

Some Aspects of Its
Phonetics and Phonology

MLBD SERIES IN LINGUISTICS

General Editor
DHANESH JAIN

Volume XI

MAITHILI

Some Aspects of Its Phonetics and Phonology

SUNIL KUMAR JHA

MOTILAL BANARSIDASS PUBLISHERS
PRIVATE LIMITED • DELHI

First Edition: Delhi, 2001

ISBN: 81-208-1320-0

Also available at:

MOTILAL BANARSIDASS

236, 9th Main III Block, Jayanagar, Bangalore 560 011
41 U.A. Bungalow Road, Jawahar Nagar, Delhi 110 007
8 Mahalaxmi Chamber, Warden Road, Mumbai 400 026
120 Royapettah High Road, Mylapore, Chennai 600 004
Sanas Plaza, 1302 Baji Rao Road, Pune 411 002
8 Camac Street, Calcutta 700 017
Ashok Rajpath, Patna 800 004
Chowk, Varanasi 221 001

Printed in India

BY JAINENDRA PRAKASH JAIN AT SHRI JAINENDRA PRESS,
A-45 NARAINA, PHASE-I, NEW DELHI 110.028
AND PUBLISHED BY NARENDRA PRAKASH JAIN FOR
MOTILAL BANARSIDASS PUBLISHERS PRIVATE LIMITED,
BUNGALOW ROAD, DELHI 110 007

To

My Parents

Shri Joganand Jha
and
Shrimati Jahan Devi Jha

with

Love and Gratitude

FOREWORD

Language is our all-encompassing medium, almost certainly the oldest means of communication and expression, one which is both central to and pervasive in the realm of all human thought. It is the basis of whatever social cohesion we can attain. Every language is said to be tri-modal—i.e. structured in three modes: phonology, grammar and lexicon. These modes are interrelated but have a considerable degree of independence and must be described in their own terms. In Nepal, there are a number of languages and dialects that still need to be described linguistically. It is good to see that Maithili—the second most widely spoken language in Nepal—has in recent years attracted the attention of our linguists and scholars.

Professor Sunil Kumar Jha's book entitled *Maithili: Some Aspects of Its Phonetics and Phonology* is a painstaking study of the central features characterising the pronunciation of Maithili. It combines a thorough analysis of the sounds of Maithili with insights into how the sound structure of the language relates to its morphological and syntactic structure. I am sure this book will prove useful to linguists and phoneticians in particular and scholars interested in Maithili and related studies in general.

Dr. Sunil Jha is a serious scholar, always producing work of fine quality. He is industrious and regularly carries research which is coloured with imagination and characterised by thoroughness. Because of his very good grounding in linguistics, his present book will be invaluable for people wishing to make a serious study of Maithili.

Tribhuvan University
Kirtipur, Kathmandu
Nepal
September 27, 1994

KEDAR B. MATHEMA
Vice Chancellor

ACKNOWLEDGEMENTS

This book is an expansion and revision of earlier works. I thank the following for allowing me to use parts of articles originally published by them: Academic Press for my articles "Acoustic analysis of the Maithili diphthongs" and "The nasal vowels in Maithili: an acoustic study" in *Journal of Phonetics* 13 (1985) and 14 (1986), respectively; Central Institute of English and Foreign Languages, Hyderabad for my article "The influence of aspiration on vowel duration" in *CIEFL Bulletin: New Series* 2 (1990); Linguistic Society of Nepal for my article "The Morphophonology of the Maithili verbs: a study on the elision of the stops in Maithili" in *Nepalese Linguistics* 5-8 (1991); and Centre for Nepal and Asian Studies for my articles "The Maithili vowels" and "The Maithili consonants" in *Contributions to Nepalese Studies* 18 (1991) and 20 (1993), respectively.

The research which has produced this book was funded by the British Council in London, and the book is a revised and refined version of my Ph.D. thesis submitted to the Department of Language and Linguistics at the University of Essex in England. I thank the British Council for its kind help.

Professor Marcel A. Tatham and Dr. Jacques M. Durand of the University of Essex supervised my Ph.D. research, and I am grateful to both of them for their constant help and encouragement. I extend my thanks also to Mr. Roger Jennings, the technician of the Phonology Laboratory of Essex University, for his generous technical assistance. I acknowledge my deep indebtedness to Tribhuvan University for granting me leave.

I owe a separate debt of thanks to G.A. Grierson, A.C. Gimson, S. Jha, G. Jha, J. Foley, N. Chomsky, M. Halle, and all those other authors whose publications have helped me in the entire process of the completion of this book. I should also like to thank my colleagues for advice and encouragement.

Finally, thanks are due to Motilal Banarsidass, publisher of this book.

SUNIL KUMAR JHA

PREFACE

This book gives an account of some phonetic and phonological aspects of a variety of the 'standard' dialect of Maithili, a modern Indo-Aryan language spoken by more than 21 million people in the northern and eastern regions of the state of Bihar in India and in the Tarai districts of Nepal. The principal informant of this study is myself. Even though the dialect being described is mine, I have made every effort to verify that the description applies to other speakers as well; their responses and judgements have been noted throughout, and they have been quite positive.

The main purpose of this study is three-fold. First, it aims to provide some materials on a number of phonetic and phonological aspects of the standard dialect of Maithili. Secondly, the analysis and description of the Maithili speech sounds and sound systems put forward in this piece of work may, it is hoped, be helpful for phonetic and phonological comparison across various languages both in India and Nepal, especially among the Indo-Aryan language groups. Thirdly, this study—since it is done when language research in Nepal as well as in most other parts of the Indian Subcontinent, for that matter, is still at a rather preliminary stage—may provide some useful hints to other researchers on methods for beginning phonetic and phonological analysis and description of various other languages.

The contents of the whole study are divided into eight chapters. In the course of this study I have attempted to establish, describe and classify the speech sounds and sound systems of Maithili using a relatively more modern phonological framework, especially using the 'standard theory' of generative phonology as presented by Chomsky and Halle in *The Sound Pattern of English* (SPE). The system as put forward in SPE is, in my opinion, sufficiently developed, sufficiently sophisticated and perhaps the best of its kind. I have found this system reasonably satisfactory in accounting for the speech sounds and sound systems in Maithili. To strengthen and support my description and classification of the phonologically distinctive speech sounds in Maithili as well as to discuss various other aspects of these speech sounds and the way they actually function in the pronunciation system of this language, I have also investigated them making use of a number of techniques of experimental phonetics, such as: the spectrographic studies of the vowels and diphthongs in Maithili as presented in chapter 4; and the electroglottographic studies of vowel duration in Maithili as put forward in chapter 5.

On the whole, in this study I think I have brought to light a number of facts on different phonetic and phonological aspects of Maithili and have concentrated primarily on the descriptive side of the discipline. I hope I have arrived at some definitive results on these phonetic and phonological aspects of my investigation. I must admit that it was simply not possible, predominantly due to time and space limitations, to include a discussion of every issue or example relevant to the various phonetic and phonological aspects of this language. I very sincerely hope that other researchers will take the work still further and thereby advance our knowledge of the various yet unexplored aspects of this language.

SUNIL KUMAR JHA

KEY TO PHONOLOGICAL SYMBOLS

Oral Vowels

i high front unrounded, as in /sir/ 'root'
e mid front unrounded, as in /ser/ 'kilogramme'
æ low front unrounded, as in /sær/ 'walk/walking'
a low central unrounded, as in /sar/ 'wife's brother'
ə mid central unrounded, as in /sər/ 'arrow'; 'sir'
ɔ low back rounded, as in /sɔr/ 'sky'
o mid back rounded, as in /sor/ 'noise'; 'to call'
u high back rounded, as in /sur/ 'tune'

Nasal Vowels

ĩ high front unrounded, as in /č^{h}ĩṭ/'garment dyed with spots'
ẽ mid front unrounded, as in /č^{h}ẽṭ/ 'surplus (e.g. of grain)'
æ̃ low front unrounded, as in /b^{h}æ̃t/'kind/type'
ã low central unrounded, as in /bãs/ 'bamboo'
ə̃ mid central unrounded, as in /'kə̃ṭgər/ 'thorny'
ɔ̃ low back rounded, as in /gɔ̃t/ '(cattle) urine'
õ mid back rounded, as in /g^{h}õṭ/ 'swallow (imp.)'
ũ high back rounded, as in /ũṭ/ 'camel'

Oral Diphthongs

əi as in /'əik^{h}ən/ 'at this time'
əu as in /əuk^{h}ən/ 'even up to this time'

Consonants

p voiceless unaspirated bilabial stop, as in /pul/ 'bridge'
p^h voiceless aspirated bilabial stop, as in /p^{h}ul/ 'flower'
b voiced unaspirated bilabial stop, as in /bul/ 'walk (imp.)'
b^h voiced aspirated bilabial stop, as in /b^{h}ul/ 'mistake'
t voiceless unaspirated dental stop, as in /tan/'pull (imp.)'
t^h voiceless aspirated dental stop, as in /t^{h}an/ 'several yards of cloth wrapped together'
d voiced unaspirated dental stop, as in /dan/ 'charity'
d^h voiced aspirated dental stop, as in /d^{h}an/ 'paddy'

ṭ	voiceless unaspirated retroflex stop, as in /ṭok/ 'ask'
$ṭ^h$	voiceless aspirated retroflex stop, as in /$ṭ^h$ok/ 'to hammer'
ḍ	voiced unaspirated retroflex stop, as in /ḍok/ 'shake and filter (imp.)'
$ḍ^h$	voiced aspirated retroflex stop, as in /$ḍ^h$ok/ 'assemble and trap (e.g. cattle)'
k	voiceless unaspirated velar stop, as in /kas/ 'a kind of large grass'
k^h	voiceless aspirated velar stop, as in /k^has/ 'particular'
g	voiced unaspirated velar stop, as in /gol/ 'round'
g^h	voiced aspirated velar stop, as in /g^hol/ 'noise'
č	voiceless unaspirated palato-alveolar affricate, as in /čor/ 'thief'
$č^h$	voiceless aspirated palato-alveolar affricate, as in /$č^h$or/ 'edge'
ǰ	voiced unaspirated palato-alveolar affricate, as in /ǰor/ 'strength'
$ǰ^h$	voiced aspirated palato-alveolar affricate, as in /$ǰ^h$or/ 'broth; soup'
s	voiceless alveolar fricative, as in /sar/ 'wife's brother'
h	voiceless glottal fricative, as in /har/ 'necklace'
m	bilabial nasal, as in /səm/ 'equal'; 'plain'
n	alveolar nasal, as in /sən/ 'like'
ŋ	velar nasal, as in /səŋ/ 'together'; 'with'
w	bilabial central approximant (glide), as in /wæh/ 'only that'
y	palatal central approximant (glide), as in /yæh/ 'only this'
r	alveolar tap, as in /har/ 'necklace'
ṛ	retroflex flap, as in /haṛ/ 'bone'
l	alveolar lateral, as in /mal/ 'cattle'; 'goods'

For ease of exposition, the present study also uses—especially in the seventh and eighth chapters—orthographic symbols such as *b, d, g,* etc., which may represent either phonetic sounds or abstract phonological elements. These letters are neither phonological elements like, for example, α1 β2 nor phonetic elements like, for example, [+ voice, - ant], but are orthographic conveniences.

LIST OF NOTATIONAL CONVENTIONS AND ABBREVIATIONS

*	asterisk: indicates a deviant word or utterance
( )	parentheses: enclose optional element(s)
{ }	braces: enclose alternative elements in a rule
[ ]	square brackets: enclose distinctive feature specifications such as [low], phonetic symbols such as [k], and surface representations such as [si:r] 'root'
//	obliques: enclose phonemic (or phonological) transcription
/	oblique: is used in context-sensitive rules or to indicate any alternative/s
→	the arrow: is placed between the input and the output of a rule. It is read "becomes"
—	the underscore: is used to indicate the location of the input in relation to the determinant
↓	downward arrow: indicates "implies" or "is also"
⇒	double arrow: is used in transformational rules
< >	angle brackets: are used to link elements of a rule which must be taken together as a condition on the application of a rule
α, β	the variable signs: are used to link features in one part of a rule with features of the same value in another
Ø	zero: indicates the absence of any element, i.e. the null symbol
=	is equal to
≠	is not equal to
>	leads to or is changed to
<	comes from or is derived from
+	marks the presence of something; also marks morpheme/stem boundary
–	marks the absence of something; also marks syllable boundary
#	marks full word boundary
underlining:	is used to indicate emphasis
~	is in free variation with
~	indicates vowel nasalization
:	indicates full length of preceding vowel/consonant
'	indicates main accentual stress or pitch prominence on following syllable

	placed over a letter indicates the weaker element of a diphthong, e.g. əŭ/əĭ
%	percent
ant	anterior
asp	aspirated
Aux	auxiliary
B.S.	Bikram Sambat
C	consonant
cf.	compare
cons	consonantal
cont	continuant
cor	coronal
del rel	delayed release
Ed.	edition
ed(s)	editor(s)
e.g.	for example
et al.	and others
etc.	etcetera
F	formant
Fn	nasal formant
Hz	hertz
ibid.	in the same place
i.e.	that is
IPA	International Phonetic Association
MIA	Middle Indo-Aryan
Ms	manuscript
ms	millisecond
N	nasal consonant
n	noun
NIA	New Indo-Aryan
p	page
pp	pages
RP	Received Pronunciation
SD	standard deviation
SIL	Summer Institute of Linguistics
son	sonorant
syll	syllabic
V	vowel
v	coefficient of variation
viz.	namely
vs	versus
vol/s	volume/s
1st	first
2nd	second
3rd	third

References in the text and notes to other works give the author, the date of publication and, where relevant, page number(s)—e.g. Catford (1977: 210); full referential details, which include only those works that are consulted and referred to, can be found on pp. 191-205.

CONTENTS

Chapter 1

INTRODUCTION

1.0 Introduction

Maithili is an Indic language belonging to the group of the modern Prakrit vernaculars. It is spoken both in Nepal and India. In this book an attempt is made to present an account of some aspects of the phonetics and phonology of a variety of the 'standard' dialect of this language, of which the author is a native speaker. Before we embark upon the description of the various aspects of the phonetics and phonology of this language, we must first present in this introductory chapter some background notes on such issues as: (1) its speakers and linguistic boundaries; (2) its genetic classification and place among modern Indo-Aryan languages; (3) linguistic and phonetic studies done on it both in India and Nepal; and (4) the emergence of a standard in Maithili and its present-day situation.

1.1 Maithili: Its Speakers and Linguistic Boundaries

Maithili is spoken mainly in the eastern and northern regions of the state of Bihar in India and in the Tarai districts of Nepal. According to some estimates (e.g. Davis, 1973: 316; R. Yadav, 1984: 1), this language is spoken by a total of more than 21 million people in India and Nepal. Map 1 shows the main languages of the Indo-Pakistan subcontinent and the geographical boundaries of their native speakers. In the map an arrow is used to show the Maithili-speaking area. The exact dimensions of the area have been fluctuating from age to age (e.g. see Mishra, 1976: 1-5, for more details); it has nevertheless managed to keep itself always distinguished in common parlance as a distinct "country with its own traditions, its own poets, and its own pride in everything belonging to itself" (Grierson, 1881: 2). Today this area is known as Tirhut or Mithilā. But in the earliest known period of history it was called Videha and it included several kingdoms in it—Mithilā and Vaishālī being the most important ones (see for more details, Sharma, 1979: 5-72).

It was about a century ago that Grierson (1883a: 16) took pains to define and demarcate in exact terms the linguistic boundaries of Maithili-speaking areas:

> Maithili was originally the language of the ancient Mithila, the kingdom of Janaka, the father of Sita, which was bounded on the west by the river Gaṇḍak, on the north by the Himālaya mountains, on the east by the Kosi, and on the south by the Ganges. It has, however, in later times been encroached upon by Bhojpuri on the west, and in revenge has itself crossed the Ganges and occupied

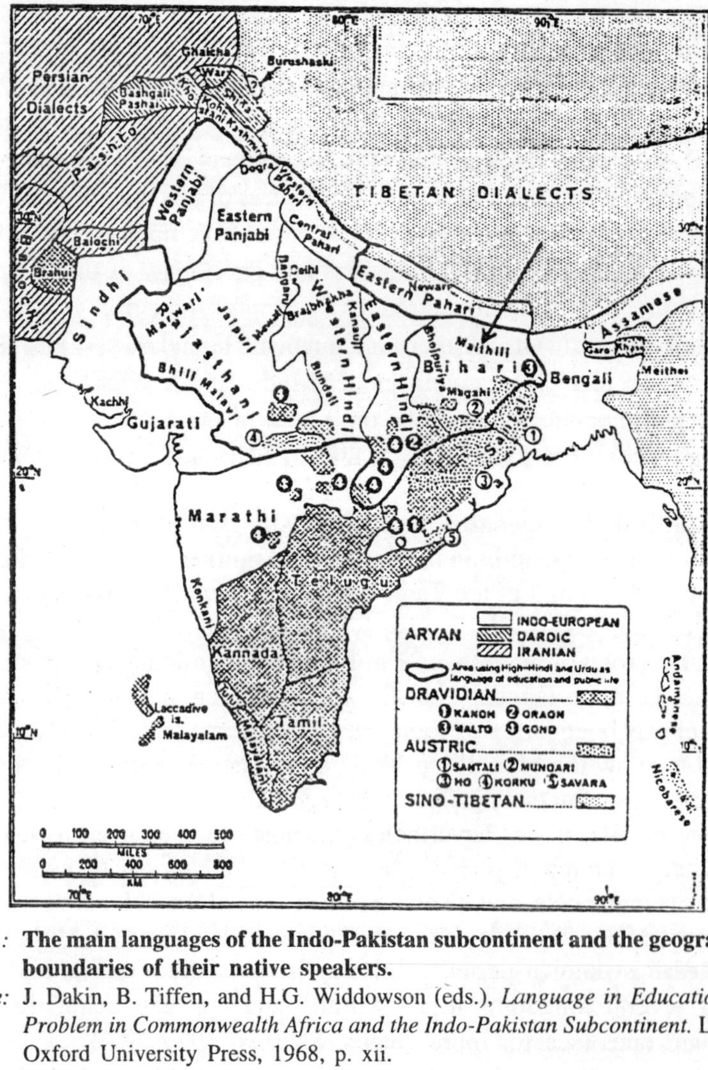

Map 1: **The main languages of the Indo-Pakistan subcontinent and the geographical boundaries of their native speakers.**

Source: J. Dakin, B. Tiffen, and H.G. Widdowson (eds.), *Language in Education: The Problem in Commonwealth Africa and the Indo-Pakistan Subcontinent.* London: Oxford University Press, 1968, p. xii.

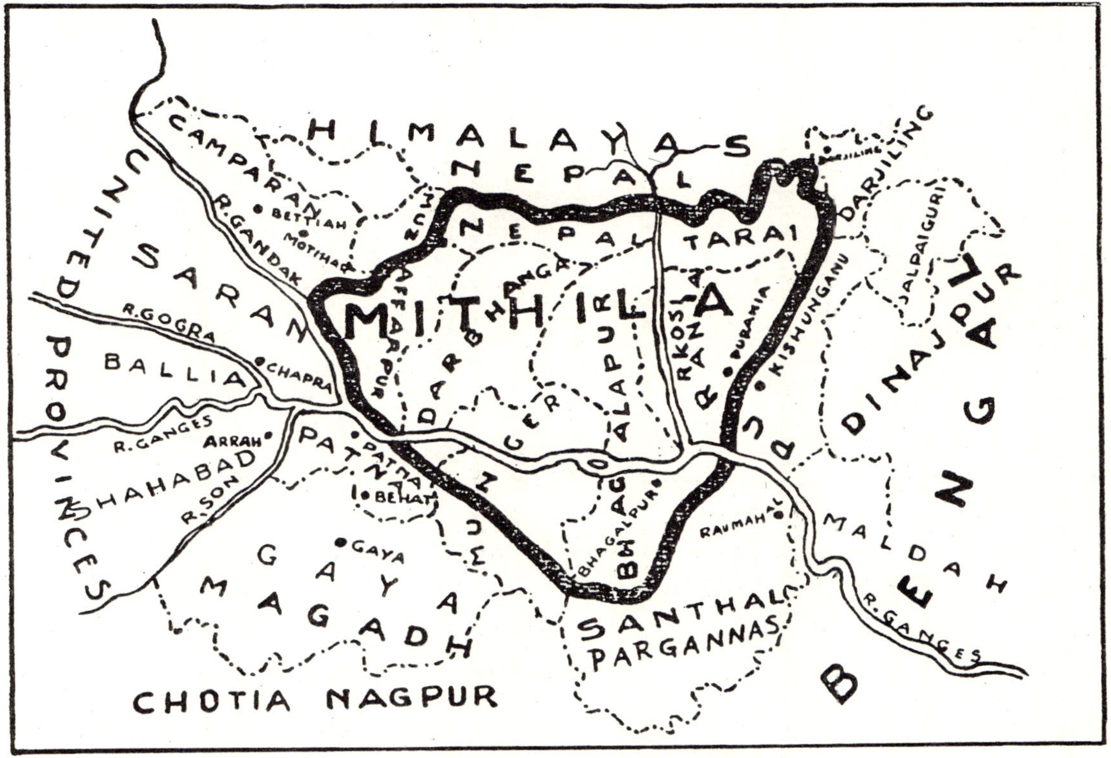

Map 2: **The existing linguistic boundaries of the Maithili-speaking community.**
Source: J. Mishra, *History of Maithili Literature*. New Delhi: Sahitya Akademi, 1976, p. viii.

North Patna and so much of the Munger and Bhagalpur districts as lie to the south of that river. It has also crossed the Kosi and occupied Purnea.

Map 2 given earlier is based on the above geographical boundary of the Maithili-speaking community and it demarcates an area of about 30,000 square miles. According to Mishra's (1976: 2) estimates, out of this total area of 30,000 square miles "roughly 10,000 square miles lie in the kingdom of Nepal (Tarai) and 20,000 square miles in India". Map 2 thus includes roughly the districts of Muzaffarpur, Sitamaṛhi, Vaishālī, Darbhanga, Madhubani, Samastipur, Saharsa, Supaul, North Munger, North Bhagalpur and parts of Champaran and Purnea in the Indian Republic, and those of Rautahaṭ, Sarlāhi, Mahottari, Dhanushā, Siraha, Saptari and Morang in the kingdom of Nepal. These geographical boundaries include all those principal areas where the main concentration of the Maithili-speaking population lies these days.

1.2 Maithili: Its Genetic Classification and Its Place Among Modern Indo-Aryan Languages

During the last one hundred years or so, various linguists have attempted to classify the Indo-Aryan languages (e.g. Grierson, 1883a and 1918; Chatterji, 1926/1970; S. Jha, 1958; G. Jha, 1974; Jeffers, 1976; Mishra, 1976). But in their classification these linguists do not always agree with one another. In some cases there still prevails a good deal of controversy, and on some points the opinions of these linguists are still divided.

To begin with, one of the earliest classifications of the modern Indo-Aryan languages is that of Grierson (1883a)—as shown in Figure 1.1—where he categorises Maithili as one of the three dialects of what he used to call the 'Bihārī' language. In his later publications, Grierson (e.g. 1918, 1919 and 1927/reprint 1967) provided a somewhat different grouping of the Indo-Aryan languages. Figure 1.2 shows Grierson's three main divisions—i.e. (1) Outer Sub-branch, (2) Mediate Sub-branch, and (3) Inner Sub-branch—that he later made of the Indo-Aryan languages (see Grierson, 1918 and 1927/reprint 1967, for more details). But even here he still grouped Maithili as a dialect of the so-called 'Bihārī' language.

Ever since Grierson's major publications on the so- called 'Bihārī' language, it has been customary—especially among western linguists-to refer to Maithili as a dialect of the 'Bihārī' language. This name (i.e. 'Bihārī') of an imaginary language seems to have been given by Grierson perhaps on his assumption that the existence of the state of Bihar in India justifies the existence of a 'Bihārī' language—in the same way perhaps

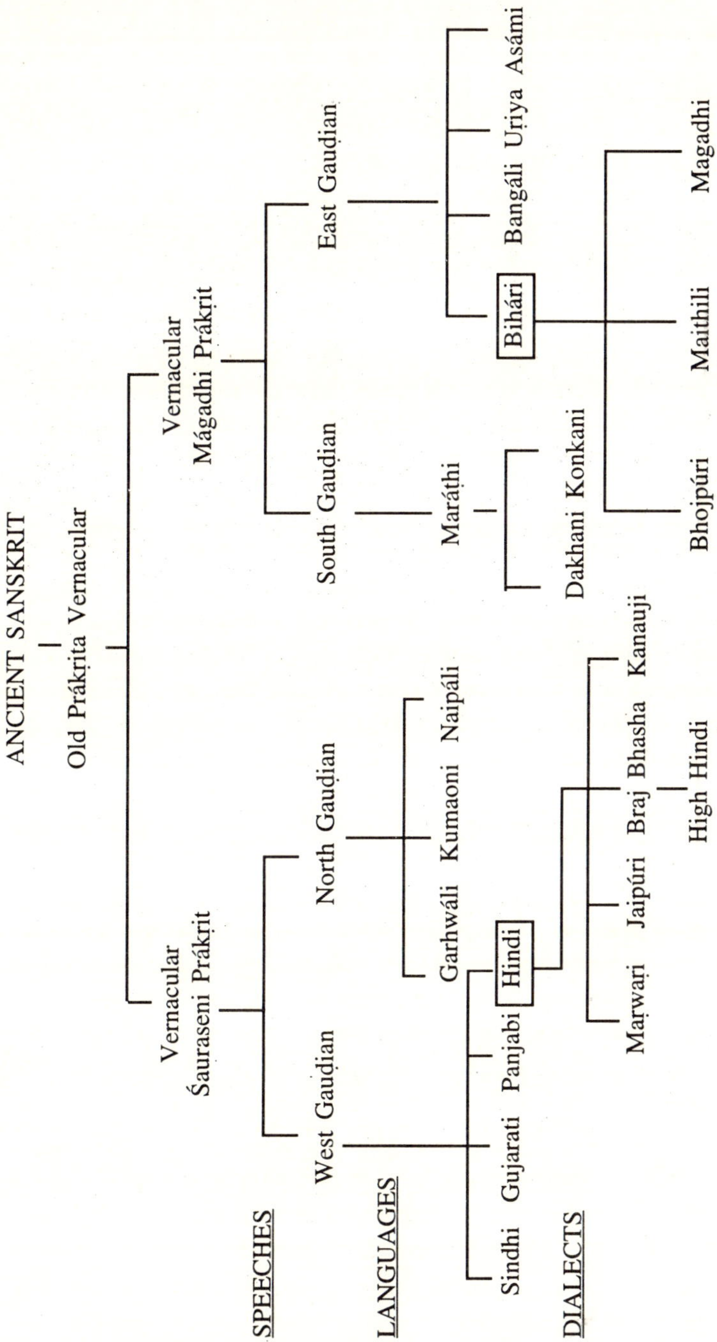

Figure 1.1: Genetic classification of the modern Indo-Aryan languages, according to Grierson (1883a).

as Gujarat has Gujarati, Punjab has Punjabi, Bengal has Bengali, or, for that matter, Nepal has Nepali. But in classifying the languages of Bihar, it was rather unfortunate that Grierson committed an error of over-generalisation. For, there never was in the past nor is there at present any 'Bihārī' language spoken either in Bihar or in Nepal. Most later writers on Maithili (e.g. S. Jha, 1958; Mishra, 1969 and 1976; G. Jha, 1974; R. Yadav, 1979a and 1981) have therefore justifiably resented the use of the term 'Bihārī' language. Mishra (1969: 270) discusses and defends the case of Maithili in his scholarly article and sums up the general feelings of modern Maithili writers in the following forceful terms:

> There never was in the past nor exists to-day a language called Bihari. There is no mention of it in any literature, any document or any record. There is not a single individual who speaks or writes in the Bihari language as defined by Grierson. It has no script, no literature, no actual existence. It is purely a creation of Grierson's mind and lives in the philological works of the scholars who thoughtlessly copy Grierson's classification.

It was very unfortunate that about a century ago even various reputed scholars sadly misunderstood the case of Maithili and grouped this language in all sorts of way. For example, Kellogg (1876/1893) and Hoernle (1880) regarded it as a dialect of Eastern Hindi; Beames (1872/reprint 1966: 84-85), on the other hand, thought of it as a dialect of Bengali; and, as stated earlier, Grierson (e.g. 1881, 1883a, 1885 and 1903/reprint 1968) grouped it as one of the three dialects of what he called the 'Bihārī' language—the remaining two dialects of 'Bihārī' being Bhojpuri and Magahi.

The criteria which are generally used, especially in historical linguistics, for the establishment of language 'sameness' or language 'split' are mainly two: (1) the notion of shared innovation, and (2) the criterion of phonological restructuring. A brief mention of the linguistic principles involved in these two criteria must be made here in order to clarify the situation concerning the position of Maithili among the modern Indo-Aryan languages.

In the first place, if innovations are shared by two or more languages in a larger family of languages, it may be tentatively assumed that, at some points in their histories, these languages shared a period of common development, and that such innovations were already a feature of some intermediate ancestor from which the languages involved may be derived. The establishment of genuine shared innovations is basic to genetic sub-

INDO-ARYAN LANGUAGES

A. OUTER SUB-BRANCH

I. North-Western Group

1. Lahanda or Western Panjābī
2. Sindhi

II. Southern Group

3. Marāṭhī

III. Eastern Group

4. Oṛiyā
5. Bihārī
6. Bangali
7. Assamese

B. MEDIATE SUB-BRANCH

IV. Mediate Group

8. Eastern Hindī

C. INNER SUB-BRANCH

V. Central Group

9. Western Hindī
10. Panjābi

11. Gujarātī
12. Bhīlī
13. Khāndēsī
14. Rājasthānī

VI. Pahāṛī Group

15. Eastern Pahāṛī of Naipali
16. Central Pahāṛī
17. Western Pahāṛī

Figure 1.2: Classfication of the Indo-Aryan languages based on Grierson (1927: 120).

grouping within a large family of languages. Many kinds of changes may represent instances of potential shared innovations. For instance, some languages—such as, Hindi, Maithili, Oṛiya, Bengali, Assamese, and so on—by virtue of being the languages of Aryan origin naturally have in them a prominence of words of Sanskrit stock, although one may find that the same word has rather different meanings in all these languages. Hence, at some higher level of generality, Maithili can be grouped with these Indic languages, which ultimately belong to the Indo-European family of languages. But it would undoubtedly be inappropriate to regard Maithili as a dialect of Hindi or Bengali (or 'Bihārī'?) simply on the basis of only a few similarities of lexicography.

Secondly, the criterion which is generally used for the establishment of language 'split' is one of phonological restructuring. Phonological restructuring occurs when the system of phonological contrasts is altered in a language. Phonological restructuring, especially phonological merger (coalescence), is for many linguists (e.g. Gumperz, 1957/ reprint 1962; Hoenigswald, 1960, 1964 and 1966; Fairbanks, 1969a) the fundamental criterion for language split, because once it has taken place the innovation is indeed irreversible. Jeffers (1976), for example, made a compa-rative study of the phonological development of Sanskrit, Maithili, Magahi, Hindi, Bhojpuri and Bengali. His study was based mainly on the strict principles of historical and comparative linguistics. The main conclusions that he finally drew are: (1) that among the so-called 'Bihārī' languages there was a split "between Bhojpuri on the one hand, and Maithilī and Magahī on the other" (Jeffers, 1976: 223); and (2) that

> As far as a split of Maithilī and Magahī is concerned, it is difficult to say much that is definite due to a lack of Magaḥī data in print. However, from the information available, it seems safe to assume that these two languages are extremely similar in their phonological development. It is in aspects of grammar other than the phonological that these two languages are differentiated.

and (3) that Maithili shares no major phonological innovations either with Hindi or with Bengali and that it has its own distinct status within the Indo-Aryan languages, "independent of the Hindi languages on the one hand, and of the Bengali languages on the other" (Jeffers, 1976: 224). Gumperz (1957/reprint 1962: 82), too, rightly came to a similar conclusion regarding the distinctiveness of the Maithili language:

> The greatest amount of linguistic difference within the Hindi-speaking area is found between Maithili and Hindi. Maithili has a . . . system of verbal inflection in which the verb is inflected for person and according to the social status of both the subject and the object, and not according to person and number as in Hindi.

It must also be pointed out that although Grierson grouped Maithili as one of the three dialects of his imaginary 'Bihārī' language, elsewhere even he firmly held (e.g. Grierson, 1881: 2) that "Maithili is a language and not a dialect. . . It differs from both Hindi and Bengali, both in vocabulary and in grammar, and is as much a distinct language from either of them as Maraṭhi or Uṛiya". This observation shows in most emphatic and unequivocal terms that Grierson did after all regard Maithili as a distinct language. But it is rather unfortunate that a great philologist like him should have grouped Maithili and Bhojpuri together as dialects of a common 'Bihārī' language—especially when he himself was aware of the fact that Bhojpuri "belongs rather to the United Provinces than to Bihar . . . and all its associations and traditions point to the west and not to the east" (Grierson, 1903/reprint 1968: 40).

The linguistic, cultural and literary traditions of Maithili and Bhojpuri are separate, and so are the geographical boundaries of their native speakers. Chatterji (1926: 99) rightly points out that

> Bhojpuriyā territory has always been under the influence of the West, and Western forms of speech, like Brajbhākā, and Awadhi, and literary Hindustani (Hindī and Urdū) in later times, have been cultivated by poets and others who spoke Bhojpuriyā at home.

In Chatterji's classification of the modern Indo-Aryan languages—as presented in Figure 1.3—Bhojpuri is therefore grouped with western languages. As for Magahi, even though ethnically Maithili and Magahi are different, yet philologically the two are so close to each other that even Grierson (1903/ reprint 1968: 40) held that Magahi "may very easily be classed as a dialect of Maithili rather than as a separate (speech)".

In his classification of the New Indo-Aryan (NIA) languages, Chatterji (1926/reprint 1970) shows that Maithili belongs to the group of Māgdhi-Apabhraṅsa. Most native Maithili scholars of the latter half of the twentieth century (e.g. S. Jha, 1958; G. Jha, 1974; Mishra, 1976; R. Yadav, 1979a and 1984) appear to have agreed to Chatterji's view—of course,

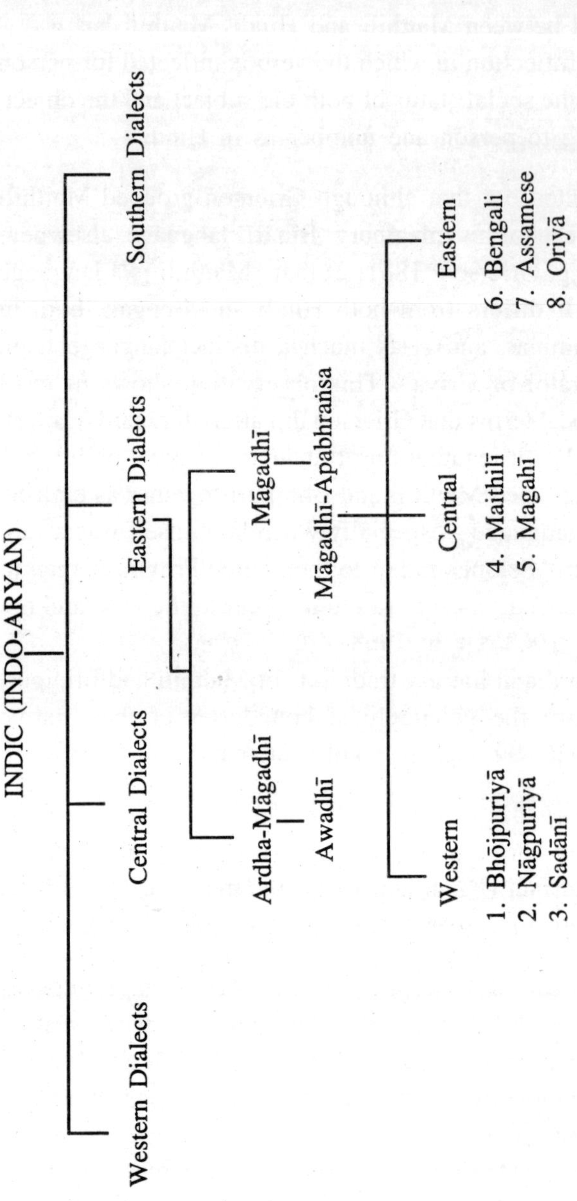

Figure 1.3: Classification of the modern Indo-Aryan languages, showing primarily the languages of North India—based on Chatterji (1926).

with a few minor modifications. For instance, S. Jha (1958: 20) holds that Maithili

> is very closely related to Bengali, Oriyā, and Assamese; like them, it has certain Māgdhan traits still present in it, all of them being the offspring of the Māgdhan Apabhraṁsa.

S. Jha's (1958: 21) classification of the modern Indo-Aryan languages is presented in Figure 1.4. Most Maithili scholars of today accept S. Jha's classification, as it helps them to emphasise, among other things, two major points of immense importance: (1) that Maithili is not a dialect either of Hindi or of Bengali; and (2) that, as Maithili is not a dialect of the so-called 'Bihārī' language either, this language should not therefore be grouped with Bhojpuri.

It should also be pointed out that Maithili does have its own script, variously known as 'Maithili Lipi', 'Mithilākṣara', or 'Tirhutā'. This script is of the same family as the scripts of Bengali, Assamese, Oṛiya and Newari (see, for example, Mishra, 1969: 268 and 1976: 24-25, for more details in this respect). It is a sad fact that the growth and development of Tirhutā has hardly been investigated in detail. But it is also a fact that in the past Maithili writers used to write in this script—as shown in Table 1.1—and we still have thousands of valuable manuscripts written in this script. Even these days on some sacred occasions several Maithili-speaking families, especially Maithil Brahmin families, use this script. It was primarily due to introducing simplicity and a sort of sameness adopted in the writing systems of most of the Indic languages that the Maithili writers later gradually started uṣing the Devanāgarī script of Sanskrit.

It must also, in addition, be mentioned that Maithili has a very rich literature, the growth and development of which follows quite closely the political and cultural history of Mithila. The antiquity of Maithili as a literary language goes back to the eighth century A.D., and it has had a continuous literary tradition during the last 700 years or so. Grierson (1882: 2) was aware of this tradition, and about a century ago he observed that "the only one of all the dialects of Eastern Hindustan which possesses any literature is Maithili, a dialect of north Bihar".

Today Maithili is recognised as a distinct language and there are provisions for it to be taught as such both in India and in Nepal. Presently,

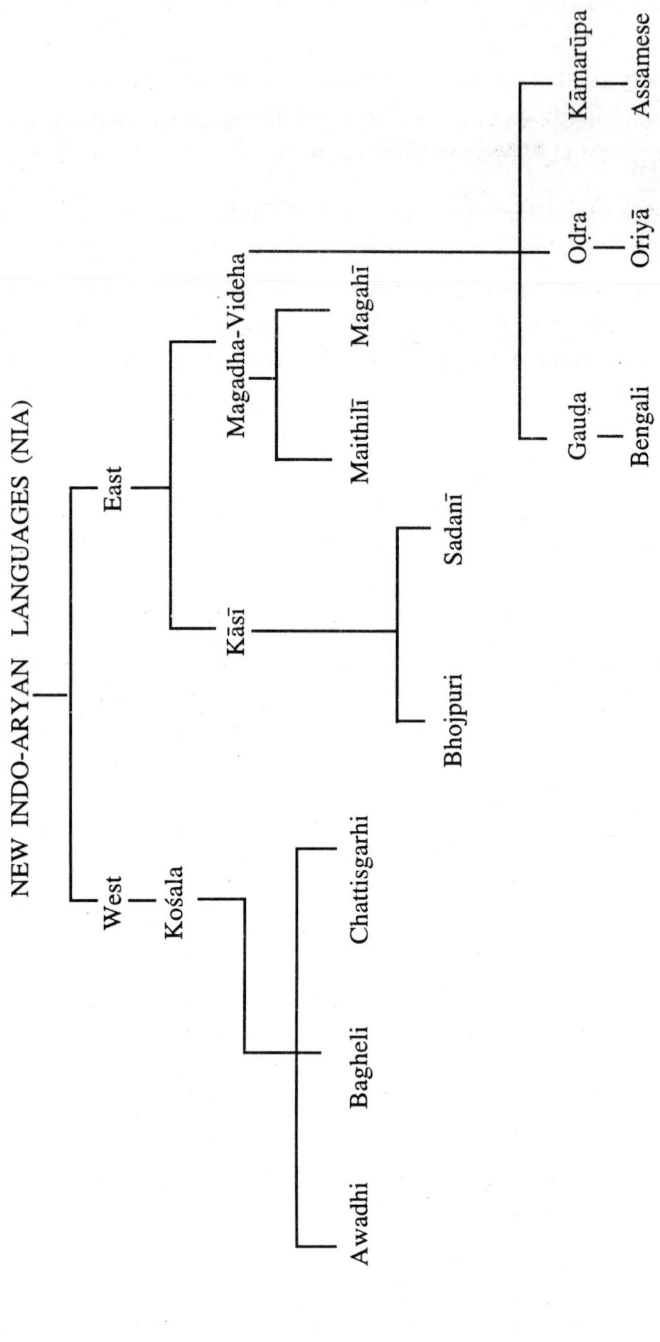

Figure 1.4: Genetic relationship of Maithili with other New Indo-Aryan languages, based on S. Jha (1958: 21).

Table 1.1: Maithili, Bengali and Devanāgarī scripts and numerals with equivalent IPA symbols and Arabic numerals-adapted from Grierson (1881: 115) and S. Jha (1958: 54-55).

Maithili	Bengali	Devanāgarī	IPA Symbols	Maithili	Bengali	Devanāgarī	IPA Symbols	Maithili	Bengali	Devanāgarī	IPA Symbols	Maithili	Bengali	Devanāgarī	IPA Symbols	Maithili	Bengali	Devanāgarī	Arabic Numerals
𑒁	অ	अ	ə	𑒎	ঔ	औ	əu	𑒙	ট	ट	ṭ	𑒤	ফ	फ	pʰ	𑓑	১	१	1
𑒂	আ	आ	a:	𑒁𑓀	অং	अं	eṁ	𑒚	ঠ	ठ	ṭʰ	𑒥	ব	ब	b	𑓒	২	२	2
𑒃	ই	इ	i	𑒁𑓁	অঃ	अः	əḥ	𑒛	ড	ड	ḍ	𑒦	ভ	भ	bʰ	𑓓	৩	३	3
𑒄	ঈ	ई	i:	𑒏	ক	क	k	𑒜	ঢ	ढ	ḍʰ	𑒧	ম	म	m	𑓔	৪	४	4
𑒅	উ	उ	u	𑒐	খ	ख	kʰ	𑒝	ণ	ण	ṇ	𑒨	য	य	y	𑓕	৫	५	5
𑒆	ঊ	ऊ	u:	𑒑	গ	ग	g	𑒛𑓃	ড়	ड़	ṛ	𑒩	র	र	r	𑓖	৬	६	6
𑒇	ঋ	ऋ	r̩	𑒒	ঘ	घ	gʰ	𑒜𑓃	ঢ়	ढ़	ṛʰ	𑒪	ল	ल	l	𑓗	৭	७	7
𑒈	ৠ	ॠ	r̩̄	𑒓	ঙ	ङ	n	𑒞	ত	त	t	𑒫	ব	व	v	𑓘	৮	८	8
𑒉	ঌ	ऌ	l̩	𑒔	চ	च	c	𑒟	থ	थ	tʰ	𑒬	শ	श	s	𑓙	৯	९	9
𑒊	ৡ	ॡ	l̩	𑒕	ছ	छ	cʰ	𑒠	দ	द	d	𑒭	ষ	ष	ṣ				
𑒋	এ	ए	e	𑒖	জ	ज	j	𑒡	ধ	ध	dʰ	𑒮	স	श	ʃ				
𑒌	ঐ	ऐ	ei	𑒗	ঝ	झ	jʰ	𑒢	ন	न	n	𑒯	হ	ह	h				
𑒍	ও	ओ	o	𑒘	ঞ	ञ	ñ	𑒣	প	प	p								

Maithili is taught and studied in various universities of both India and Nepal. Demographically, Maithili is the second most widely spoken language of Nepal. And, according to the International P.E.N. (Poets, Essayists and Novelists), it is the sixteenth major language of India.

1.3 Linguistic and Phonetic Studies on Maithili: A Brief Sketch

Maithili is clearly a member of the North Indian group of Indo-Aryan languages which includes Nepali, Hindi, Gujarati, Punjabi, Bengali, and so on, and its development has been closely related to the changes which have occurred in all these languages. Yet there is a great paucity of early written materials in Maithili, and it would indeed be true to say that the reconstruction of Maithili linguistic history still involves a great deal of speculation. In this section an attempt is made to put forward a brief survey of linguistic and phonetic studies done on Maithili both in India and Nepal.

1.3.1 *Studies on Maithili done in India*

Up to a few centuries ago there was no unanimously agreed one particular name for the language of Mithila. For example, at some periods it used to be called 'Avahaṭṭha' or 'Mithila-Apabhraṁsa', at other periods as 'Desh-Bhāṣā' or 'Tirhutiā' (e.g. see, Mishra, 1976: 16-18, for more details). According to Mishra (1976: 16), it was Colebrooke who for the first time named the language of Mithila as Maithili in 1801—although this language was then spelt as 'Mithelee' or 'Mythili'. It was in fact Grierson who finally and permanently fixed the name of this language as *Maithili*, with its present spelling in the early 1880s.

In India it was indeed Grierson who for the first time began serious studies on Maithili linguistics and published a series of scholarly papers and books on this language. In 1881 he published: *An Introduction to the Maithili Language of North Bihar*, Part 1, 'Grammar'. This piece of work is divided into four parts; it is the first elaborate synchronic description of Maithili, although the whole description is based upon only a few Maithili forms obtained from translations of a few Hindi and Sanskrit passages by "the Pundits, Village School Masters and educated Native Gentlemen of Northern Mithila" (Grierson, 1881: 1). Later, in 1882 Grierson published: *An Introduction to the Maithili Language of North Bihar*, Part 2, 'Chrestomathy and Vocabulary'. This piece of work includes perhaps the earliest published word-list of the Maithili language and, to put it in Grierson's (1882: 1) words, "nearly all the Maithili Literature I have been able to collect". Still later—i.e. between 1883 and 1887—Grierson published: *Seven Grammars of the Dialects and Subdialects of the Biharī Language.* This piece of work is divided into eight parts, each of which presents an extensive dialectal survey of what he called 'Biharī'. During this period, Hoernle and Grierson also published in two parts: *A Comparative Dictionary of the Biharī Language* (Part 1, 1885; Part 2, 1889). Afterwards, quite a few years later, Grierson (1903/reprint 1968) again published: *Linguistic Survey of India 5:2,* which includes a detailed summary of Grierson's major findings on Maithili and on some other Indian languages as well.

Another earliest publication, which includes some phonological interpretations on Maithili as well, is Kellogg's (1876/1893) *A Grammar of the Hindi Language.* Although Kellogg here treats Maithili as a dialect of Hindi, the importance of his work lies in the various illustrations that he gives from Maithili, together with several insightful phonological notes. It must, however, be stated that throughout his book Kellogg presents lengthy discussions primarily on Hindi rather than on Maithili.

Quite a few years later in 1941 there appeared an elaborate article by S. Jha on Maithili phonetics in a journal, *Indian Linguistics,* where the author presents mainly a phonemic summary of the so-called 'standard' dialect of the Maithili language. Again, in 1958 appeared S. Jha's book: *The Formation of the Maithili Language.* This book gives a very exhaustive diachronic description of Maithili: it is indeed the first most detailed attempt to trace the history of Maithili from the Old Indo-Aryan (OIA) period. Based on thorough acquaintance with the Maithili language itself and with its antecedents, S. Jha's (1958) publication did make a significant advance in furthering our knowledge of Maithili. However, it is to be regretted that, as the author himself points out, the book

> was begun in 1935 and during the period of about twenty-two years that have elapsed in the meantime many changes have taken place in the circumstances. Consequently on so many points the present work has already become out of date (S. Jha, 1958: vi).

In his review of S. Jha's (1958) book , Southworth (1961) makes some fair comments and criticisms and he rightly sums up his opinion by stating that S. Jha's (1958) book

> as a research tool would have been enhanced by the addition of a word index and a bibliography, as well as English glosses of the Maithili words cited in the text. The lack of glosses for most of these words not only impairs the value of Jha's work as a source of material for historical-comparative research, but also makes it difficult to evaluate his etymologies (Southworth, 1961: 169).

Nevertheless, as far as the early materials on Maithili are concerned, S. Jha's (1958) book still remains as a significant source of material for historical-comparative research.

In 1958 there also appeared G. Jha's article on the conjugation of verbs in Maithili. In this article G. Jha (1958) made an attempt to trace out the origin and development of some verb forms in Maithili. Quite later in 1974 appeared G. Jha's book: *Maithilī Bhāṣā kā Vikās* (The Development of the Maithili Language). This piece of work is written in Hindi: it presents a brief history of the development of Maithili and also gives a glimpse of some of its synchronic descriptions. Still later in 1979 appeared G. Jha's book: *Ũccatar Maithili Vyākaraṇa* (A Higher Grammar of Maithili). This book is written in Maithili and it gives an account of some grammatical aspects of this language.

In addition to these studies, there have also been some other comparatively less exhaustive studies on the origin and development of the Maithili language (e.g. Sh. Jha, 1957). On the origin and development of the Maithili script, too, there have been some studies (e.g. R. Jha, 1971). Relatively recently, there have been some comparative studies on some grammatical aspects of Maithili together with other Indo-Aryan languages (e.g. Junghare, 1972; Jeffers, 1976; Singh and Bandhopadhyay, 1978). Following some transformational-generative approaches, there have also been a few studies on some aspects of the Maithili syntax (e.g. Singh, 1979a, 1979b and 1980).

In the 1970s quite a few publications have come out on the history and development of Maithili literature (e.g. Mishra, 1976; Chaudhary, 1976; D. K. Jha, 1979). There have also been some comparative studies of Maithili linguistics and of the history and culture of its native speakers (e.g. V. Jha, 1977; Sharma, 1979). Most of these works have concentrated on the study of documents and inscriptions. A great deal of useful information about the history of Maithili and Mithila as well as about the relationship between Maithili and other modern Indo-Aryan languages can now be obtained from these studies carried out primarily in India.

1.3.2 *Studies on Maithili done in Nepal*

The 1971, 1981 and 1991 census reports of Nepal list up to 37 languages spoken in this country. All these 37 languages can be grouped in one or the other of the following four language families—i.e. (i) Indo-European (Indo-Aryan Group), (ii) Sino-Tibetan (Tibeto-Burman Group), (iii) Austro-Asiatic (Munda Group), and (iv) Dravidian (Northern Kudux Group)—as shown in Figure 1.5. All census reports clearly show that Nepali is the main language of Nepal and Maithili is the second most widely spoken language in the country.

It is only from the previous three decades or so that serious linguistic and phonetic studies on Maithili have begun in Nepal. For example, in 1973 two encouraging papers were published (i.e. Davis, 1973; Williams, 1973) by the Summer Institute of Linguistics (SIL) on Maithili syntax, both written in the tagmetic framework. In the same year, the SIL also published a detailed word-list (Trail, 1973a), which includes a fairly large number of Maithili words. Later, in 1973-74 the Royal Nepal Academy published *Paryāyavācī Shavdakosha* (Dictionary of Synonyms), which includes the words of Maithili together with those of some 13 other languages of Nepal. Afterwards, R. Yadav (1976) published a paper on the aspirated consonants of colloquial Maithili. A few years later, Ingemann and Yadav (1978) published a scholarly article in which they discuss the results of their study of the voiced aspirated consonants of a number of languages, including those of Hindi and Maithili. A year later R. Yadav (1979a) submitted his doctoral dissertation on Maithili phonetics and phonology at the University of Kansas, and he published his dissertation in 1984. R. Yadav's (1979b, 1979c, 1980a, 1980b, 1981, 1982 and 1991) other studies contain much interesting work with findings which will prove useful to linguists and phoneticians in general, as well as to those working in the area of Maithili and related studies.

Another dedicated scholar working on Maithili, Y.P. Yadav (1981, 1982a, 1982b and 1984) has also published a number of articles, each of which deals with areas concerning Maithili syntax. Y.P. Yadav (1983) also submitted his doctoral dissertation at Hyderabad in which he made a comparative study of Movement Rules in Maithili and English. In 1984 B.K. Jha also submitted his doctoral dissertation entitled "A Descriptive

THE LANGUAGES OF NEPAL

Indo-European
Indo-Aryan Group
1. Nepali
2. Maithili
3. Bhojpuri
4. Tharuwani
5. Awadhi
6. Danuwar
7. Darai
8. Bhote
9. Majhi
10. Kumhale
11. Rajbansi

Sino-Tibetan
Tibeto-Burman Group
1. Tamang
2. Newari
3. Magar
4. Rai-Kirati
5. Gurung
6. Limbu
7. Sherpa
8. Tibetan
9. Loke
10. Sunwar
11. Thakali
12. Pahari
13. Chepang
14. Dhimal
15. Raji
16. Bayu (Hayu)
17. Byasi
18. Kham
19. Kaike (Lhomi)
20. Lepcha
21. Rautya
22. Meche

Austro-Asiatic
Munda Group
1. Satar
2. Santhali
3. Kusunda

Dravidian
Northern Kudux Group
1. Jhangad

Figure 1.5: The languages of Nepal divided into four main groups in accordance with their respective language families.

Study of Maithili Language of Nepal" at Poona University. Baidyanath Jha is another researcher currently engaged in ongoing doctoral research on Maithili. The present author (S.K. Jha, 1984) submitted his doctoral dissertation at the University of Essex; his study presents an account of some phonetic and phonological aspects of a variety of the standard dialect of Maithili. In addition, S.K. Jha (1985, 1986, 1990, 1991a, 1991b, 1992, 1993, 1994 and 1999) also published a number of articles on different phonetic and phonological aspects of this language. At present various other scholars are working on different aspects of Maithili at Tribhuvan University as well as at a number of other universities in other countries.

1.4 The Emergence of a Standard in Maithili and Its Present-day Situation

An exhaustive survey of Maithili dialects has not yet been published, and few dialects have been analysed by linguists. For this reason, most dialects remain undefined and no system for their classification has yet proved widely acceptable. The standardisation of the Maithili language was seriously begun a little more than a century ago. In that entire process of standardisation the contributions of G.A. Grierson and his associates are undoubtedly immense. After some considerable research and survey carried out more than a century ago, Grierson (1881: 2) observed that Maithili

> . . . is emphatically a spoken language. There is no standard to which it can be referred, and hence no form can be put aside as vulgar or impure. It is hoped, not only by myself, that the publication of a treatise like the present will tend to fix a standard ... The dialect which I have adopted as a standard is that of the Madhubani Sub-division, which is centrally situated, and which is admitted by all . . . to be the head-quarters of Mithila.

In his later publications on Maithili, Grierson (e.g. 1882, 1883a, 1883b, 1884b, 1885, 1886, 1887a, 1887b, 1909/reprint 1967) concentrated on the above-mentioned standard dialect of this language. It is that same dialect of Maithili which S. Jha (1941: 39) also regarded as the standard one:

> It is the 'sista-bhāsā', the language of the highest groups of Mithilā, and has been described as the Standard Form of Maithilī, as it has been adopted by speakers of all the other Maithili dialects as the

most elegant form of their mother tongue; and, moreover, it is the only accepted literary form of the language.

The speakers of Maithili are today particularly sensitive to variations in the pronunciation of their language. The 'wrong accent' may still be an impediment to social intercourse or to advancement or entry in certain professions. There is now very little controversy regarding the written form of standard Maithili—the spelling of this form was largely fixed by the end of the first half of this century (e.g. Grierson, 1882; D. Jha, 1952); the conventions of grammatical forms and constructions (e.g. Grierson, 1881, 1883a, 1883b, 1883c, 1884a, 1884b, 1885, 1886, 1887a and 1887b) as well as of the greater part of the vocabulary of Maithili have for the last five decades or so been accepted and adhered to by the majority of educated Maithili speakers. Although written Maithili is now quite standard, like any other language, there has always existed a great diversity in the spoken realisations of this language, in terms of the speech sounds used in different parts and by different sections of the Maithili-speaking community.

With such publications as S. Jha's (1941 and 1958) article and book on Maithili phonetics and philology, G. Jha's (1958, 1974 and 1979) article and books on Maithili grammar, J. Mishra's (1969 and 1976) publications on the Maithili language and literature, with the spread of education in the Maithili-speaking community, and with the advent of radio and television broadcasts in Maithili by some radio and television stations of both India and Nepal, what has been of immense significance—social as well as linguistic—is the attitude of the Maithili-speaking communities both in India and Nepal, which regards a certain set of speech sound values as more acceptable, even more 'beautiful' than another. Judgements of this kind suggest that there is some kind of 'standard' for comparison; and it is clear that such a standard pronunciation of Maithili does exist, although it has never been explicitly imposed by any official body, whether in India or in Nepal, nor has it so far been clearly and elaborately described by any Indian or Nepalese linguists. A consideration of the origins and present nature of this unofficial standard of Maithili goes some way towards explaining the controversies and emotions which it arouses at the present day. Whatever the controversies, it cannot be denied that great prestige is still attached to this implicitly accepted social standard of the pronunciation of Maithili.

It must be emphasised that the variant of Maithili implicitly accepted by the majority as the standard form of this language is the result of a social judgement rather than of any explicit official decision or inherent reason as to what is 'correct' or 'wrong'. This standard has become more widely known and accepted through the advent of radio and television. The Indian and Nepali radio stations broadcasting in Maithili formerly recommended this form of pronunciation for its announcers mainly because it was the type which was most widely understood and which excited least prejudice of a regional kind. Indeed, it is said that attempts to use announcers who had a mild regional (i.e. 'non-standard') accent provoked protests even from the region whose accent was used.

Thus, over the last five decades or so, the standard pronunciation of Maithili often became identified in the public mind with the pronunciation of that form of the language which the Indian, and of late even the Nepali, radio stations and print media have been using, and which the Indian and Nepali educational institutions have been using for the teaching of this language. It is this form of the language that has led to its being the standard form of pronunciation in Maithili. Apart from Grierson's publications, D. Jha's (1952) lexicographic work entitled *Maithilī Bhāsā Kos* (Maithili Dictionary) further established the spelling system of this language by bringing the spelling closer to pronunciation. At present Maithili grammar is reasonably well standardised. It would therefore be true to say that written Maithili is now almost entirely standard in its grammatical structure, spelling and vocabulary throughout Nepal and India.

1.5 Summary

Maithili is a modern Indo-Aryan language spoken by more than 21 million people in India and Nepal. Up to the early 20th century, the place of this language among the modern Indo-Aryan languages was very much misunderstood and misrepresented. But today Maithili is recognised as a distinct language and it is being taught and studied as such both in India and Nepal. Demographically, it is the second most widely spoken language in Nepal, and it is regarded as the 16th major language of India, according to the International P.E.N.

In the past there have been some substantial diachronic studies on Maithili, but synchronic studies on this language really started from the 1970s only. The present author is a native speaker of a variety of the standard dialect of Maithili, and in this book he presents a detailed description of some phonetic and phonological aspects of that dialect, basing his study on his own pronunciation.

Chapter 2

THE MAITHILI VOWELS

2.0 Introduction

Vowels can be defined in terms of both phonetics and phonology. Phonetically, they are sounds articulated without a complete closure in the mouth or a degree of narrowing which would produce audible frication; the air escapes evenly over the centre of the tongue. If air escapes solely through the mouth, the vowels are said to be oral. If, on the other hand, some air is simultaneously released through the nose, the vowels are said to be nasal. From a phonological point of view, vowels are those units which function as the focus of syllables.

Vowel segments are a great deal more difficult to describe than consonant segments. Almost all consonant segments, as we shall see later in the third chapter, are made with a stricture involving contact of relatively large areas of active as well as passive articulators. Since the contacts involved in the production of any given consonant can be ascertained fairly easily, such contacts usually provide a convenient basis for consonant description. But vowel segments are usually made with 'open approximation' of the articulators. For this reason, they involve little contact, sometimes none at all. They are therefore, literally, less 'tangible' than consonants.

Articulatorily, vowels may be described and classified in terms of such main factors as: (1) vertical tongue position (high-low), (2) horizontal tongue position (front-back), (3) lip position (rounded-unrounded), and (4) velic closure (oral-nasal). Maithili has sixteen phonologically distinctive vowel segments—i.e. eight oral vowels: /i.e. æ a ə ɔ o u/ and eight nasal vowels:/ ĩ ẽ æ̃ ã ə̃ ɔ̃ õ ũ / as well as two phonologically distinctive oral diphthongs: /əi/ and /əu/. The acoustic characteristics of these 18 vowels and diphthongs are discussed later in Chapter 4. This chapter presents the description, classification and phonemic analysis of these vowels and diphthongs.

2.1 Description, Classification and Phonemic Analysis of the Maithili Vowels

The length of vowels is not phonologically distinctive in Maithili, although the Devanagari script in which this language is now written does provide some separate graphemes for 'long' and 'short' vowels. At the level of surface phonology, however, Maithili does have instances of long and short vowels. That is to say, variations in the length of vowels, whether oral or nasal, are completely allophonic in Maithili: the long allophonic variants occur mainly in stressed syllables, while the short ones occur in unstressed syllables. In this section we shall classify and describe the Maithili vowels and shall also present their phonemic analysis.

2.1.1. *The Oral Vowels in Maithili*

The Maithili oral vowels /i e æ a ə ɔ o u / may be classified into the following three main categories: (1) front vowels, (2) central vowels, and (3) back vowels.

2.1.1.1 *The Front Vowels in Maithili*

Maithili has three front vowels —/i/, /e/ and /æ/:

/i/

The Maithili /i/ may be described as a high front unrounded oral vowel. It has two major allophonic variants at the surface phonological level—i.e. [i:] and [i]. In the production of the Maithili [i:] the front of the tongue is raised to a height slightly below and behind the close front position; the lips are spread; the soft palate is in a raised position; the tongue is tense, with the side rims making a firm contact with the upper molars. [i], on the other hand, is the short allophonic variant of the Maithili /i/, and it is pronounced with a part of the tongue nearer to centre than to front raised just above the half-close position; the lips are loosely spread; the soft palate is in a raised position; the tongue is relatively lax, with the side rims making a light contact with the upper molars. Both [i:] and [i] occur in all word positions: initial, medial and final.

/e/

The Maithili /e/ may be described as a mid front unrounded oral vowel.

In the pronunciation of its long allophonic variant [e:], the front of the tongue is raised almost half-way towards the hard palate; the lips are unrounded; the soft palate is in a raised position; the tongue is fairly tense, the side rims making a contact with the upper molars. [e:] occurs in all word positions. But in pronouncing the short allophonic variant [e], the front of the tongue is raised between the half-open and half-close positions; the lips are loosely spread and are slightly wider apart than for [i]; the soft palate is in a raised position; the tongue is relatively lax, the side rims making a light contact with the upper molars. [e] does not occur word-finally.

/æ/

The Maithili /æ/ may be described as a low front unrounded oral vowel. In pronouncing its long allophonic variant [æ:], the mouth is slightly more open than for [e:]; the front of the tongue is raised just below the half-open position, with the side rims making a contact with the back upper molars; the lips are neutrally open; the soft palate is in a raised position. [æ:] occurs in all word positions, and there is a tendency to diphthongise it. The short allophonic variant [æ], on the other hand, is drawn towards the central position. In pronouncing [æ], the opening between the jaws is medium; the lips are unrounded; the soft palate is in a raised position; the tongue is somewhat retracted and lax, with the side rims making a very slight contact with the back upper molars. [æ] does not occur word-finally.

The three front vowels in Maithili, /i e æ/, show full phonological opposition in all word positions: initial, medial and final. For example:

Initial	Medial	Final
/is/ 'expression of pain'	/git/ 'song'	/ki/ 'what'
/æs/ 'luxury'	/gæt/ 'will sing'	/kæ/ 'vomit'
/'ila/ 'bring this'	/piṭ/ 'beat (imp.)'	/ǰi/ 'yes'
/'ela/ 'came'	/peṭ/ 'stomach'	/ǰe/'which; that'
/'æna/'looking glass'	/ǰæb/ 'will go'	/gæ/ 'cow'
/'ena/ 'like this'	/ǰeb/ 'pocket'	/ge/'hi! (feminine)'

Of all these three front vowels in Maithili, /æ/ is the least frequent. The short allophonic variants of these front vowels occur only in unstressed syllables. [i] occurs in all word positions; [e] and [æ], on the other hand, occur only word-initially and word-medially. For example:

Initial	Medial	Final
[ij̆'la:s]'court'	[bi'na:] 'without'	['ra:ti] 'night'
[e'kə:r] 'his/her'	[ke'na:] 'how'	------
[æ'la:]' '(he) came'	[pæ'ta:] '(he) will get'	------

2.1.1.2 *The Central Vowels in Maithili*

Maithili has two central vowels—/a/ and /ə/:

/a/

The Maithili /a/ may be described as a low central unrounded oral vowel. In the articulation of its long allophonic variant [a:], there is a considerable separation of the jaws and the lips are neutrally open; the soft palate is in a raised position; a part of the tongue between the centre and back is in the open position, and no contact is being made between the rims of the tongue and the upper molars. The Maithili [a:] is really a central vowel, and it is not as open as the English (RP) /a:/. The Maithili [a:] occurs in all word positions—initial, medial and final. The short allophonic variant [a], on the other hand, is slightly higher than [a:]. In the pronunciation of [a], the opening between the jaws is narrower than what it is in the case of the long [a:]; and a part of the tongue between the centre and back is raised up. In articulating both [a:] and [a], the tongue is rather lax, and there is no diphthongising tendency noticeable. [a] does not occur word-finally.

/ə/

The Maithili /ə/ may be described as a mid central unrounded oral vowel. Its long allophonic variant [ə:] has the quality of a central vowel with neutral lip position. [ə:] occurs in all word positions. The short allophonic variant [ə], on the other hand, has a very high frequency of occurrence in unstressed syllables. It is also pronounced with a neutral lip position, having a tongue-raising between half-open and half-close, and it seems to advance to some extent towards the front, though basically it is also a central vowel. [ə], too, occurs in all word positions.

Both /a/ and /ə/ show full phonological contrast in all word positions: initial, medial and final. For example:

Initial	Medial	Final
/an/ 'bring'	/kal/ 'time; enemy'	/'paṛa/ 'a buffalo calf'
/ən/ 'grain'	/kəl/ 'machine'	/'paṛə'/ 'dig (imp.)'

It should be mentioned that the frequency of occurrence of /ə/ is much more in non-final word positions, and that in the word-final position /ə/ occurs mainly in the imperative construction. In the above examples it is the long allophonic variants of /a/ and /ə/ which have occurred. As stated above, these central vowels also have their short allophonic variants, [a] and [ə], and both of them occur mainly in unstressed syllables. [a] does not occur word-finally; [ə], on the other hand, occurs in all word positions. For example:

Initial	Medial	Final
[a'ka:rə] 'shape'	[ba'ča:lə]'eloquent'	------
[ə'mə:rə] 'immortal'	[ǰə'di:] 'if'	['pu:lə]'bridge'

2.1.1.3 *The Back Vowels in Maithili*

Maithili has three back vowels— /ɔ/, /o/ and /u/:

/ɔ/

The Maithili /ɔ/ may be described as a low back rounded oral vowel. Its long allophonic variant [ɔ:] is articulated with medium lip-rounding; the back of the tongue is raised between the half-open and half-close positions, no contact is being made between the tongue and the upper molars. [ɔ:] occurs in all word positions. In the articulation of the short allophonic variant [ɔ], the raising of the tongue, in so far as the height is concerned, is almost the same as in the case of [ɔ:], but the raised part is nearly the middle of the tongue rather than its back; the rounding of the lips is a little greater in the case of [ɔ] than in [ɔ:]. [ɔ] does not occur word-finally.

/o/

The Maithili /o/ may be described as a mid back rounded oral vowel. Its long allophonic variant [o:] is articulated by raising the mid part of the back of the tongue towards the soft palate; the lips are rounded; the soft palate is in a raised position. The short allophonic variant [o] seems to be advanced midway between the back and the central positions. The lips are rounded to a greater extent in the case of [o] than in that of [o:]. In articulating both [o:] and [o] the opening between the jaws is narrow and no contact is being made between the tongue and the upper molars. The two variants occur in all word positions.

/u/

The Maithili /u/ may be described as a high back rounded oral vowel. Its long allophonic variant [u:] is a back close vowel. It is pronounced with the back of the tongue raised up; the lips tend to be closely rounded; the soft palate is in a raised position; the tongue is rather tense, though no firm contact is made between the tongue and the upper molars. The short allophonic variant [u], on the other hand, is pronounced with a part of the tongue nearer to the centre than to back raised just above the half-close position; the lips are closely but loosely rounded; the soft palate is in a raised position; the tongue is relatively lax, no firm contact being made between the tongue and the upper molars. Both [u:] and [u] occur in all word positions.

All these three back vowels in Maithili, /ɔ o u/, show full phonological opposition in all word positions: initial, medial and final. For example:

Initial	Medial	Final
/ɔṛ^{h}/'out of sight'	/kɔr/ 'morsel'	/hɔ/ 'whoa!'
/oṛ^{h}/'wrap (imp.)'	/kor/ 'edge'	/ho/ 'also'
/oṭ^{h}/ 'lip'	/b^{h}oǰ/ 'feast'	/'p^{h}ero/'again'
/uṭ^{h}/ 'get up (imp)'	/b^{h}uǰ/ 'fry (imp.)'	/'p^{h}eru/ 'turn aside'
/o'sar/ 'verandah'	/b^{h}or/ 'morning'	/ko'ṛo/ 'bamboo pole'
/u'sar/'retreat (imp.)'	/b^{h}ur/ 'hole'	/ko'ṛu/ '(please) dig'

Of all these three back vowels, /ɔ/ is the least frequent—especially in non-medial positions. It is the long allophonic variants of /ɔ o u / which have occurred in the above examples. But these vowels also have their short allophonic variants, which occur in unstressed syllables. [ɔ] does not occur word-finally; [o] and [u], on the other hand, occur in all word positions. For example:

Initial	Medial	Final
[ɔ'ta:] 'will come'	[kɔ'ra:] 'food given to a dog'	- - - -
[o'kə:r] 'his/her'	[ko'da:ri] 'spade'	['to:ro] 'yours too'
[u'sa: sə] 'consolation'	[nu'kæ: lə] 'hidden'	['mə: d^{h}u] 'honey'

2.1.1.4 *The High, Mid and Low Vowels in Maithili*
Maithili has three degrees of vowel height, which may be termed as: high, mid and low. The high vowels are /i/ and /u/, and they show full phonological opposition in all word positions: initial, medial and final. For example:

Initial	Medial	Final
/i'nar/'well(n)'	/kiṭ/ 'fix (imp.)'	/'tari/'palm juice'
/u'nar/'unbalanced'	/kuṭ/'hard cover (e.g. of a book)'	/'taru/ '(please) fry'

The mid vowels in Maithili are /e ə o/ and they also show full phonological contrast in all word positions. For example:

Initial	Medial	Final
/e'na/ 'like this'	/'kera/'banana'	/he/ 'hai!'
/o'na/ 'like that'	/'kora/ 'lap'	/ho/ 'become'
/e'kəṛ/ 'acre'	/peṛ/ 'tree'	/'mare/ 'many'
/ə'kəṛ/ 'boast'	/pəṛ/ 'lie down (imp.)'	/'marə/ 'beat (imp.)'

The low vowels in Maithili are /æ a ɔ/ and they, too, show full phonological contrast in all word positions. For example:

Initial	Medial	Final
/æs/ 'luxury'	/pær/ 'leg'	/b^{h}æ/ 'brother'
/as/ 'hope'	/par/ 'across'	/b^{h}a/ 'pretension'
/ɔ'ta/ 'will come'	/sɔr/ 'sky'	/sɔ/ 'hundred'
/a'ta/ 'a kind of fruit'	/sar/ 'wife's brother'	/sa/ 'a musical note'

Based on the above description, the Maithili oral vowels are charted on the 'standard' vowel diagram in Figure 2.1. It should be mentioned here that it is purely on an impressionistic basis that these oral vowels have been charted on the diagram presented in Figure 2.1. The impressions, however, include those of other trained phoneticians (e.g. S. Jha, 1941: 40 and 1958: 65; G. Jha, 1974: 58 and 1979: 7; R. Yadav, 1979a: 149) as well. The acoustic analysis of these vowels is done in the fourth chapter of this study, and in the same chapter the average frequency

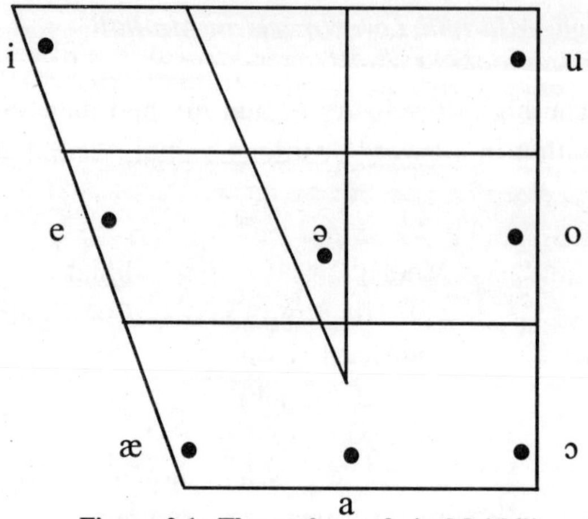

Figure 2.1: The oral vowels in Maithili.

values (in Hz) of F_1 and F_2 for these vowels spoken in different contexts are also plotted on a number of formant charts. All eight Maithili oral vowels and their major allophonic variants are summarised and presented in Figure 2.2 below:

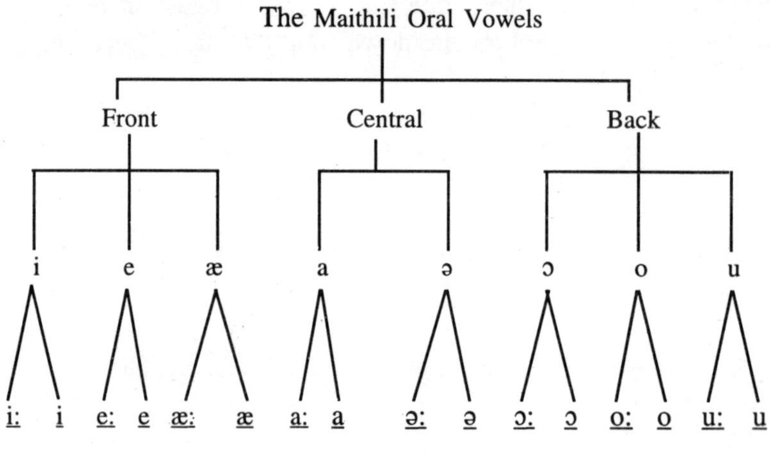

Figure 2:2: The Maithili oral vowels and their major allophonic variants.

2.1.2 *The Nasal Vowels in Maithili*

The term 'nasal' is traditionally used in the phonetic classification of speech sounds on the basis of their manner of articulation. In the production of nasal sounds the velum is lowered and the nasal cavity is thus linked with the vocal tract below it. An airstream from the lungs may then pass through the 'nasal port' into the nasal cavity. Simultaneously, the airstream also enters the oral cavity. Modifications of the airflow by action of the tongue, teeth and/or lips may later give rise to various kinds of nasal sounds. In Maithili both consonants and vowels may be articulated in this way. In the case of nasal vowels, air escapes through both the nose and the mouth simultaneously. The nasal vowels are transcribed with [~] above the symbol—e.g. [ĩ], [ẽ], and so on

Like many other languages—e.g. French, Portuguese, Hindi and Gujarati—in Maithili nasal vowels are opposed to oral vowels. Nasality is therefore an essential identifying feature of the vowel sounds in Maithili. All the eight oral vowels of Maithili have their phonologically distinctive nasal counterparts, too—i.e. /ĩ ẽ æ̃ ã ə̃ ɔ̃ õ ũ /. These nasal vowels are produced almost exactly like their oral counterparts with the exception that during their production the soft palate is in a lowered position so that air escapes even through the nose. The acoustic analysis of these nasal vowels is done in the fourth chapter of this study.

The nasal vowels of some languages like Slavic and French, for example, are said (e.g. see, Lightner, 1970; Ruhlen, 1973, for more details) to be realisations of underlying vowel plus nasal (VN) sequences. Unlike Slavic and French, the nasal vowels in Maithili are truly phonemic. That is to say, in current Maithili there are plenty of words where nasal vowels occur in non-nasal consonantal environments. And even in the same consonantal contexts they all show full phonological contrasts with their oral counterparts. In other words, whether it be the case of slow, formal or less formal speech, a nasal vowel in Maithili occurring in environments of non-nasal consonants exists as a phonologically distinct nasal vowel, and not as a sequence of vowel plus nasal (for historical details of the nasal vowels of some modern Indo-Aryan languages, including Maithili, see, for example, Chatterji, 1926/1970 and 1960; S. Jha, 1958). This does not, however, mean that the phonetic nasalisation of vowels does not occur in Maithili. In fact, as discussed at some length in the seventh chapter of this study, a derived level non-nasal vowel in Maithili is phonetically nasalised at the surface level, whenever the vowel in question occurs in the vicinity of any nasal consonants.

The oral and nasal vowels in Maithili show phonological opposition in all word positions: initial, medial and final. For example:

2.1.2.1 *Initial Position*

/i'ṭa/ 'only this'
/ĩ'ṭa/ 'brick'

/ə'hi/ 'only this (place/thing)'
/ə̃'hĩ/ 'only you'

/ek/ 'one'
/ẽṛ/ 'heel'

/ɔt/ 'will come'
/ɔ̃ṭ/ 'boil (imp.)'

/æ/ 'expression of contempt'
/æ̃/ 'what'

/o/ 'he/she'
/õ/ 'a groaning sound'

/aṭ^h/ 'eight'
/ãṭ/ 'courage'

/uṭ^h/ 'awake'; 'get up'
/ũṭ/ 'camel'

2.1.2.2 *Medial Position*

/č^{h}iṭ/ 'scatter'
/č^{h}ĩṭ/ 'garment dyed with spots'

/'kəṭgər/'commendable; adequate'
/'kə̃ṭgər/ 'thorny'

/b^{h}eṭ/ 'see'; 'get in touch'
/b^{h}ẽṭ/'a kind of water plant'

/gɔt/ 'will sing'
/gɔ̃t/ '(cattle) urine'

/b^{h}æt/ 'will become'
/b^{h}æ̃t/ 'kind; type'

/g^{h}oṭ/ 'mix (imp.)'
/g^{h}õṭ/ 'swallow'

/bas/ 'shelter; dwelling place'
/bãs/ 'bamboo'

/sur/ 'brave (person)'
/sũṛ^h/' (elephant's) trunk'

2.1.2.3 *Final Position*

/kə'hi/'(I/you) say'
/kə̃'hĩ/ '(what) if'

/hə/ 'oh!'
/hə̃/ 'yes'

/me/ 'May'
/mẽ/ 'in'

/b^{h}ɔ/ 'price'
/b^{h}ɔ̃/ 'eyebrow'

/sæ/ 'thus'; 'that way'
/sæ̃/ 'husband'

/kə'so/'get tightened (imp.)'
/kə'sõ/ 'small hole from which water leaks in the field'

/kə'ha/ 'make someone say'
/kə'hã/ 'where'

/kə'hu/ '(you) say'
/kə'hũ/ 'somewhere'; 'in case'

Of the eight nasal vowels in Maithili, /ĩ ə̃ õ ũ/ have both long and short allophonic variants: the long variants occur mainly in stressed syllables; the short ones occur in unstressed syllables. The short [ĩ] and [ũ] occur in all word positions: initial, medial and final. For example:

Initial	Medial	Final
[ĩ'ǰo: tə] 'light'	[hĩ'sa: bə] 'account'	['bã: hĩ] 'arm'
[ũč'ka:] 'the high one'	[sũ'ṛiani:] 'a hamlet of brewers'	[kəh'lə̃: hũ] '(I) said'

But the short [ə̃] occurs mainly word-initially and word-medially, whereas [õ] occurs primarily in the word-medial position. For example:

Initial	Medial
[ə̃'hĩ:] 'only you'	[kə'hĩ:] '(what) if'
- - - -	[ṭõṭi'æ:1] 'seedling becoming apparent'

The remaining four nasal vowels, i.e. /ẽ æ̃ ã ɔ̃/, occur primarily in stressed syllables and they all have only one variant each. All the Maithili nasal vowels and their major allophonic variants are summarised and presented in Figure 2.3 below:

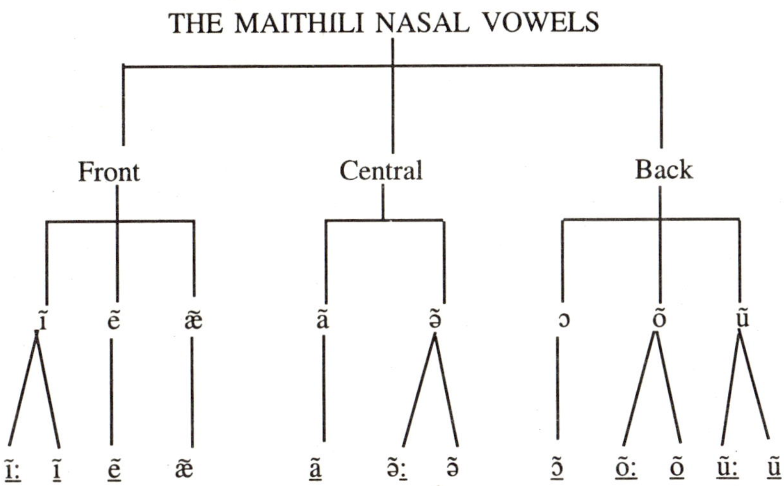

Figure 2.3: The Maithili nasal vowels and their major allophonic variants.

2.1.3 *The Diphthongs in Maithili*

Like many other languages, Maithili has some vowel segments whose quality is not constant. That is to say, it changes continually while the vowel is being uttered. The technical term for a vowel of continually changing quality is a 'diphthong'. Maithili has two such diphthongs, /əi/ and /əu/, and both of them are phonologically distinctive. They can be described and identified in terms of their beginning and ending points, which form a glide within one and the same syllable. Both Maithili diphthongs have their first element in the region of [ə] and their second element is either in the region of [i] or in that of [u]. Most of the stress associated with these diphthongs is concentrated on the first element, whereas the second element is only lightly sounded, although it is usually longer than the first element. The two diphthongs may briefly be described in the following way:

/əi/

For the production of the Maithili /əi/, the mouth remains in a position between half-close and half-open. The tongue glide begins at a central position, and then moves in the direction of the Maithili /i/, there being a slight closing movement of the lower jaw. The lips change from a neutral to a loosely spread position; the soft palate is in a raised position and as a result air escapes only through the oral cavity.

/əu/

For the production of the Maithili /əu/, the mouth position remains between half-close and half-open. The tongue glide begins at a central position, and then moves in the direction of the Maithili /u/, there being a slight closing movement of the lower jaw. The lips are neutral for the first element, i.e. for [ə], but they have a tendency to round on the second element: [u]. During the production of this diphthong the soft palate remains in a raised position and as a result air escapes only through the oral cavity.

The two Maithili diphthongs, /əi/ and /əu/, show full phonological contrast in all word positions. For example:

Initial	Medial
/'əik^{h}ən/ 'at this time'	/kəil/ 'of white colour'
/'əuk^{h}ən/ 'even at this time'	/kəul$^{(h)}$/ 'small mill'

Final
/kəhəl'kəi/ 'someone said (something to a third person)'
'kəhəl'kəu/ 'someone said (something to a second person)'

The acoustic analysis of these diphthongs is done in the fourth chapter of this study.

2.2 Summary

To summarise, Maithili has a total of eighteen phonologically distinctive vowel segments: i.e. eight oral vowels, eight nasal vowels, and two oral diphthongs. The length of vowels is not phonemic in this language, but the language does use both long and short allophonic variants of all its eight oral vowels and also of the following four of its nasal vowels [ĩ ə̃ õ ũ]. The long allophonic variants occur primarily in stressed syllables; the short ones occur in unstressed syllables. A final summary of the Maithili oral and nasal vowels as well as of their major allophonic variants is given in Figure 2.4.

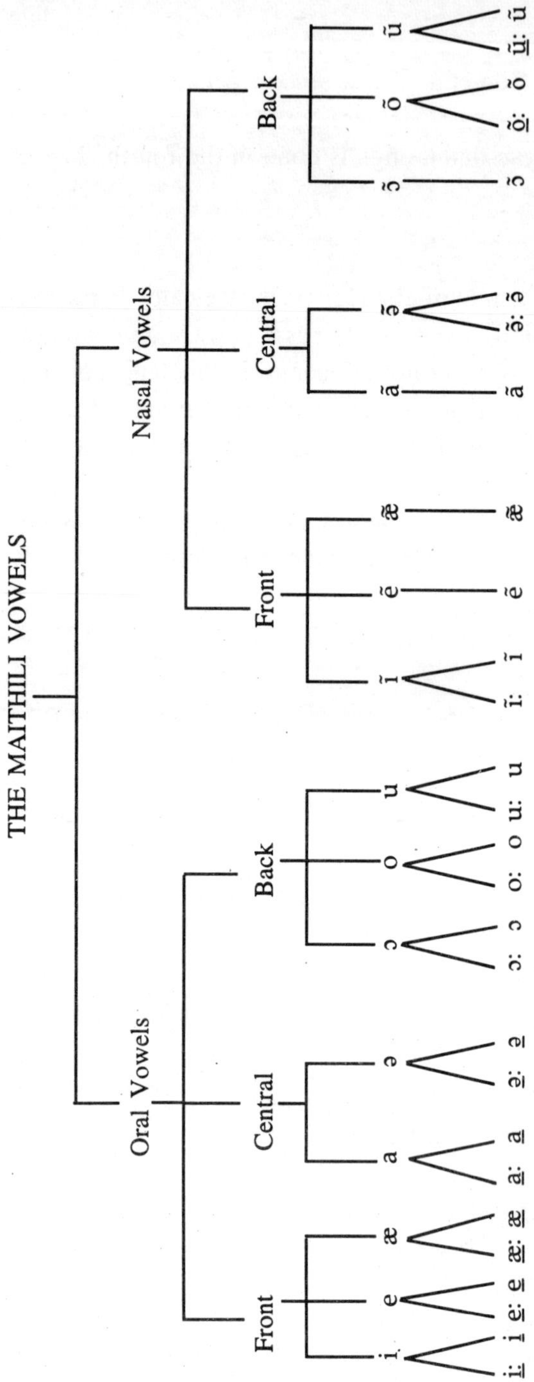

Figure 2.4: The Mithili oral and nasal vowels and their major allophonic variants.

Chapter 3

THE MAITHILI CONSONANTS

3.0 Introduction

Consonants can be defined in terms of both phonetics and phonology. Phonetically, consonants are sounds made by a closure or narrowing in the vocal tract so that the air flow is either completely blocked or so restricted that some audible frication is produced. Consonant articulations are relatively easy to feel and determine by such means as palatography or x-rays, and as a result are most conveniently described in terms of place and manner of articulation. From a phonological point of view, consonants are those units which typically function at the margins of syllables, either singally or in clusters. The present chapter looks into all types of phonologically distinctive consonant sounds in Maithili and puts forward their description, classification and phonemic analysis.

3.1 Description, Classification and Phonemic Analysis of the Maithili Consonants

Like the consonants of other languages, the Maithili consonants are formed when the airstream through the vocal tract is obstructed in some way. These consonants can therefore be described and classified primarily according to the place and manner of this articulation. When classified according to their places of articulation, the Maithili consonants can be grouped into eight main categories: (1) bilabial, (2) dental, (3) alveolar, (4) retroflex, (5) palate-alveolar, (6) palatal, (7) velar and (8) glottal; when classified according to their manner of articulation, these consonants can be grouped into five main categories: (1) stops, (2) affricates, (3) fricatives, (4) nasals and (5) approximants.

3.1.1 *The Stops in Maithili*

Stops refer to any speech sound which is produced by a complete closure in the vocal tract, and thus traditionally includes the class of plosives. The complete articulation of stop consonants consists of three stages: (1) the *closing* stage, (2) the *compression* stage, and (3) the *release* or *explosion* stage. The closing stage is the one during which the articulating organs move together in order to form the obstruction; the compression stage is the one during which lung action compresses the air behind the closure—this stage may or may not be accompanied by vibration of the vocal cards; the release or explosion stage is the one during which the organs forming the obstruction part rapidly, allowing the compressed air to escape abruptly. The stops in Maithili may be grouped into four main categories in accordance with their different places of articulation in the vocal tract: i.e. bilabial, dental, retroflex and velar.

3.1.1.1 *The Bilabial Stops*

Bilabial consonants are those that are produced by a combined movement of both lips—i.e. in their articulation the two lips closely approach or touch each other. There are four phonologically distinctive bilabial stops in Maithili: /p/, /p^h/, /b/ and /b^h/. In the production of each one of them the soft palate is raised and the nasal resonator is shut off, the primary obstruction to the airstream is provided by the closure of the lips. Lung air is compressed behind this closure, during which stage the vocal cords are held wide apart for /p/ and /p^h/, but they vibrate for all or part of the compression stage for /b/ and b^h/ according to their situation in the utterance. The air escapes with force when the lip closure is released. All the four bilabial stops / p p^h b b^h/ show full phonological contrast in all word positions: initial, medial and final. For example:

Initial	Medial	Final
/par/'end'; 'across'	/ə'pər/ 'upper'	/sap/ 'snake'
/p^{h}ar/ 'ploughshare'	/ə'p^{h}ər/ 'suffocate'	/sap^h/ 'clean'
/bar/ 'light (imp.)'	/sə'bək/ 'task'	/ǰib/ 'soul'; 'live'
/b^{h}ar/ 'weight'	/sə'b^{h}ək/ 'of everyone'	/ǰib^h/ 'tongue'

3.1.1.2 *The Dental Stops*

Dental consonants are those that are produced with the tip and/or blade of the tongue touching the upper front teeth and alveolar ridge. There are four phonologically distinctive dental stops in Maithili: /t/, /t^h/, /d/ and /d^h/. In the articulation of these dental stops the velum is raised and the nasal resonator is shut off, the primary obstruction to the airstream is formed by a closure made between the tip, blade and rims of the tongue and the upper front and side teeth and the alveolar ridge. Lung air is compressed behind this closure, during which stage the vocal cords are wide apart for /t/ and /t^h/, but they vibrate for all or part of the compression stage for /d/ and /d^h/ according to their situation in the utterance. All the four dental stops in Maithili show full phonological contrast in all word positions: initial, medial and final. For example:

Initial	Medial	Final
/tan/ 'pull'	/'patər/ 'thin'	/pat/ 'leaf'
/t^{h}an/ 'roll of cloth'	/'pat^{h}ər/ 'stone'	/pat^h/'shape (imp.)'
/dan/ 'charity'	/u'dar/'generous'	/bad/ 'after'
/d^{h}an/ 'paddy'	/u'd^{h}ar/ 'on credit'	/bad^h/'land surrounding a village'

3.1.1.3 *The Retroflex Stops*

Retroflex consonants are those that are made when the tip of the tongue is curled back in the direction of the front part of the hard palate—i.e. just behind the alveolar ridge. There are four phonologically distinctive retroflex stops in Maithili: /ṭ/, /ṭ^h/, /ḍ/ and /ḍ^h/. In the articulation of these stops the velum is raised and the nasal resonator is shut off, the primary obstruction to the airstream is formed by a closure made between the tip and rims of the tongue and the upper hard palate and side teeth. Lung air is compressed behind this closure, during which stage the vocal cords are wide apart for /ṭ/ and /ṭ^h/, but they vibrate for all or part of the compression stage for /ḍ/ and /ḍ^h/ according to their situation in the utterance. Of the four retroflex stops in Maithili, /ṭ/ and /ṭ^h/ show full phonological contrast in all word positions, but the remaining /ḍ/ and /ḍ^h/ show phonological opposition mainly word-initially. For example:

Initial	Medial	Final
/ṭop/'helmet'	/'paṭi/ 'wooden board'	/kaṭ/ 'cut (imp.)'
/ṭ^{h}op/'drop (n)'	/'paṭ^{h}i/ 'she goat'	/kaṭ^h/ 'wood'
/ḍah/'jealousy'	- - - -	- - - -
/ḍ^{h}ah/'knock down (imp.)'	- - - -	- - - -

It has to be mentioned that even though /ḍ/ and /ḍ^h/ do not show phonological contrast in word-medial and word-final positions, /ḍ/ does nevertheless occur in those word positions. Moreover, be it word-medially or word-finally, /ḍ/ is always preceded by the nasal consonant /n/, which is assimilated to the retroflex place of articulation of /ḍ/. For example:

Medial	Final
/'ənḍa/ 'egg'	/'kanḍ/ 'canto'
/'pənḍa/ 'a priest'	/'kʰənḍ/ 'part'; 'piece'
/'gənḍa/ 'useless'	/'pinḍ/ 'homage to the dead'

3.1.1.4 *The Velar Stops*

Velar consonants are those that are made by the back of the tongue against the soft palate. There are four phonologically distinctive velar stops in Maithili: /k/, /kʰ/, /g/ and /gʰ/. In the articulation of these stops the velum is raised and the nasal resonator is shut off, the primary obstruction to the airstream is formed by a closure made between the back of the tongue and the soft palate. Lung air is compressed behind this closure, during which stage the vocal cords are wide apart for /k/ and /kʰ/, but they vibrate for all or part of the compression stage for /g/ and /gʰ/ according to their situation in the utterance. All the four velar stops in Maithili show full phonological contrast in all word positions. For example:

Initial	Medial	Final
/kas/ 'a kind of grass'	/sə 'kar/ 'confession'	/sik/ 'reed'
/kʰas/ 'special'	/sə'kʰar/ 'big box'	/sikʰ/ 'learn (imp.)'
/gam/ 'village'	/'ugrəl/ 'surplus'	/bag/ 'garden'
/gʰam/ 'sweat'	/'ugʰrəl/'unveiled'	/bagʰ/ 'tiger'

3.1.2 *The Affricates in Maithili*

The term 'affricate' refers to a speech sound that is made when the air-pressure behind a complete closure in the vocal tract is gradually released; the initial release produces a plosive, but the separation which follows is sufficiently slow to produce audible frication—i.e. frication sufficiently audible to be used contrastively in the phonology—and there is thus a fricative element in this kind of speech sound. However, the duration of the frication is usually not as long as would be in the case of an independent fricative consonant. It is thus the combination of plosion and frication which identifies an affricate. There are four phonologically distinctive affricate consonants in Maithili: /č/,/č^{h}/, /ǰ/ and /ǰ^{h}/.

In the articulation of these Maithili affricates the velum is raised and the nasal resonator is shut off, the obstruction to the airstream is formed by a closure made between the tip, blade, and rims of the tongue and the palato-alveolar region and side teeth. At the same time, the front of the tongue is raised towards the hard palate in readiness for the fricative release. The closure is released slowly, and the air escapes in a diffuse manner over the whole of the central surface of the tongue with frication occurring between the blade/front region of the tongue and the plato-alveolar section of the roof of the mouth. During both stop and fricative stages, the vocal cords are wide apart for /č/ and /č^{h}/, but they vibrate for all or part of /ǰ/ and /ǰ^{h}/ according to their situation in the utterance. All the four affricates in Maithili show full phonological contrast in all word positions. For example:

Initial	Medial	Final
/čor/ 'thief'	/ə'čar/ 'pickle'	/bič/ 'centre'
/č^{h}or/ 'edge'	/ə'č^{h}ar/ 'shower'	/bič^{h}/ 'pick up (imp)'
/ǰor/ 'strength'	/'baǰəl/ 'spoke'	/biǰ/ 'seed'
/ǰ^{h}or/ 'soup'	/'baǰ^{h}əl/ 'trapped'; 'entangled'	/biǰ^{h}/ 'rust'

3.1.3 *The Fricatives in Maithili*

A fricative consonant is one that is made when two speech organs come so close together that the airstream escaping between them produces frication sufficiently audible to be used contrastively in the phonology. There is no complete closure between the organs. Indeed, there is simply a stricture, or narrowing of the organs. Maithili has two phonologically distinctive fricative sounds: i.e. the alveolar fricative /s/ and the glottal fricative /h/.

In the articulation of the Maithili alveolar fricative /s/ the velum is raised and the nasal resonator is shut off, the tip and blade of the tongue make a light contact with the upper alveolar ridge, and the side rims of the tongue make a close contact with the upper side teeth. The airstream escapes by means of a narrow groove in the centre of the tongue and causes frication between the tongue and the alveolar ridge. There is very little opening between the teeth and the frication is voiceless.

In the articulation of the Maithili glottal fricative /h/ the air is expelled from the lungs with considerable pressure, causing some frication throughout the vocal tract, the upper part of which is shaped in readiness for the articulation of the following vowel. In other words, as regards the position of the tongue, lips, soft palate, and the configuration of the pharynx, the Maithili /h/ is simply the voiceless counterpart of the following speech sound. Thus differing types of frication will be heard for /h/ in the Maithili words with such sequences as, for example: /hit/ 'benefit', /hatʰ/ 'hand', /hur/ 'thrust', and so on. The frication is therefore largely of the mouth cavity type—in most cases, associated with the nature of the following vowel.

The Maithili fricatives /s/ and /h/ show full phonological contrast in all word positions. For example:

Initial	Medial	Final
/saṭ/ 'paste (imp.)'	/o'sar/ 'corridor'	/kas/ 'a kind of grass'
/haṭ/ 'market'	/o'har/ 'cover (n)'	/kah/ 'dirt'

3.1.4 *The Nasals in Maithili*

The term 'nasal' refers to those speech sounds that are produced while the soft palate is lowered to allow an audible escape of air through the nose. Both consonants and vowels may be articulated in this way. Nasal consonants occur when there is a complete closure in the mouth, and all the air escapes through the nose. There are three phonologically distinctive nasal consonants in Maithili: /m/, /n/ and /ŋ/. In the articulation of /m/, /n/ and /ŋ/, the closures occur in bilabial, alveolar and velar positions, respectively.

In the articulation of the Maithili bilabial nasal /m/ the lips form a closure as for /p b/; the soft palate is lowered, adding the resonance of the nasal cavity to those of the pharynx and the mouth chamber closed by the lips; the tongue generally anticipates or retains the position of the adjacent speech sound. In the articulation of the Maithili alveolar nasal /n/ the tip and rims of the tongue form a closure with the upper alveolar ridge just behind the teeth ridge and upper side teeth; the soft palate is lowered, adding the resonance of the nasal cavity to those of the pharynx and of that part of the mouth chamber behind the alveolar closure; the lip position depends upon that of adjacent vowels. In the articulation of the Maithili velar nasal /ŋ/ a closure is formed in the mouth between the back of the tongue and the velum as for /k g/. The actual point of closure will depend on the type of vowel preceding /ŋ/; the soft palate is lowered, adding the resonance of the nasal cavity to that of the pharynx and the above-mentioned part of the mouth chamber behind the velar closure; the lip position depends upon that of the preceding vowel.

Of the three nasal consonants in Maithili, /m/ and /n/ show full phonological opposition in all word positions. For example:

Initial	Medial	Final
/mam/ 'mother's brother'	/'nami/'famous'	/tam/ 'copper'
/nam/'name'	/'nani/'mother's mother'	/tan/ 'pull'

But the velar nasal /ŋ/ shows phonological opposition with /m/ and /n/ only in two positions: i.e. word-medially and word-finally. For example:

Medial	Final
/'kəŋhi/ 'comb'	/səŋ/ 'together'; 'with'
/'kəmhi/ 'the period of being away from work'	/səm/ 'equal'; 'like'
/kənhi/ 'a one-eyed female'	/sən/ 'similar'

3.1.5 *The Approximants in Maithili*

'Approximant' is a general term used by some phoneticians (e.g. Ladefoged, 1971 and 1975/1982) in the classification of speech sounds on the basis of their manner of articulation, and corresponding to what in other approaches (e.g. Abercrombie, 1967; Gimson, 1970) would be called 'frictionless continuant'. The term is based on the articulations involved, in that one articulator approaches another, but the degree of narrowing involved does not produce audible frication. Approximant consonants may be classified into two further groups: 'central' and 'lateral'. Maithili has both central and lateral approximant consonants.

A central approximant is one that is made by the approach of one articulator towards another, but without the oral tract being narrowed to such an extent that a turbulent airstream is produced,. There are four phonologically distinctive approximant consonants in Maithili: /w/, /y/

/r/ and /ṛ/. Of these, /w/ and /y/ are semi-vowels; /ṛ/ is a tap and /ṛ/ is a flap.

Semi-vowels are sometimes called glides because they are produced by gliding the tongue toward or away from a more prominent adjacent vowel. Maithili has two phonologically distinctive semi-vowels: i.e. the bilabial /w/ and the palatal /y/. Their articulation involves a constriction of the oral cavity which is greater than that for the highest vowels (i.e. /i/ and /u/) but not great enough to produce frication. In the articulation of /w/ the tongue assumes the position for a back half-close to close vowel—depending upon the degree of openness of the following speech sound—and moves away immediately to the position of the following speech sound; the lips are rounded; the soft palate is raised and the vocal cords usually vibrate. In the articulation of /y/ the tongue assumes the position for a front half-close to close vowel—depending on the degree of openness of the following speech sound—and moves away immediately to the position of the following speech sound; the lips are generally neutral or spread, but may anticipate the lip-rounding of the following vowel; the soft palate is raised and the vocal cords usually vibrate.

Both /w/ and /y/ show phonological opposition in word-initial and word-medial positions. For example:

Initial	Medial
/war/ 'strike'; 'hit'	/pwar/ 'straw'
/yar/ 'friend'	/pyar/ 'love'

It should be made clear that both /y/ and /w/ are used mostly by educated Maithili speakers. In colloquial speech, however, most uneducated native speakers often replace the pronunciation of /y/ by /ǰ/ and of /w/ by /b/ or /o/. There are three main phonological contexts in which /y/ is realised as /ǰ/: i.e. (1) when it occurs word-initially, as /yəs/ ~[ǰə:s] 'fame'; (2) when it occurs immediately after /r/, as /'kəryə/~['kə:rǰə] 'debt'; and (3) when it occurs immediately after /h/, as /'səhyə/ ~ ['sə:hǰə] 'bearable'. All these cases where /y/ is realised as /ǰ/ can in fact be stated by means of just one informal rule as given below:

(1)

$$y \text{----------} > \check{j} / \left\{ \begin{array}{l} \# \text{---------} \\ r \text{---------} \\ h \text{---------} \end{array} \right\}$$

Similarly, whenever /w/ is spoken in colloquial speech, it is usually realised either as [b], such as /'widya/ ~ ['bidya:] 'learning, education', or as [o], if the words where it occurs are of non-Sanskrit origin, such as /wə'kil/ ~[o'ki:1] 'a lawyer'. But whenever /w/ occurs in words of CwV syllable structure, it is always realised as [w].

The Maithili tap, /r/, is produced by an obstruction which the tongue makes in a single tap against the alveolar ridge; the Maithili flap, /ṛ/ , is produced by a single rapid contact of the tongue with the retroflex. Both /r/ and /ṛ/ show phonological contrasts in word-medial and word-final positions. For example:

Medial	Final
/'kəru/ '(please) do'	/har/ 'necklace'
/'kəṛu/ 'hot (e.g. food)'	/haṛ/ 'bone'

The term 'lateral' refers to a consonant sound which is articulated by means of a partial closure, on one or both sides of which the airstream is able to escape through the mouth. In Maithili /l/ is a phonologically distinctive consonant segment. In the articulation of the Maithili /l/ the soft palate is in a raised position, shutting off the nasal resonator, the tip and blade of the tongue come in contact with the alveolar ridge, allowing the air to escape on both sides or, in the case of a unilateral tongue-rim closure on the upper side teeth, on one side. Both /l/ and /r/ show full phonological opposition in all word positions. For example:

Initial	Medial	Final
/laǰ/ 'shame'	/mala/ 'garland'	/mal/ 'cattle'; 'goods'
/raǰ/ 'nation, state'	/mara/ 'a kind of fish'	/mar/ 'beat (imp.)'

3.2 Summary

Thus, we have established in this chapter that Maithili has a total of thirty consonant phonemes: /p pʰ b bʰ t tʰ d dʰ ṭ ṭʰ ḍ ḍʰ k kʰ g gʰ č čʰ ǰ ǰʰ s h m n ŋ w y r ṛ l/. These Maithili consonants are summarised and presented in a chart given in Figure 3.1. The customary chart includes: (1) the place of articulation parameter shown horizontally, (2) the manner of articulation parameter shown vertically, and (3) a pairing of consonantal types to show the voiceless variety on the left and the voiced variety on the right.

Table 3.1.: Chief Maithili consonantal articulations.

Manners of Articulation \ Places of Articulation			Bilabial	Dental	Alveolar	Retroflex	Palato-alveolar	Palatal	Velar	Glottal
Stops		Unaspirated	p b	t d		ṭ ḍ			k g	
		Aspirated	pʰ bʰ	tʰ dʰ		ṭʰ ḍʰ			kʰ gʰ	
Affricates		Unaspirated					č ǰ			
		Aspirated					čʰ ǰʰ			
Fricatives					s					h
Nasals		Unaspirated	m		n				ŋ	
		Aspirated								
Approximants	Central	Unaspirated	w		r	ṛ		y		
		Aspirated								
	Lateral	Unaspirated			l					
		Aspirated								

Chapter 4

ACOUSTIC ANALYSIS OF THE MAITHILI VOWELS

4.0 Introduction

There has been a long tradition among phoneticians (e.g. Bell, 1867; Sweet, 1877; Jones, 1956a; Ladefoged, 1964, 1967, 1971 and 1975/ 1982; Abercrombie, 1967; Gimson, 1970; Robins, 1971; Catford, 1977) to describe the vowels of a language both impressionistically and in terms of articulatory movements—e.g. the height of the body of the tongue, the front-back position of the tongue, the raised-lowered position of the velum, and the degree of lip rounding. It is generally acknow-ledged (e.g. Ladefoged, 1967: 62-75; Catford, 1981) that the 'traditional' classification of vowels in terms of 'horizontal' and 'vertical' tongue-position was invented by Melville Bell (1867) and further developed and popularised by Henry Sweet (1877). It is this 'Bell-Sweet' model of vowel production and system of classification that underlies most modern description of vowels, including the system of Cardinal Vowels developed by Daniel Jones and used by the International Phonetic Association (IPA).

Daniel Jones' system of cardinal vowels is a set of standard reference points to provide a precise means of identifying the vowel sounds of a language. It is primarily based on a combination of both articulatory and auditory judgements, and it also has its validity when judged on an acoustic scale (e.g. Catford, 1981: 27). Despite some marginal inadequacies (e.g. see Ladefoged, 1967: 75-103, and 1975: 194-199; Catford 1981, for more details), the cardinal vowel system works fairly successfully, and it has allowed the vowels of a large number of languages to be described with far greater precision than has any other method.

However, with the emergence of various instrumental methods of investigation, especially with the advent of refined methods of acoustic analysis of speech, various phoneticians (e.g. Russell, 1928 and 1936; Joos, 1948; Ladefoged, 1967 and 1976) have criticised the tongue-position model of vowel description and classification. Like Russell (1928), Ladefoged (e.g. 1976) criticised the tongue-position model on the basis of its non-correspondence with x-ray data. A good deal of evidence apparently supporting this type of criticism has also been presented by Sidney Wood (1975 and 1977). But relatively recent evidences (e.g. Lindau, 1978) suggest that linguistic phonetic aspects of vowels may in fact be described in both articulatory and acoustic terms. In a recent publication, Ladefoged (1980: 485) has now modified his earlier position (i.e. the position held in Ladefoged, 1967: 84-85, and 1971: 69-71) by saying that "linguistic phonetic aspects of languages can be described in terms of about 17 articulatory parameters, and/or a similar number of acoustic parameters". In other words, Ladefoged now holds that both sets of parameters are essential for necessary linguistic phonetic descriptions.

In the second chapter we have described all the phonologically distinctive oral and nasal vowels and oral diphthongs in Maithili mainly by stating how they are made. But it is also possible to describe them in terms of what we can hear. The way in which we hear a sound largely depends on its acoustic structure. In the present chapter an attempt is made to put forward an acoustic description of all the oral and nasal vowels as well as of the two phonologically distinctive oral diphthongs in Maithili. The main objectives of the present study are to determine: (1) the frequencies of the first three formants of the oral and nasal vowels and diphthongs in Maithili; (2) the duration of these vowels and diphthongs in various contexts; (3) the effect of nasalisation on vowel formants; and (4) the similarities and differences between the acoustic properties of these oral and nasal vowels. Before we embark upon our discussions on these areas, a few words must first be said about the experimental method used to carry out the present acoustic study.

4.1 Experimental Method

4.1.1 *Test Utterances*

As stated earlier in the second chapter, Maithili has a total of 18 phonologically distinctive vowel phonemes: i.e. 8 oral vowels, 8 nasal vowels and 2 oral diphthongs. Since the phoneme is primarily an abstract concept, it cannot be analysed acoustically. However, the main acoustic realisations of the phoneme can be analysed, and one can determine the acoustic correlates of such abstract units. In order to carry out an analysis of the main acoustic realisations of the Maithili vowels, a list of these oral and nasal vowels as well as of the oral diphthongs was prepared, keeping the vowels and diphthongs both in isolation and in word contexts. The words were mainly monosyllabic and of the CV(C) type. Each test utterance was put in a sentence context (the frame of the sentence being /'pʰero. . . 'uččaṛəṇ kə'ru/ 'Please pronounce . . . again') and it was spoken at a normal conversational speed. All the test utterances used in this study are listed in Table 4.1. It should also be stated that most of the Maithili vowels in isolation are used as morphemes, and in principle each one of them can be used as a 'free' or 'bound' morpheme in this language.

4.1.2 *Apparatus Used*

Nine tokens of each test utterance were recorded in a soundproof studio of Essex University. All these recordings were made on a Revox B 77 tape-recorder. Of the nine tokens of each test utterance, the first two as well as the last two tokens were ignored, and all the remaining five tokens from the middle were used to obtain visual records in the form of spectrograms. Wideband spectrograms and wideband 'sections' (i.e. short-term spectrum) of each of the five tokens were made on a Sona-Graph 6061-B Sound Spectrograph.

4.1.3 *Formant Frequency and Duration Measurements*

The formant frequency of each token was measured from wideband spectrograms, since these were found to offer the most convenient way of locating the centre frequency of each formant. In determining the centre of F_1 of some of the tokens of vowels / æ a ɔ/ some difficulties were encountered, mainly because of the presence of high amplitudes at lower frequencies. In cases presenting such difficulties, the formant frequency was determined by a comparison between the wideband spectrograms and the wideband 'sections'.

Duration measurements were made from all the five tokens of each test utterance as recorded in various contexts and speaking rates. Formant frequency and duration measurements were made to the nearest 20 Hz and 5 ms, respectively. In the remainder of this chapter, we shall present our results of and discussions on this spectrographic study. Our main conclusions are summarised at the end of this chapter.

Table 4.1: List of the Maithili vowels spoken in isolation and in words.

1 Vowels in isolation		2 Vowels in words		3 Oral and nasal vowels contrasted in words
<u>Oral:</u>		<u>Oral:</u>		
/i/	/e/	/sir/ 'root'	/ser/ 'kilogramme'	/čʰiṭ/ 'scatter'
/æ/	/a/	/sær/ 'walk'	/sar/ 'wife's brother'	/čʰĩṭ/ 'garment dyed with spots'
/ə/	/ɔ/	/sər/ 'arrow'; 'sir'	/sɔr/ 'sky'	/bʰeṭ/ 'see'; 'get in touch'
/o/	/u/	/sor/ 'noise'	/sur/ 'brave'; 'tune'	/bʰẽṭ/ 'a kind of flower-seed'
<u>Nasal:</u>		<u>Nasal:</u>		
/ĩ/	/ẽ/	/čʰĩṭ/ 'garment dyed with spots	/čʰẽṭ/'surplus (e.g. of grain)'	/bʰæt/ 'will become' /bʰæ̃t/ 'kind'; 'type'
/æ̃/	/ã/	/sæ̃/ 'husband; lover'	/hãs/ 'goose'	/bas/ 'shelter'; 'dwelling place'
/ə̃/	/ɔ̃/	/hə̃s/ 'laugh (imp.)'	/sɔ̃/ 'from'	/bãs/ 'bamboo'
/õ/	/ũ/	/ḍʰõṛʰ/ 'a kind of snake'	/ḍʰũṛʰ/ 'search (imp.)'	/'kəṭgər/ 'commendable; adequate' /'kə̃ṭgər/ 'thorny'
<u>Diphthongs:</u>		<u>Diphthongs:</u>		
/əi/	/əu/	/'əikʰən/ 'at this time'	/'əukʰən/ 'even at this time'	/gɔt/ 'will sing' /gɔ̃t/ '(cattle) urine'
		/kəil/ 'of a white colour'	/kəul⁽ʰ⁾/'small mill'	/gʰoṭ/ 'mix (imp.)' /gʰõṭ/ 'swallow (imp.)'
		/dəl'kəi/ 'someone gave (something to a 3rd person)'	/del'kəu/ 'someone gave (something to a 2nd person)'	/kə'hu/ '(please) say' /kə'hũ/ 'somewhere'; 'in case'

4.2 Results and Discussions

For a systematic presentation of the results of this spectrographic study as well as of our discussions on these results, the contents of the present section are grouped into three categories. In the first category, we deal with the oral vowels in Maithili; in the second, we deal with its nasal vowels; and in the third, we deal with its oral diphthongs.

4.2.1 *The Oral Vowels in Maithili*

Our results and discussions of the present sub-section concern: (1) the formant frequency measurements, and (2) the duration measurements of the oral vowels in Maithili.

4.2.1.1 *Formant Frequency Measurement Results and Discussions*

In this study the formant frequency measurements of all Maithili vowels are done in Hz. Table 4.2 displays the average frequencies, i.e. frequency values averaged between the five tokens of each vowel, of the first three formants for the Maithili oral vowels spoken in isolation. The broken lines shown at the end of Table 4.2 indicate that it was not possible to ascertain the frequencies of F_3 in any of the five tokens for the vowel /u/. Table 4.3 presents the average frequency values of the first three formants for these oral vowels spoken in words.

The average frequencies of F_1, F_2 and F_3—as given in Tables 4.2 and 4.3 below—are represented graphically in Figures 4.1 and 4.2, and in doing this some slight degree of approximation is introduced. In both

Table 4.2: The average frequency values of the first three formants for the Maithili oral vowels spoken in isolation (in Hz).

Vowel	F_1	F_2	F_3
/i/	258	2456	3260
/e/	412	2284	3114
/æ/	646	1674	2410
/a/	672	1280	2328
/ə/	480	1088	2350
/ɔ/	568	870	2264
/o/	410	774	2378
/u/	308	626	------

Table 4.3: The average frequency values of the first three formants for the Maithili oral vowels spoken in words (in Hz).

Vowel	Word with gloss	F_1	F_2	F_3
/i/	/sir/ 'root'	310	2494	3450
/e/	/ser/ 'kilogramme'	418	1920	2578
/æ/	/sær/ 'walk'	664	1670	2458
/a/	/sar/ 'wife's brother,	688	1398	2448
/ə/	/sər/ 'arrow'; 'sir'	514	1322	2486
/ɔ/	/sɔr/ 'sky'	596	906	2538
/o/	/sor/ 'noise'	432	896	2404
/u/	/sur/ 'brave'; 'tune'	328	852	2368

figures the vertical scale shows the frequencies in Hz and the horizontal scale lists the vowels. As the figures show, each oral vowel in Maithili is sufficiently distinguished from the others by the first two characteristic formants—i.e. F_1 and F_2. The overall pattern of these average frequencies is very similar in both figures. That is, in both figures the F_2 frequency goes downwards throughout the series / i e æ a ə ɔ o u/. The F_1 frequency goes up for the first four vowels /i e æ a/, and then down for the last three / ɔ o u/. Similarly, the F_3 frequency goes downwards for the vowels /i e æ a/ in that order, and then again down for the last three / ɔ o u/ in that order.

Although these overall patterns are there in both figures, the actual average-frequency values do differ in the two figures. The actual frequency values for all the vowels in Figure 4.1 differ from those in Figure 4.2 in that the latter shows the effects of the consonantal environments, i.e. /s—r/, on these vowels as they occur in the Maithili words: /sir/, /ser/, /sær/, /sar/, /sər/, /sɔr/, /sor/ and /sur/, respectively. The average frequency values of F_1 for all the vowels spoken in isolation are slightly less than what they are when the same vowels are spoken in the above words. Except the vowels /e/ and /æ/, the F_2 frequencies for the remaining six vowels / i a ə ɔ o u/ remain relatively higher when they are spoken in words than when spoken in isolation. As for the average frequency values of F_3, the differences in both figures are such that any significant generalisations do not seem to be possible.

The average frequency values of F_1 and F_2 for all the vowels in Tables

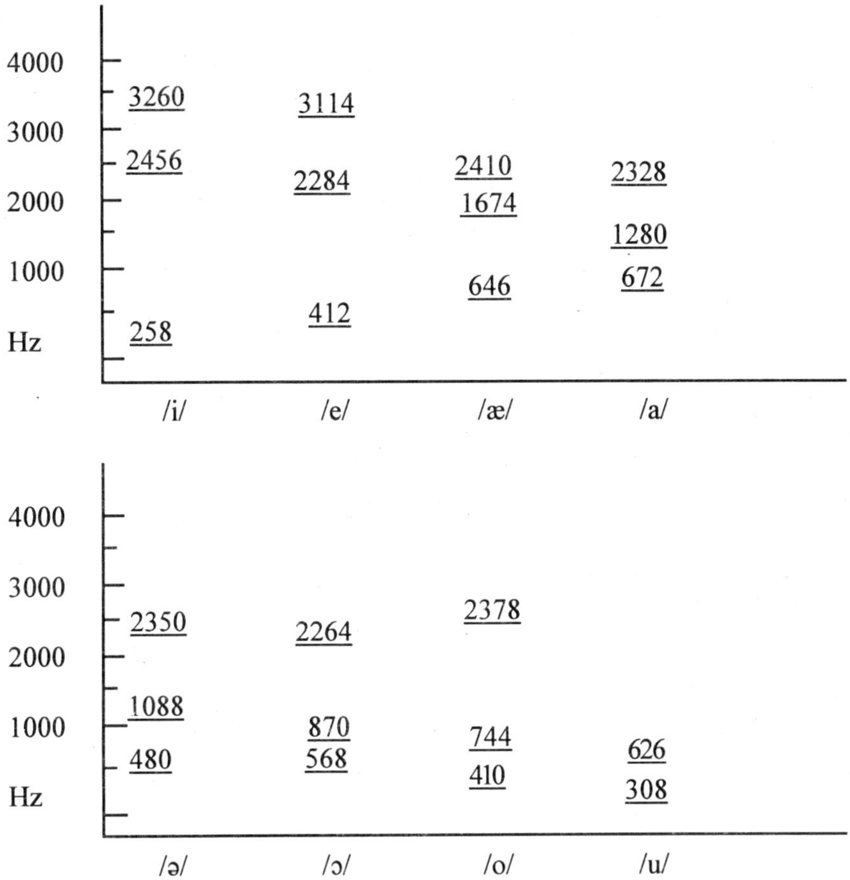

Figure 4.1: The average frequency values for the first three formants for the eight oral vowels in Maithili spoken in isolation.

4.2 and 4.3 are also plotted on a formant chart in Figure 4.3 for a comparison between these vowels spoken both in isolation and in words. Since the F_1 frequency is inversely related to vowel height, in Figure 4.3 the F_1 frequency for all the vowels is plotted on the vertical axis with the frequency of F_2 on the horizontal axis. The dots linked in the figure by connected lines are for the vowels spoken in isolation, while those linked by broken lines are for the same vowels spoken in words. The figure shows more 'peripheral extreme' (i.e. less centralised) articulation

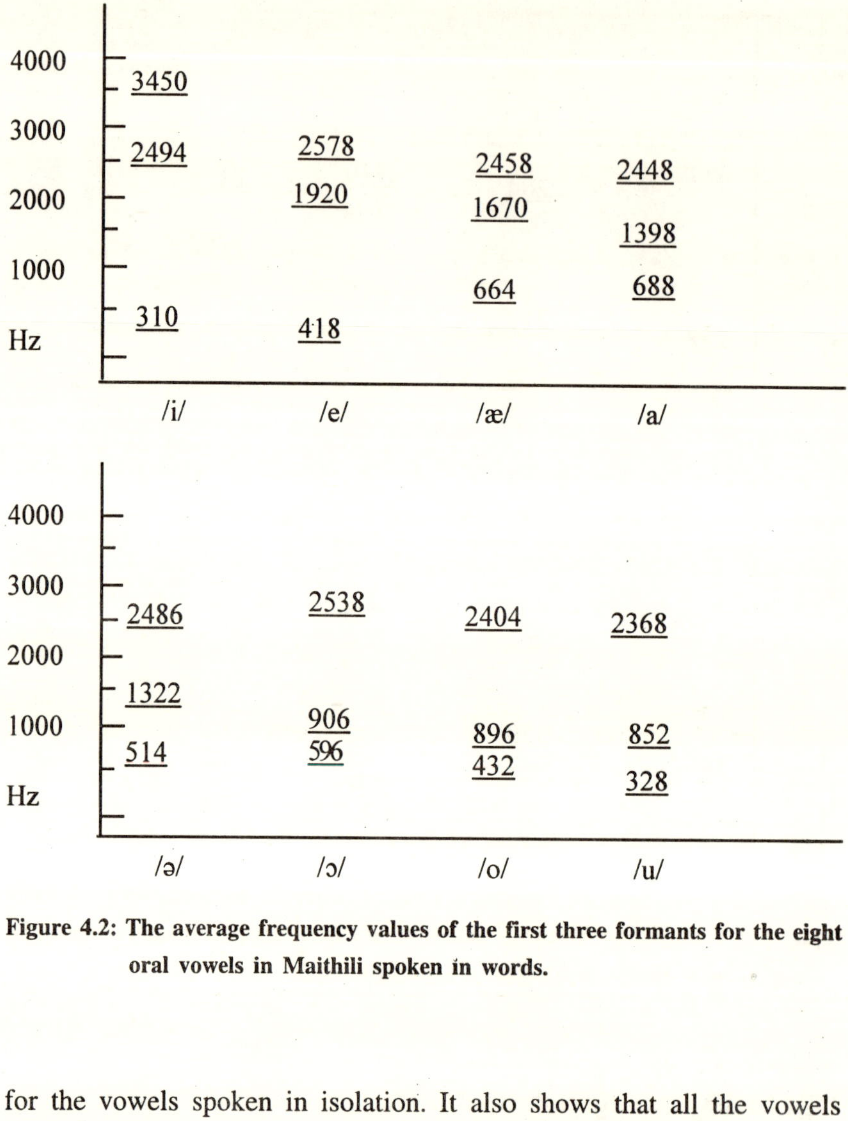

Figure 4.2: The average frequency values of the first three formants for the eight oral vowels in Maithili spoken in words.

for the vowels spoken in isolation. It also shows that all the vowels maintain relatively higher 'vowel height' when spoken in isolation than when spoken in words. In other words, the F_1 frequency for each vowel is slightly less when spoken in isolation than when spoken in words. Except /e/ and /æ/, the F_2 frequencies for /i a ə ɔ o u/ remain relatively lower when spoken in isolation than when spoken in words. Thus, the major effects of the consonantal environments (i.e. /s—r/) on the positioning of these vowels (when spoken in words) are:

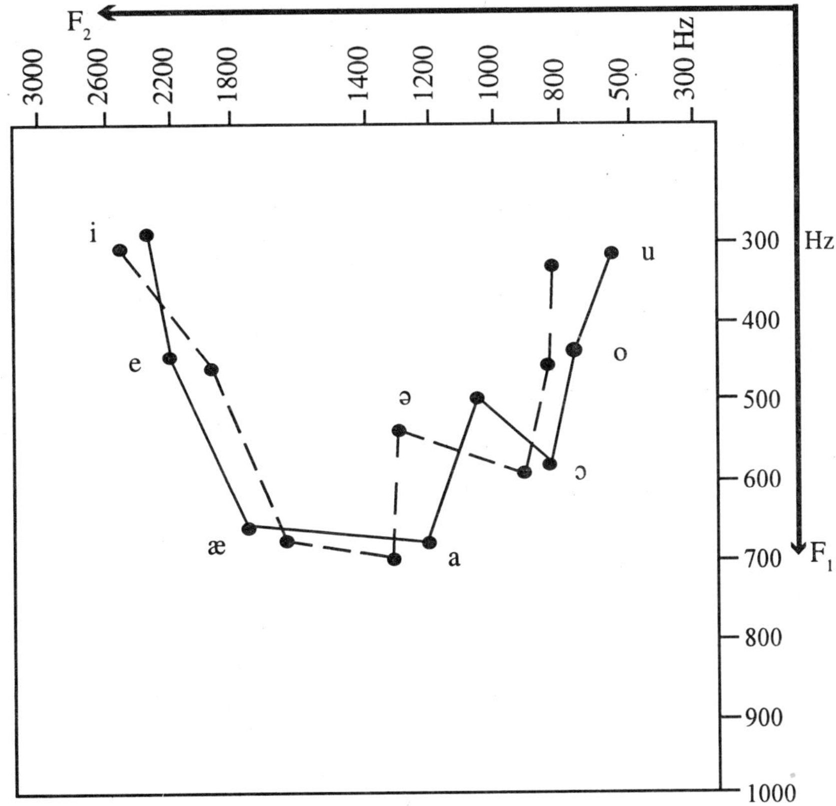

Figure 4.3: The average frequency values (in Hz) of F_1 and F_2 of the Maithili oral vowels spoken both in isolation (connected lines) and in words (broken lines).

(i) the 'height' of each of these vowels lowers slightly;
(ii) except /i/, the front vowels /e æ/ become less fronted;
(iii) the central vowels /a ə/ become more central—i.e. more fronted and less back; and
(iv) the back vowels /ɔ o u/ become less back.

Ladefoged (1967: 88-89) reports the fundamental frequency values as well as the frequency values of the first three formants for 31 sets of cardinal vowels as pronounced by 11 phoneticians of the School of Daniel

Table 4.4: The average frequency values of F_1 and F_2 for the 31 sets of cardinal vowels as reported in Ladefoged (1967: 88-89).

Formants \ Vowels	i	e	ɛ	a	ɑ	ɔ	o	u
F_1	360	489	707	949	807	622	487	354
F_2	1738	1669	1548	1377	981	889	796	718

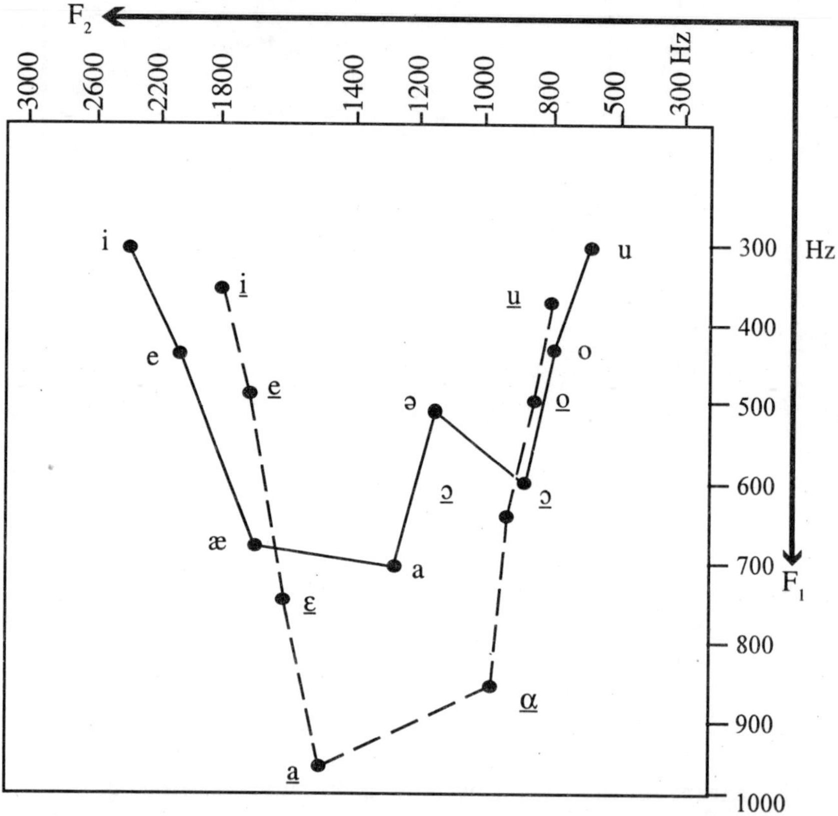

Figure 4.4: The average frequency values of F_1 and F_2 for the Maithili vowels spoken in isolation (connected lines) and those for the cardinal vowels (broken lines) as reported in Ladefoged (1967: 88-89).

Jones. The average frequency values of the first two formants for those 31 sets of cardinal vowels are made in Table 4.4. In Figure 4.4 a comparison is made between the average F_1 and F_2 frequencies for the Maithili vowels as given in Table 4.2 and those for the cardinal vowels as presented in Table 4.4. As Figure 4.4 shows, the F_1 frequencies for all cardinal vowels remain much higher than what they are for the Maithili vowels. Despite this difference there is, however, some similarity between the overall F_1 frequency-patterns of the Maithili front and back vowels, and those of the first three and last three cardinal vowels, respectively. That is to say, the proportion in which the F_1 frequencies of these Maithili vowels and cardinal vowels differ is very similar.

In a relatively recent study, Dave (1977: 215) presents the average frequency values of F_1 and F_2 for the Gujarati oral vowels as shown in Table 4.5 below:

Figure 4.5 presents a comparison between these average F_1 and F_2 frequency values for the Gujarati oral vowels (broken lines) and those for six of the eight Maithili oral vowels (connected lines). As the figure

Table 4.5: The average frequency values of F_1 and F_2 for the Gujarati oral vowels as reported in Dave (1977: 215).

Vowels / Formants	i	e	a	ə	o	u
F_1	263	420	747	603	493	313
F_2	2358	2200	1409	1330	770	721

shows, the F_1 frequency values for the Gujarati vowels are relatively higher than the F_1 frequency values for the Maithili vowels. The figure also shows that the Gujarati vowels /a ə o u/ have relatively higher F_2 frequency values, too, than what their Maithili counterparts have. In spite of these small differences, the overall pattern of the acoustic data for the vowels of the two languages is still very similar.

Mittal and Gupta (1971: 130) also studied the main acoustic realisations of the Hindi vowels. They present (*ibid.*) the average frequency values of F_1 and F_2 for the Hindi oral vowels /i e a ə ɔ o u/ spoken in words; their F_1 and F_2 frequency patterns are very similar to the patterns of the Maithili vowels shown earlier.

R. Yadav (1979a) has also done a spectrographic study of some di-

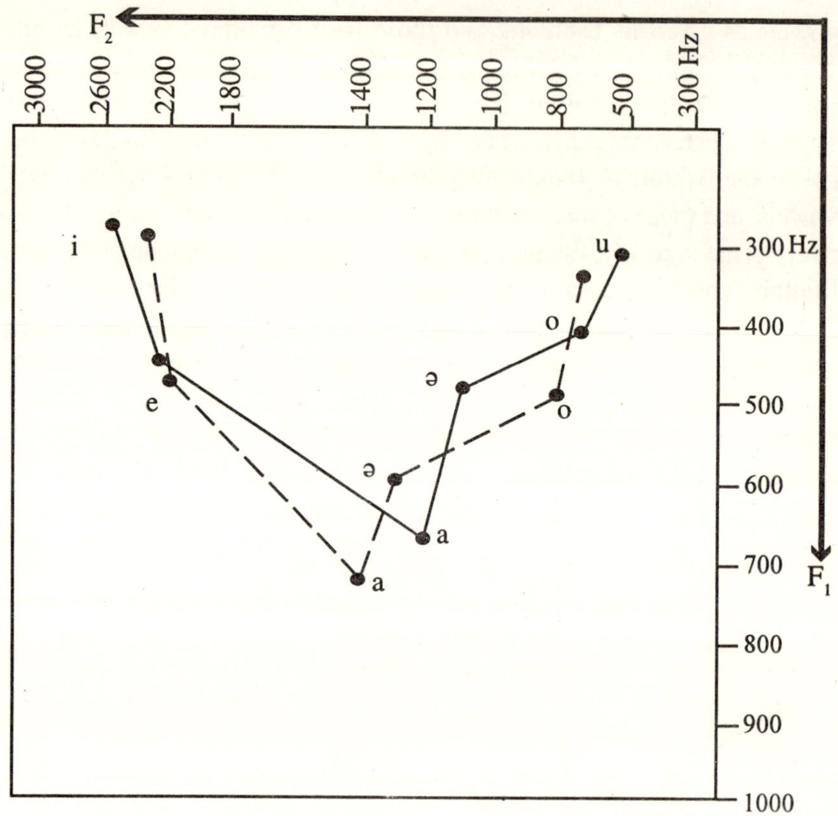

Figure 4.5: Average frequency values of F_1 and F_2 for the six of the eight Maithili oral vowels spoken in isolation (connected lines) compared with those for the Gujarati oral vowels spoken in isolation (broken lines) as reported in Dave (1977: 215).

alect—he does not specify which—of the Maithili vowels. He presents the average frequency values of F_1 and F_2 for the Maithili oral vowels spoken in isolation as given in Table 4.6. A comparison between these F_1 and F_2 frequency values (broken lines) and those of the present study (connected lines) is done in Figure 4.6.

Figure 4.6 shows that the overall pattern of the acoustic data in both studies has a good deal of similarity, although in R. Yadav the vowels

/æ a ə/ maintain relatively lower 'vowel height' than what the same vowels do in our study.

Table 4.6: The average frequency values of F_1 and F_2 for the Maithili oral vowels as reported in R. Yadav (1979a: 147).

Vowels / Formants	i	e	æ	a	ə	ɔ	o	u
F_1	277	430	843	847	777	542	445	330
F_2	2583	2223	1843	1277	1237	847	777	777

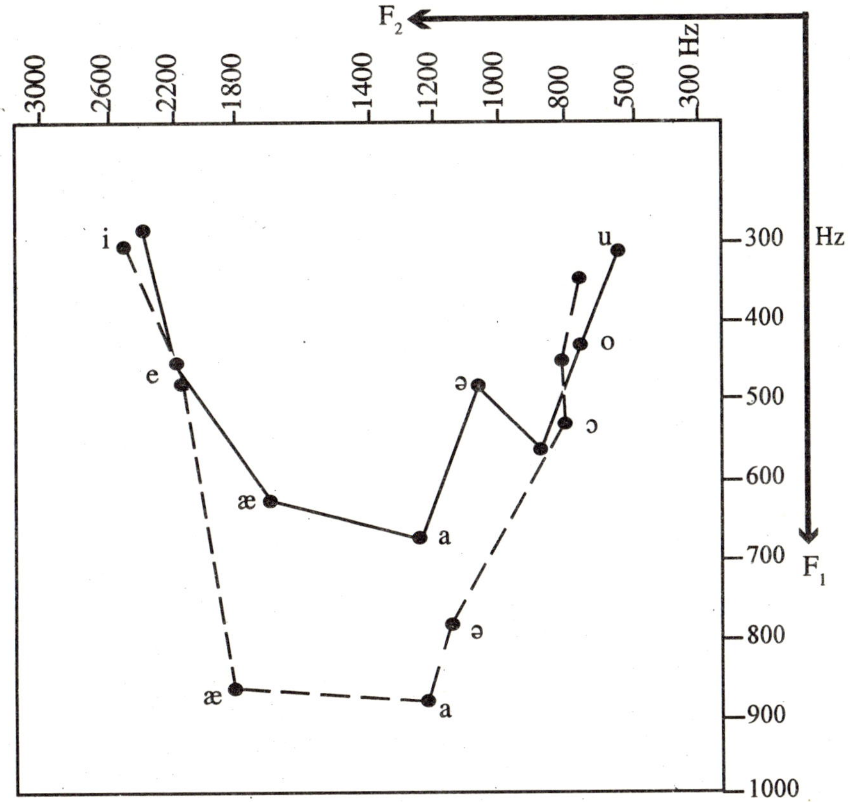

Figure 4.6: Our average frequency values of F_1 and F_2 for the Maithili oral vowels (connected lines) compared with those as reported in R. Yadav (1979a: 147).

4.2.1.2 *Duration Measurement Results and Discussions*

The results of a detailed electroglottographic study on the duration of vowels in Maithili are presented and discussed in the fifth chapter. In this sub-section we concentrate simply on the duration of the Maithili oral vowels spoken both in isolation and in words. The test utterances used for this purpose were the same as listed for these vowels earlier in Table 4.1; the experimental method used for this study was the same as outlined earlier in the first section (4.1). Table 4.7 shows the average duration (in ms) of these vowels spoken in isolation. Table 4.8, on the other hand, gives the average duration of these vowels as spoken in words, together with the average-percentage of vowel duration within each overall utterance.

Table 4.7: Average duration of the Maithili oral vowels spoken in isolation (in ms).

Vowels	i	e	æ	a	ə	ɔ	o	u
Duration	220	235	253	261	130	257	240	210

The average durations of these vowels, as given in Tables 4.7 and 4.8, are also plotted graphically in Figure 4.7. This figure presents a comparison between the average durations of these vowels as spoken both in isolation (connected lines) and in words (broken lines). As Tables 4.7

Table 4.8: Average duration (in ms) of the Maithili oral vowels spoken in words, together with the percentage of vowel duration within the overall utterance.

Vowels	i	e	æ	a	ə	ɔ	o	u
Duration	191	204	219	228	104	220	206	184
% of vowel duration	47	50	53	55	33	51	50	47

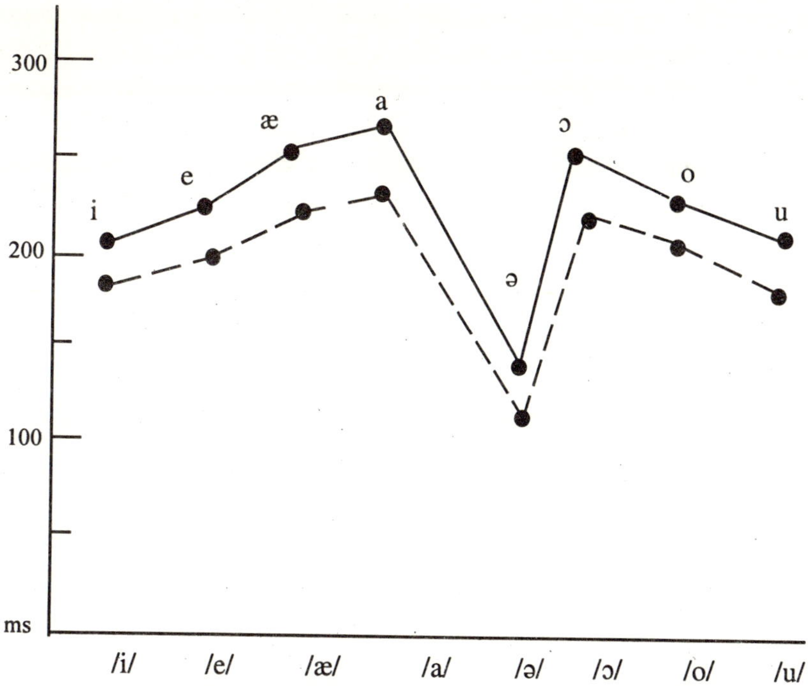

Figure 4.7: Average duration of the Maithili oral vowels spoken both in isolation (connected lines) and in words (broken lines).

and 4.8, as well as the above figure show, /a/ has the longest duration while /ə/ has the shortest duration in Maithili. Whether spoken in isolation or in words, the overall duration-patterns of these vowels remain very similar. In general, the average durations of all these vowels remain higher when spoken in isolation than when spoken in words. Moreover, other things being equal, our data also show that in general open vowels maintain longer durations than close vowels.

4.2.2 *The Nasal Vowels in Maithili*

At one point or another, every theory of speech production has to contend with the transition from discrete phonological units or categories to "continuously varying phonetic dimension", as Benguerel and Lafargue (1981: 309) put it. Similarly, every theory of speech perception has to contend with the inverse transition—i.e. from the phonetic continuum to the discreteness of the phonological level. The use of a certain phonetic dimension in a given language may or may not reflect a corresponding contrast in the phonology of that language. Vowel nasalisation, for example, is a phonetic phenomenon which does not reflect a phonological contrast in, say, English, although this phonetic phenomenon is often present to some extent whenever a derived level non-nasal vowel occurs between nasal consonants. But there are other languages, e.g. French, Portuguese, Gujarati, Urdu, Hindi and Maithili, in which vowel nasalisation does mark a phonological contrast.

Various studies on vowel nasalisation (e.g. Lightner, 1970; Ruhlen, 1973; Ferguson, 1974; Cagliari, 1977) point out that many languages show long phonetic vowels in place of underlying VN sequences. Like Hindi and Urdu (e.g. see Narang and Becker, 1971; Bhatia and Kenstowicz, 1972), or like Gujarati (e.g. Dave, 1977), Maithili has phonologically distinctive nasal vowels. Even *Varnaratnākara* (Chatterji and Mishra, eds. 1940: xi)—one of the earliest, fourteenth century written texts available in Maithili—bears witness to the existence of phonologically distinctive nasal vowels in Maithili. In the second chapter we have already discussed the phonological status of the Maithili nasal vowels /ĩ ẽ æ̃ ã ə̃ ɔ̃ õ ũ/; in the present section we shall analyse the main acoustic realisations of these nasal vowels. To do so, we shall focus our attention on two main areas: (1) on their F_1, F_2, F_3 and nasal formant (Fn) measurement results as well as our discussions on those results; and (2) on their relative duration measurement results along with our discussions on them.

4.2.2.1 *Formant Frequency Measurement Results and Discussions*

Following the experimental methods outlined earlier in the first section of this chapter, spectrographic recordings of all the nasal vowels in Maithili were made. The vowels were spoken both in isolation and in words. The test utterances used for this purpose were the same as given earlier in Table 4.1. The phonetic evidences gathered from the spectrograms of these recordings strengthen the fact that all the nasal vowels in Maithili are unit sounds, and not sequences of an oral vowel plus a nasal consonant. The acoustic analysis given in this section is based on this fact.

Table 4.9 presents the average frequencies of the first 3 formants as well as of the Fn for the nasal vowels spoken in isolation; Table 4.10, on the other hand, lists the average frequencies of F_1, F_2, F_3 and Fn for these nasal vowels spoken in words. In Figure 4.8 a comparison is made between the average F_1, F_2 and F_3 frequency values of these nasal vowels (connected lines) and those of their oral counterparts (broken lines) as spoken in isolation. As Tables 4.9 and 4.10 as well as Figure 4.8 show, each nasal vowel in Maithili is sufficiently distinguished by the first two formants. Whether spoken in isolation or in words, the F_2 for all nasal vowels goes downwards throughout the series: /ĩ ẽ æ̃ ã ə̃ ɔ̃ õ ũ/. The F_1 goes up for the front vowels /ĩ ẽ æ̃/, and then down for the back vowels /ɔ̃ õ ũ/ in that order. The F_1 for /ã/, whether spoken in isolation or in words, always remains higher than what it is for /ə̃/.

The average F_1 and F_2 frequencies for these nasal vowels as given in Tables 4.9 and 4.10 are also plotted on a formant chart in Figure 4.9 for a comparison between these vowels spoken both in isolation and in

Table 4.9: The average frequency values of F_1, F_2, F_3 and Fn for the Maithili nasal vowels spoken in isolation (in Hz).

Vowel	F_1	F_2	F_3	Fn
/ĩ/	288	2636	3236	962
/ẽ/	448	2354	3104	1274
/æ̃/	708	1752	2682	1084
/ã/	718	1256	2682	1534
/ə̃/	514	1068	2778	1178
/ɔ̃/	580	856	2536	1336
/õ/	432	726	2792	1140
/ũ/	322	614	2786	1070

Table 4.10: The average frequency values of F_1, F_2, F_3 and Fn for the Maithili nasal vowels spoken in words (in Hz).

Vowel	Word	F_1	F_2	F_3	Fn
/ĩ/	/čʰĩṭ/	330	2638	3490	952
/ẽ/	/čʰẽṭ/	436	1944	2608	1068
/æ̃/	/sæ̃/	750	1728	2598	1126
/ã/	/hãs/	736	1294	2480	974
/ə̃/	/hə̃s/	534	1246	2542	1722
/ɔ̃/	/sɔ̃/	610	894	2576	1486
/õ/	/ḍʰõṛʰ/	442	770	2764	1484
/ũ/	/ḍʰũṛʰ/	338	634	2566	1092

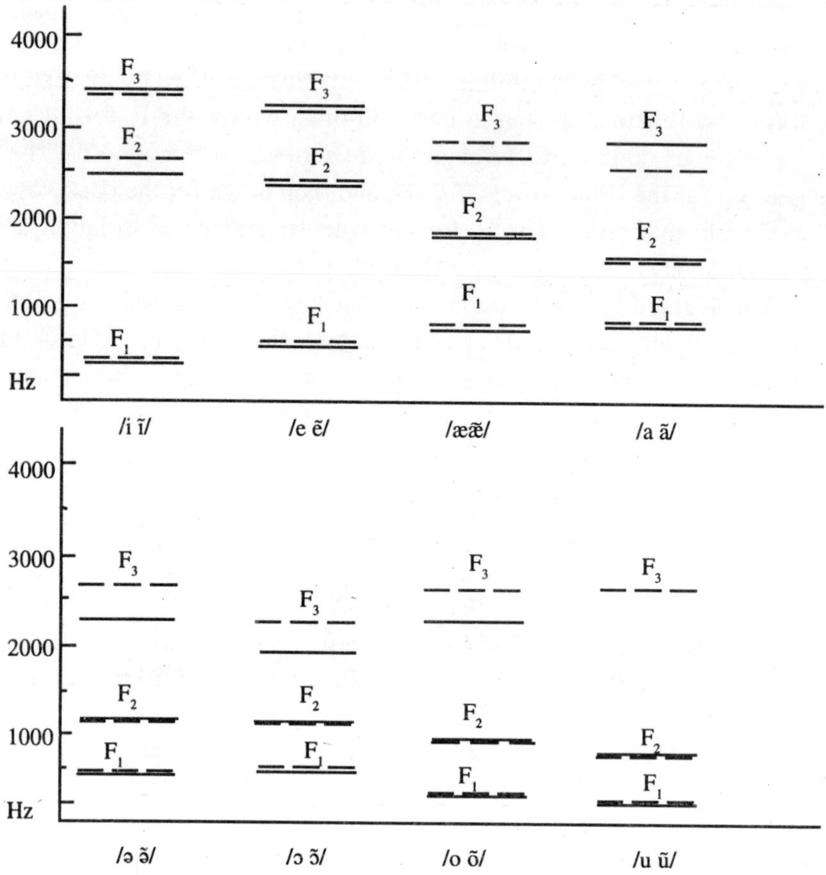

Figure 4.8: A comparison between the average frequency values of F_1, F_2 and F_3 for the Maithili oral vowels (connected lines) and for their nasal counterparts (broken lines) spoken in isolation.

words. In Figure 4.9 the actual frequency values shown by broken lines differ from those shown by connected lines in that the former display the effects of the consonantal environments in which the nasal vowels were spoken. Figure 4.9 clearly shows that, except /ẽ/, the remaining nasal vowels /ĩ æ̃ ã ə̃ ɔ̃ õ ũ/ maintain relatively lower vowel heights when

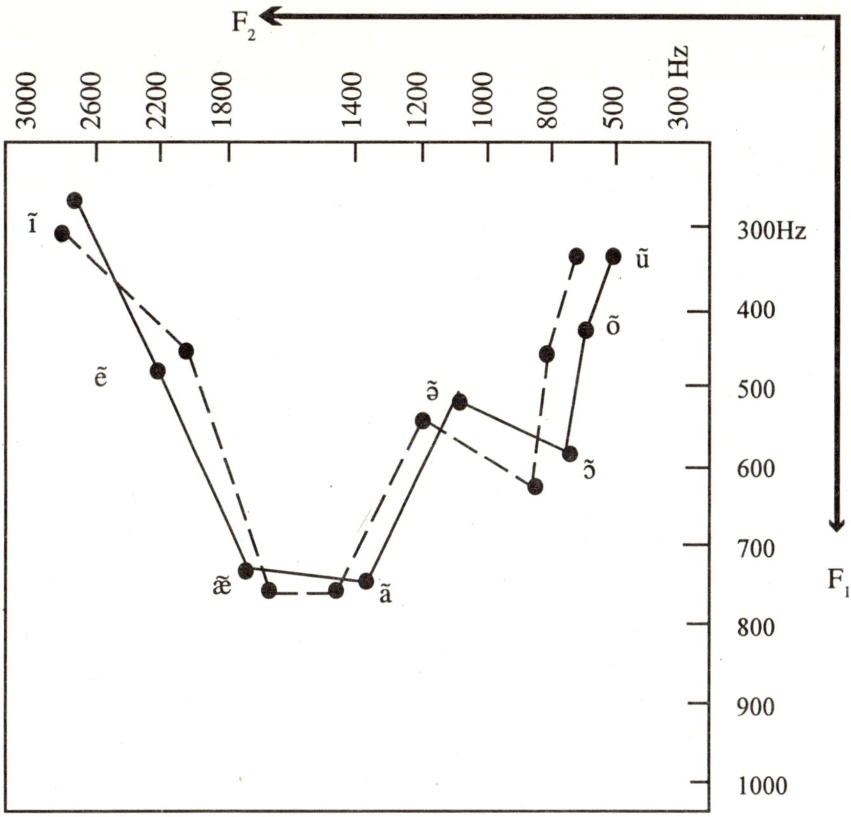

Figure 4.9: Average frequency values of F_1 and F_2 for the Maithili nasal vowels spoken both in isolation (connected lines) and in words (broken lines).

spoken in words than when spoken in isolation. In addition, when spoken in words:

(i) the front nasal vowels /ẽ æ̃/become less fronted;
(ii) the central nasal vowels /ã ə̃/ become more central—i.e. more fronted and less back; and
(iii) the back vowels /ɔ̃ õ ũ/ become less back.

Figure 4.10 makes a graphic representation of both the oral (connected lines) and the nasal (broken lines) vowels in Maithili as spoken in isolation. The figure shows a good deal of similarity between the overall

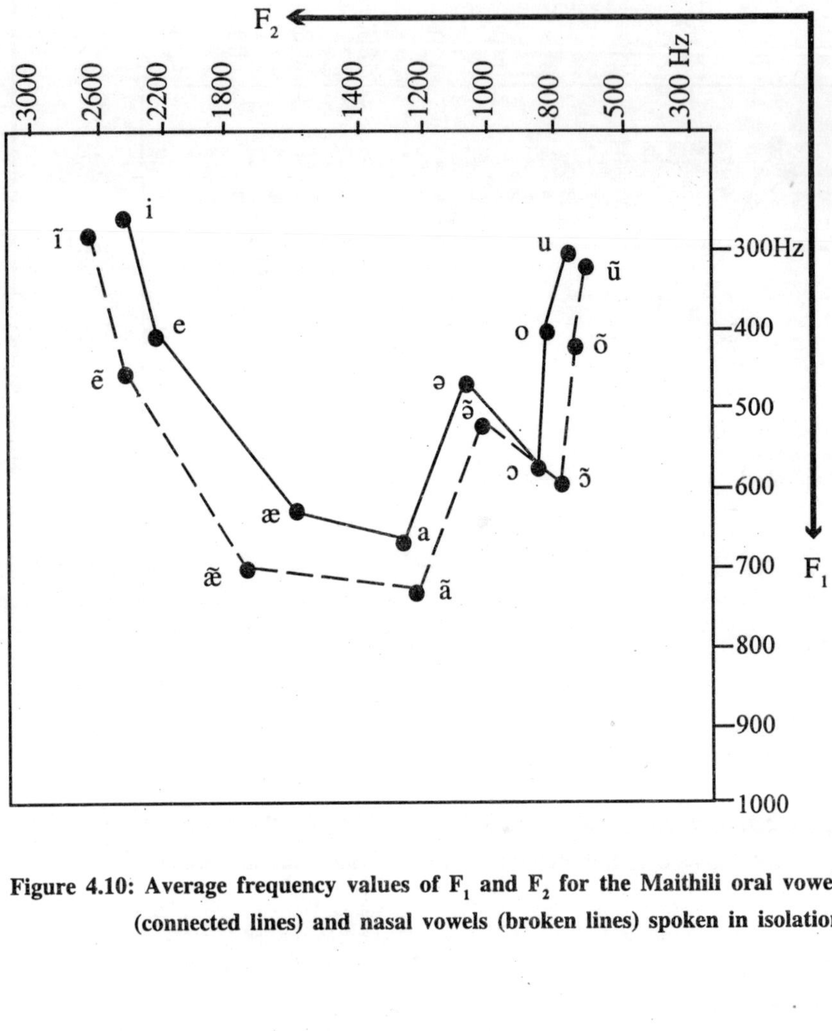

Figure 4.10: Average frequency values of F_1 and F_2 for the Maithili oral vowels (connected lines) and nasal vowels (broken lines) spoken in isolation.

frequency patterns of these oral and nasal vowels. It also shows that the nasal vowels maintain relatively lower vowel heights than their oral counterparts. In addition, the above figure also shows that, when compared with their oral counterparts:

(i) the front nasal vowels /ĩ ẽ æ̃/ are more fronted;

(ii) the central nasal vowels /ã ə̃/ become less central—i.e. less fronted

Table 4.11: Average frequency values of F_1, F_2 and F_3 for the Maithili oral and nasal vowels spoken in words of the same stress and consonantal environments.

Vowel	Word	F_1	F_2	F_3
/i/ /ĩ/	/cʰiṭ/ /čʰĩṭ/	310Hz 330	2430 Hz 2638	3408Hz 3490
/e/ /ẽ/	/bʰeṭ/ /bʰẽṭ/	424 450	1935 1962	2578 2626
/æ/ /æ̃/	/bʰæt/ /bʰæ̃t/	680 751	1679 1724	2460 2572
/a/ /ã/	/bas/ /bãs/	683 753	1366 1232	2450 2402
/ə/ /ə̃/	/'kəṭgər/ /'kə̃ṭgər/	523 543	1314 1218	2636 2522
/ɔ/ /ɔ̃/	/gɔt/ /gɔ̃t/	631 648	907 857	2552 2570
/o/ /õ/	/gʰoṭ/ /gʰõṭ/	429 443	812 740	2450 2764
/u/ /ũ/	/kə'hu/ /kə'hũ/	318 324	776 613	2352 2448

and more back; and

(iii) the back nasal vowels /ɔ̃ õ ũ/ become more back.

In order to make a further comparison between these oral and nasal vowels, each one of them was also recorded in words of the same stress and consonantal environments. Table 4.11 gives the average frequency values of the first three formants for these oral and nasal vowels. The F_1 and F_2 frequency values for these oral and nasal vowels are also graphically plotted on a formant chart in Figure 4.11.

Thus, to summarise, the acoustical measurements displayed in all the tables and figures of this section, and close inspections of formant amplitudes as well as of the relative intensity of the first three formants of

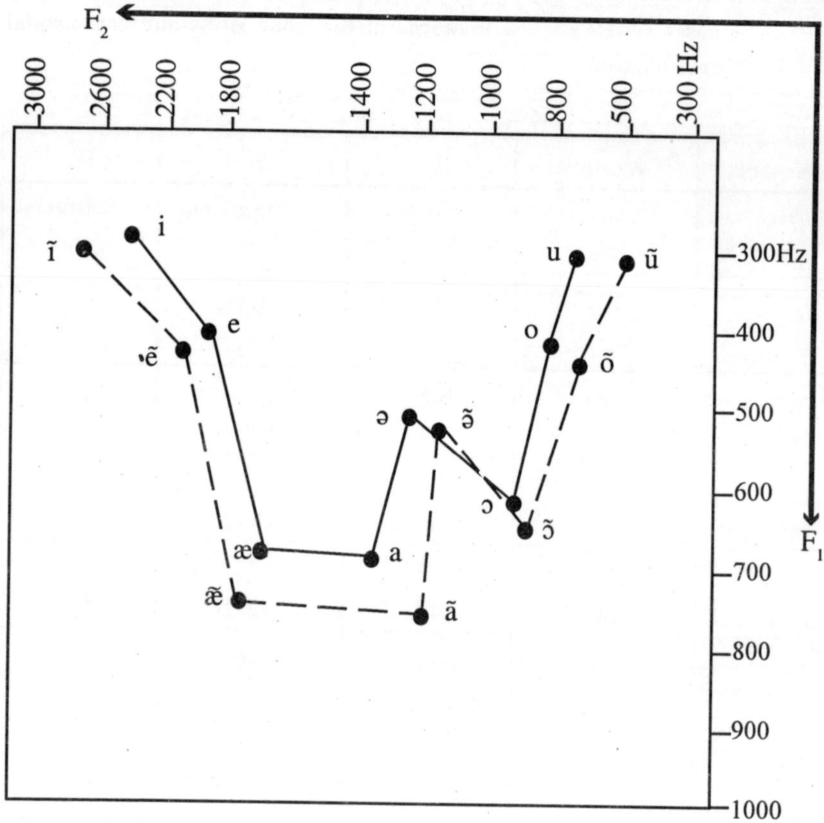

Figure 4.11: Average frequency values of F_1 and F_2 for the Maithili oral vowels (connected lines) and nasal vowels (broken lines) spoken in words of the same stress and consonantal environments.

all the oral and nasal vowels in Maithili lead to the following main observations.

First, our results support the observation of most previous investigators of nasal vowels (e.g. House and Stevens, 1956: 225; Fant, 1960: 148-49; Kongsdal, 1967: 59-66; Dave, 1977: 62-68; R. Yadav, 1979a: 173-74) that the major attributes for these vowels lie in the region of F_1. Our study reveals that there are three major attributes for nasal vowels in the F_1 region: i.e. F_1 frequency, F_1 intensity and F_1 amplitude. The results of our F_1 frequency-measurements show that on average all the nasal vowels in Maithili maintain relatively higher frequency values, and therefore relatively lower 'vowel height', than their oral counterparts. A close study of all spectrograms investigated in this study indicates that in the nasal vowels, when compared with their oral counterparts, the F_1 loses much of its intensity in favour of the F_2. In addition, our results also show that the F_1 amplitude for the nasal vowels remains relatively lower than that of their oral counterparts.

Secondly, our results also show a good deal of similarity between the overall frequency-patterns of the Maithili oral and nasal vowels. But, on the whole, when compared with their oral counterparts:

(i) the front nasal vowels /ĩ ẽ æ̃/ are more fronted;
(ii) the central nasal vowels /ã ə̃/ are less central—i.e. they tend to be positioned more toward the back than the front; and
(iii) the back nasal vowels /ɔ̃ õ ũ/ are more back.

As a result, the Maithili nasal vowels occupy relatively more extreme positions in the formant charts than their oral counterparts. Dave (1977: 63) also reports a similar finding for the Gujarati oral and nasal vowels.

Thirdly, almost all spectrograms investigated in this study show that the relative intensity of F_3 remains much weaker in the Maithili nasal vowels than in their oral couterparts.

Finally, the appearance of nasal formants has also been said (e.g. Joos, 1948; Fant, 1960; Delattre, 1969; Ladefoged, 1975/1982; Cagliari, 1977; Dave, 1977) to be an important attribute of nasal vowels. According to Smith (1951), nasal formants usually occur in nasal vowels at around 1000 Hz. Our Fn measurement-results support Smith's claim, but only partly. Although it does not always seem easy to state the exact Fn frequency of nasal vowels, our results show that the average Fn frequency region for the Maithili nasal vowels has a range between 952 Hz and 1722 Hz. This (952 Hz-1722 Hz) range should not be taken as surprising because Ladefoged (1975: 173), too, reports the presence of "pseudoformants" for some American English vowels at around 1700 Hz "due to a slight degree of nasalization", and Dave (1977: 67) also reports the presence of 'extra formants' for some Gujarati nasal vowels "in the region of 1000 to 2500 cps".

4.2.2.2 *Duration Measurement Results and Discussions*

To determine the relative duration of the Maithili oral and nasal vowels, duration measurements of all these vowels were made from spectrograms. Following the experimental method outlined earlier in the first section of this chapter, the duration of these vowels was measured in ms. The test utterances used for this purpose were the same as given earlier in Table 4.1.

Table 4.12 lists the average duration of the Maithili nasal vowels spoken in isolation:

Table 4.12: Average duration of the Maithili nasal vowels spoken in isolation (in ms).

Vowels	ĩ	ẽ	æ̃	ã	ə̃	ɔ̃	õ	ũ
Duration	241	253	270	280	150	275	256	235

Table 4.13 lists the average duration of these vowels as spoken in words. The average duration values of these tables are also plotted on a chart as displayed in Figure 4.12 in which the dots linked by connected lines represent the nasal vowels spoken in isolation, while those linked by broken lines represent the same vowels spoken in words.

Table 4.13: Average duration of the Maithili nasal vowels spoken in words (in ms).

Vowels	ĩ	ẽ	æ̃	ã	ə̃	ɔ̃	õ	ũ
Duration	160	196	255	227	102	231	211	196

The figure clearly shows that the nasal vowels spoken in isolation have longer durations than when spoken in words. It also shows that open nasal vowels tend to maintain longer durations than less open and close ones.

The relative durations of these oral and nasal vowels as spoken in isolation are compared in Figure 4.13. The figure clearly shows that all the nasal vowels maintain longer durations than their oral counterparts. Table 4.14 presents the average durations of all these vowels spoken in words of the same stress and consonantal environments. The average duration values for these vowels as given in Table 4.14 are also graphically plotted in Figure 4.14.

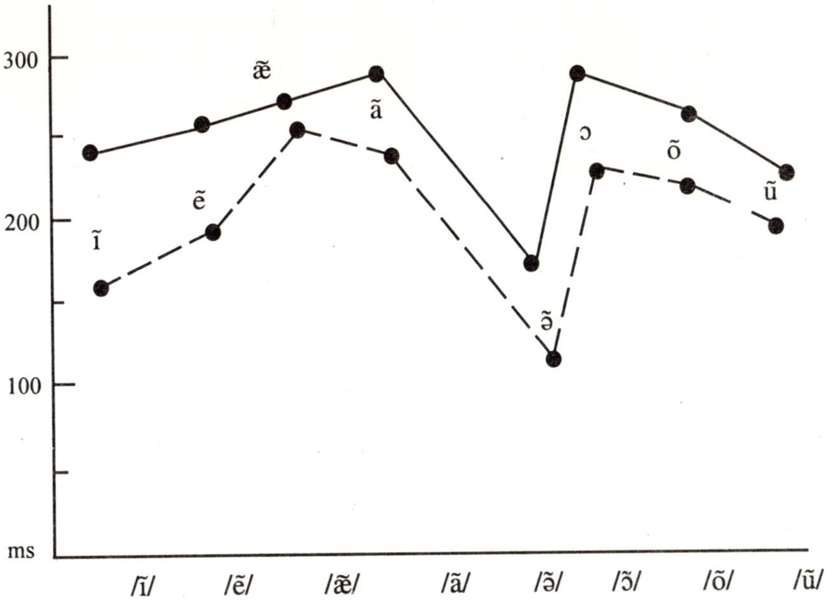

Figure 4.12: Average duration of the Maithili nasal vowels as spoken both in isolation (connected lines) and in words (broken lines).

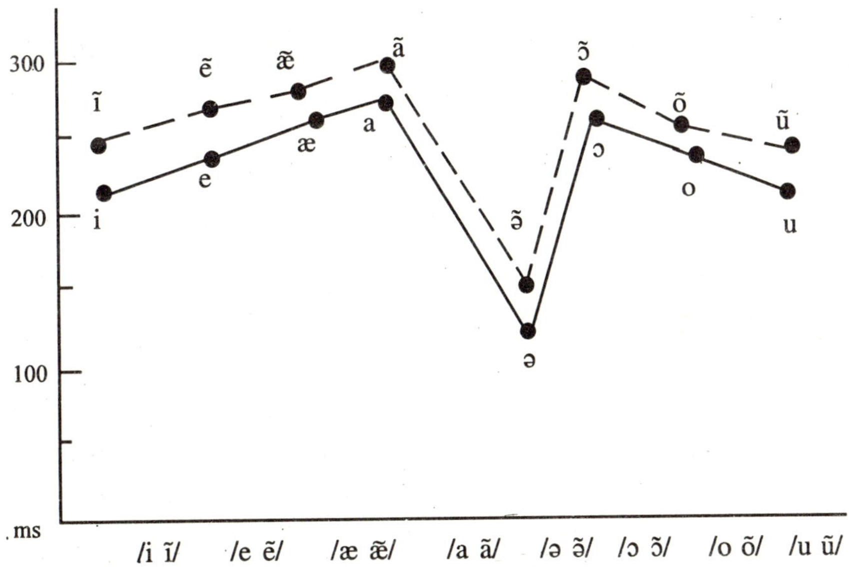

Figure 4.13: Average duration of the Maithili oral vowels (connected lines) and nasal vowels (broken lines) spoken in isolation.

As Figure 4.14 shows, there is a good deal of similarity between the overall duration-patterns of these oral and nasal vowels. In general, even

Table 4.14: Average duration (in ms) of the Maithili oral and nasal vowels spoken in words of the same stress and consonantal environments, together with the average duration of overall utterance and the average percentage of vowel duration within the overall utterance.

Vowel	Word	Vowel duration	Duration of overall utterance	% of vowel duration within the overall utterance
/i/	/čʰiṭ/	132	278	47
/ĩ/	/čʰĩṭ/	160	310	51
/e/	/bʰeṭ/	159	306	52
/ẽ/	/bʰẽṭ/	202	342	59
/æ/	/bʰæt/	197	419	47
/æ̃/	/bʰæ̃t/	231	455	51
/a/	/bas/	218	424	51
/ã/	/bãs/	247	448	55
/ə/	/'kəṭgər/	59	436	14
/ə̃/	/'kə̃ṭgər/	80	449	18
/ɔ/	/gɔt/	221	411	54
/ɔ̃/	/gɔ̃t/	260	428	61
/o/	/gʰoṭ/	207	404	51
/õ/	/gʰõṭ/	242	438	55
/u/	/kə'hu/	326	440	74
/ũ/	/kə'hũ/	352	456	77

when spoken in words of the same stress and consonantal environments, the nasal vowels remain longer in duration than their oral counterparts—the length of this duration-difference ranging between 3 and 7 percent within the overall utterance. Pathak (1976: 314) carried out an electrokymographic study of phonetic nasalisation in Bagheli—a dialect of Hindi spoken in eastern India—and he also came to a similar conclusion: i.e. "the nasalized vowels in Bagheli have a little longer duration

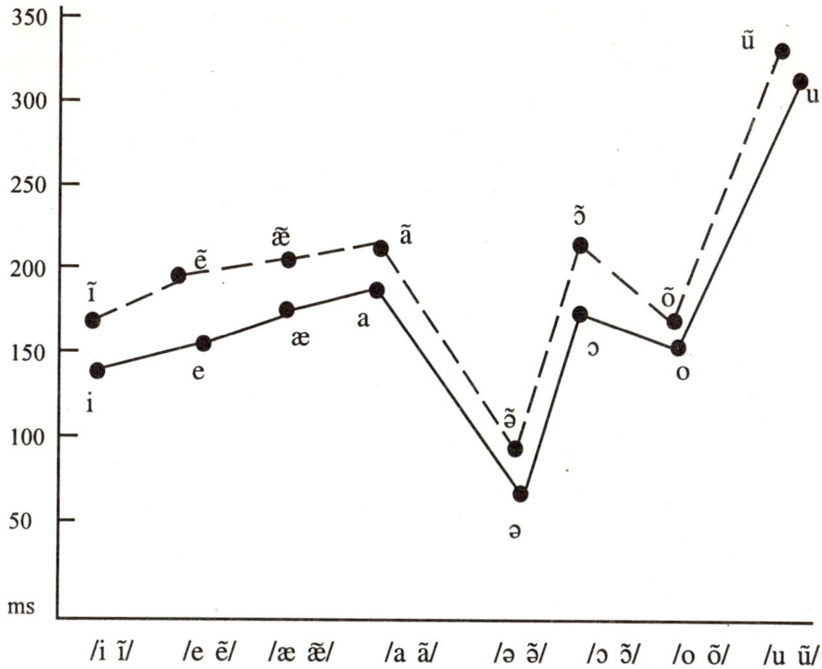

Figure 4.14: Average duration of the Maithili oral vowels (connected lines) and nasal vowels (broken lines) spoken in words of the same stress and consonantal environments.

than their oral counterparts". Our results shown in Table 4.14 and graphically displayed in Figure 4.14 indicate quite clearly that the presence of the nasal vowel lengthens the overall utterance. That is to say, in almost each test utterance of Table 4.14 there is no compensation (for the increased length of the nasal vowel) taking place elsewhere in the utterance. And, in general, these data also confirm that, other things being equal, in Maithili open vowels remain longer in duration than close vowels.

4.2.3 *The Oral Diphthongs in Maithili*

There have been various studies on diphthongs (e.g. Hibbitt, 1948; Trager and Smith, 1951; Gleason, 1955; Lehiste and Peterson, 1961; Malmberg, 1963; Gay, 1968; Gerber, 1972) during the previous five decades or so. But the interpretations and definitions of diphthongs given by different researchers do not always agree. For example, some researchers (e.g.

Hibbitt, 1948; Gleason, 1955; Catford, 1977) hold that a diphthong is a blend of two perceptually different vowels within one and the same syllable; others (e.g. Trager and Smith, 1951) hold that it is a sequence of vowel and semi-vowel; while still others (e.g. Lehiste and Peterson, 1961; Malmberg, 1963; Gay, 1968; Gerber, 1972) hold that it is a vocalic syllable nucleus containing two 'target' positions.

It is primarily due to the different criteria followed in the investigation of diphthongs—whether articulatory, perceptual, acoustic, or some combination of these—that different researchers have resorted to different definitions of what a diphthong is. On the whole, most researchers seem to agree that in point of fact a diphthong may, indeed, consist of two discrete 'elements', with a relatively rapid transition between them. According to most of them, a diphthong may be described and identified in terms of its beginning and ending points, using the categories for monophthongs with the assumption that the articulators, in their movement, take the shortest path between these points. It is more or less in this way that we described and identified the Maithili diphthongs earlier in the second chapter (2.1.3).

But the question is: Is a diphthong really a pair of monophthongs, end-to-end? It seems that in the articulatory domain a diphthong is a single event characterised by the change of articulator position. In the perceptual domain, however, there is the question whether diphthongs are identified as single events—i.e. as individual vocalic syllable nuclei—or as dual events. Put slightly differently, the question still is: Is the perceived diphthong different from the perception of a pair of vowels? It is with the help of some attributes gathered from the results of a spectrographic study of the Maithili diphthongs that we shall make an attempt to find out some possible answers to this question.

As mentioned earlier in the second chapter, Maithili has two phonologically distinctive oral diphthongs: /əi/ and /əu/. In this section we shall put forward the results of a spectrographic study intended to characterise these two diphthongs recorded under three different speaking rates: (1) at a slow speed (i.e. recorded in isolation); (2) at a moderate speed (i.e. recorded in words); and (3) at a fast speed (i.e. recorded in words put in a normal conversational sentence context, the frame of the sentence being: /'pʰero . . .'uččaṛəṇ kə'ru/ 'Please pronounce . . .again'.

Following the experimental methods outlined earlier in the first section of this chapter, spectrographic recordings of the two Maithili diphthongs were made in the above-mentioned three different speaking rates. The test utterances used for this purpose were the same as given earlier in Table 4.1. Formant frequency and duration measurements were done in the same way as outlined earlier in the first section (4.1.3). The two main objectives of this study were to determine:

(1) the average frequency of F_1 and F_2 for each of the two elements (i.e. of the 'onset' and 'offset' steady-state) as well as the rate of change of F_2 for each diphthong as recorded under the three speaking rates; and
(2) the duration of the onset and offset steady-state, the duration of the F_2 transition from the initial element to the final element as well as the overall duration of the two diphthongs in each one of the three speaking rates.

The 'steady-state' was defined as the time interval during which formants remained parallel to the time axis; the 'transition state' was considered in terms of the rate of change of the formant frequency in a given time interval (i.e. Hz per ms).

4.2.3.1 *Formant Frequency Measurement Results and Discussions*
The average frequency values for the onset and offset steady-state of the two diphthongs as well as the rate of F_2 for each diphthong are all given in Table 4.15. The table shows the effects of duration conditions on F_1 and F_2 target frequencies. For both diphthongs, there is little consistent change in onset frequency positions for the three duration conditions. But both F_1 and F_2 offsets show consistent changes in frequency levels across changes in duration. For /əi/, F_1 offset frequency values are higher and F_2 offset frequency values are lower as the diphthong duration decreases under the three conditions of speaking rate; for /əu/, both F_1 and F_2 offset frequency values are higher for conditions of shorter duration. Another important point to note is that the rate of change of F_2 for each diphthong is relatively constant across changes in duration. This rate of change of F_2 for the diphthong /əi/ has a range between 12.33 and 12.95 in Hz/ms; for /əu/ the rate of change has a range between 4.50 and 4.78 in Hz/ms.

To show the effects of these changes on the identity of the 'targets', we first plot in Figure 4.15 the average F_1 and F_2 frequency values for the three steady-state vowels /ə i u/, as given earlier in Table 4.2. In

Table 4.15: Average formant frequencies (in Hz) for the onset and offset steady-state of the Maithili diphthongs and their F_2 rate of change for the three conditions of speaking rate.

Diph-thong	Rate of speaking	F_1 Onset	F_1 Offset	F_2 Onset	F_2 Offset	F_2 rate of change (in Hz ms^{-1})
/əi/	slow	485	255	1090	2450	12.95
	moderate	480	310	1120	2170	12.35
	fast	475	360	1140	1880	12.33
/əu/	slow	475	310	1080	650	4.78
	moderate	470	350	1100	775	4.64
	fast	465	395	1110	840	4.50

Figure 4.15 the three steady-state vowels are shown by three bold dots. The average F_1 and F_2 frequency values for the steady-state onset and

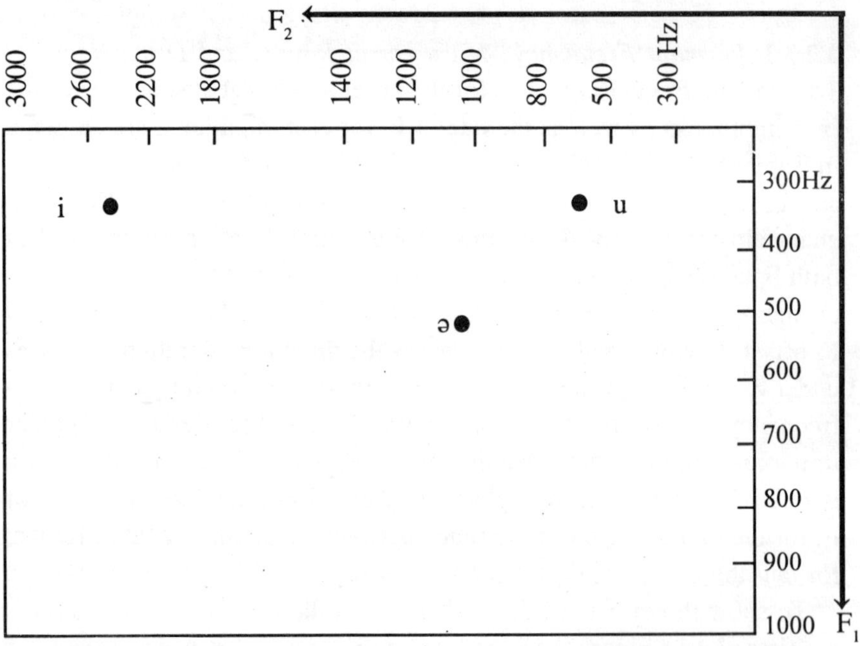

Figure 4.15: Average frequency values of F_1 and F_2 for the three Maithili steady-state vowels: /ə i u/.

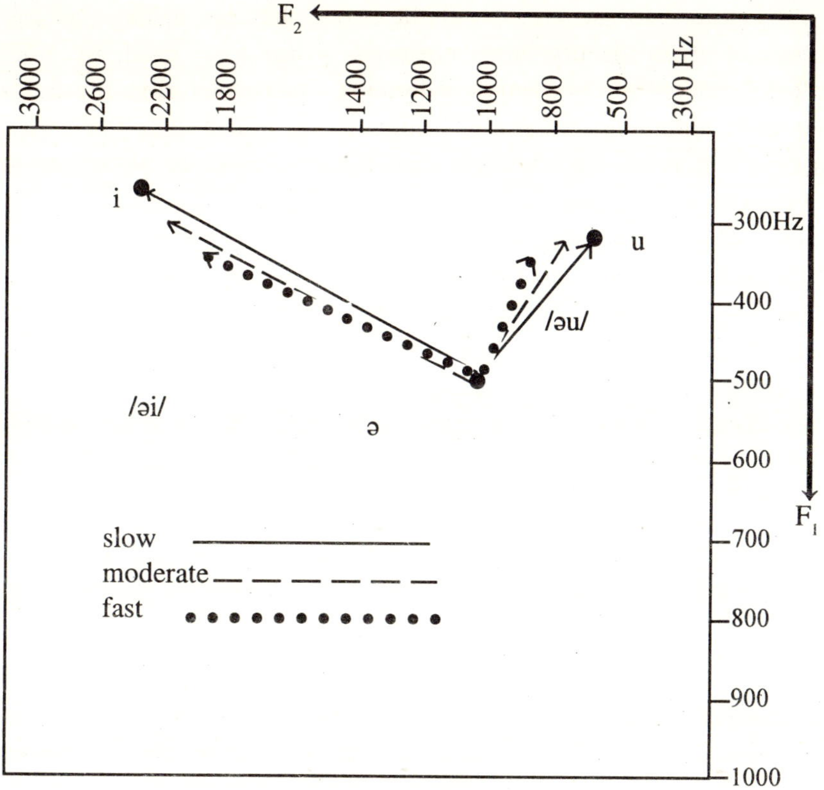

Figure 4.16: Average F_1 and F_2 values for the steady-state onsets and offsets of the Maithili diphthongs /əi/ and /əu/ as recorded under the three conditions of speaking rate plotted on an F_1-F_2 grid against the three boldly dotted positions of the steady-state Maithili vowels: /ə i u/.

offset positions of the diphthongs /əi/ and /əu/ as spoken under the three conditions of speaking rate are plotted on an F_1-F_2 grid in Figure 4.16 against the three boldly dotted positions of the steady-state vowels: /ə i u/. Figure 4.16 embodies:

(i) 'corresponding' start 'target': ə;
(ii) 'corresponding' end 'target': i or u;
(iii) direction of movement: ——→ ;
(iv) amount of movement: i.e. length of ——→; and
(v) variation of rate of movement: i.e. connected——→ vs broken ·····→ vs dotted ····→ lines.

As Figure 4.16 shows, each of the two diphthongs displays a clear change of offset identity; onset positions, on the other hand, are more or less preserved across changes in duration. The figure further illustrates that each diphthong follows a similar displacement-direction across changes in duration with the shorter utterances terminating before reaching their targets. In other words, the plots in Figure 4.16 clearly display that it is only in conditions of 'slow' speaking rate that the offset 'targets' of the diphthongs /əi/ and /əu/ are reached, while in conditions of both 'moderate' and 'fast' speaking rates the offset targets are never quite reached. In general, the faster the conditions of speaking rate, the quicker the termination of the offset displacement-direction of each diphthong.

In short, the results of our spectrographic study show that the Maithili diphthongs /əi/ and /əu/ are each characterised by two attributes:

(1) a comparatively fixed onset steady-state; and
(2) continuously as well as systematically changing glide elements, the main property of this *systematic* continuous change being a very similar rate of change of F_2 across changes in the three duration conditions.

Offset steady-states are found least prominent in these diphthongs—in fact, each diphthong displays a clear change of offset identity across changes in duration conditions. Hence, if we assume—as the symbols traditionally used to write the diphthongs /əi/ and /əu/ would suggest—that the offset targets of /əi/ and /əu/ are the steady-state vowels /i/ and /u/, respectively, then it is only in conditions of slow speaking rate that these offset targets are reached, while in faster conditions of speaking rate the offset displacement-direction of each diphthong always terminates before reaching its target.

4.2.3.2 *Duration Measurement Results and Discussions*

In addition to the frequency of vowel formants, other parameters involved in the perception of the Maithili diphthongs—like the diphthongs of other languages, for that matter—concern their duration. Therefore, studies on the duration of the two Maithili diphthongs were also made. The results of these duration measurements are given in Table 4.16. This table shows average durations (in ms) of the onset steady-state, the offset steady-state, the F_2 transition as well as the total duration of the two

Table 4.16: Average durations (in ms) of the onset steady-state, the offset steady-state, the F_2 transition and the total duration of the two Maithili diphthongs as recorded under the three conditions of speaking rate.

Diphthong	Rate of speaking	a Onset	b F_2 transition	c Offset	Total
/əi/	slow	50	105	80	235
	moderate	25	85	40	150
	fast	10	60	20	90
/əu/	slow	40	90	60	190
	moderate	20	70	30	120
	fast	10	60	15	85

diphthongs as recorded under three conditions of speaking rate: slow, moderate and fast.

To show exactly what these measurements refer to, Figure 4.17 given below displays spectrograms of two words—['əikʰə̃n] 'at this time' and [kəhi'yəu] '(please) say'—containing the two diphthongs. Both words were spoken at a moderate speed. A time scale (with an arbitrary starting

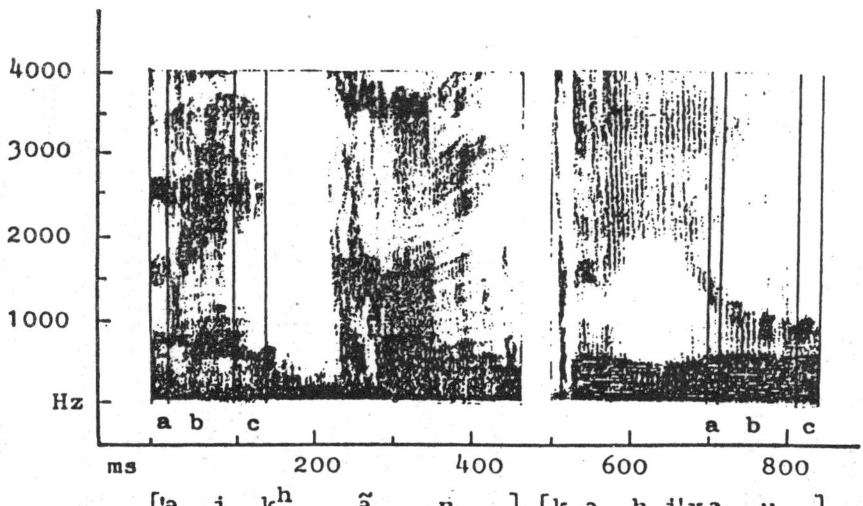

Figure 4.17: Spectrograms of two words, ['əikʰə̃n] and [kəhi'yəu], spoken at a moderate speed.

point) is shown in ms along the bottom of the horizontal axis; the vertical axis shows the frequencies in Hz. In the above figure:

(i) 'a' embodies onset steady-state;
(ii) 'b' embodies F_2 transition; and
(iii) 'c' embodies offset steady-state.

The average F_2 frequency values for the two diphthongs given earlier in Table 4.15 and the average durations for the same diphthongs given in Table 4.16 are graphically illustrated in Figure 4.18.

In this figure, too, 'a', 'b' and 'c' embody onset steady-state, F_2 transition and offset steady-state, respectively. Connected lines of the figure show the two diphthongs spoken at a slow speed; broken lines show them

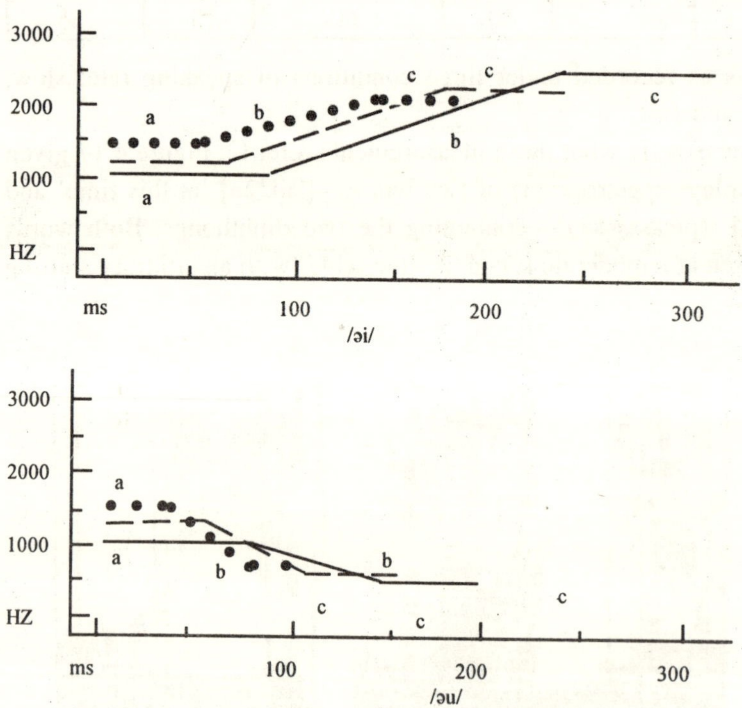

Figure 4.18: Average F_2 frequencies and average durations of the onset steady-state, the F_2 transition and the offset steady-state of the two Maithili dipthongs recorded under three conditions of speaking rate: slow (connected lines), moderate (broken lines) and fast (dotted lines).

as spoken at a moderate speed; and dotted lines show the same diphthongs as spoken at a fast speed.

All the above tables and figures concerning the two diphthongs show that a change in the speaking rate from slow to fast brings about a reduction in the total duration ranging between 38 and 64%. The data also show that the onset durations for both diphthongs are less than their offset durations. Although both onset steady-state and F_2 transition durations decrease as the speaker's rate of production increases, the significant point to note about our data is that the decrease in F_2 transition duration is always accompanied by an increase in F_1 offset frequency and a decrease in F_2 offset frequency for /əi/ but an increase in F_2 offset frequency for /əu/. And there is no distinct modification of the rate of change of F_2 either in /əi/ or in /əu/, as spoken in all three conditions of speaking rate. This stability is a fact of the production. It seems that the speaker maintains the stability here because he believes this section of the diphthong to be that most relevant for diphthong-perception.

When recorded under moderate and fast speaking rates, both diphthongs were placed in all word positions: initial, medial and final. The formant frequency and duration measurements of these diphthongs do not indicate any consistent initial or terminal consonant effects on target frequency levels, or initial consonant effects on duration. However, there was some slight terminal consonant voicing-effect on duration (see S.K. Jha, 1984: 334-35, for more information). The increased duration of /əi/ and /əu/ preceding a voiced consonant—i.e. in the Maithili words: /kəil/ 'of a white colour' and /kəul$^{(h)}$/ 'small mill'—is accomplished primarily by a lengthening of the steady-state onset. F_2 transition and steady-state offset durations are also slightly longer.

Our analysis of the acoustic characteristics of the two Maithili diphthongs reveals a certain movement along the particular path between the zones corresponding to two different vowels—i.e. between /ə/ and /i/ or /u/—in the vowel space. It has been observed that in a consonant-diphthong-consonant context this movement is performed in five steps:

(i) transition from the consonant to the initial element of the diphthong;
(ii) steady-state (or 'target') of the initial element—i.e. onset steady-state;
(iii) transition from the initial target-element to the final target-element of the diphthong;

(iv) steady-state (or 'target') of the final element—i.e. offset steady-state; and

(v) transition from the final target-element of the diphthong to the following consonant.

These steps are more evident in a slow speaking rate; when the speaking rate is increased, they tend to shorten.

Thus, from the point of view of the production, it may be inferred that the articulatory gesture for the Maithili diphthongs begins at a rather fixed position in the vowel space, which is very similar to the position held by the Maithili steady-state vowel /ə/. This position is held for a particular length of time (relative time, that is), the absolute duration of which is determined mainly by the rate of speaking and/or the presence or absence of a following voiced consonant. The articulators then begin to move toward a final target position at a given speed, the final target position being similar to the one that the steady-state vowel /i/ or /u/ has. If the rate of speaking is slow, the final target is reached and the gesture is completed; if, on the other hand, the rate of speaking is fast, the movement, while still on course, is cut off before reaching the final target.

Hence, if we recall our earlier question: Is a diphthong really a pair of monophthongs, end-to-end?, our spectrographic evidences from Maithili suggest an answer which could be put as *yes* and *no: yes,* if the speaking rate is slow; *no, not really*, if the speaking rate is fast. These evidences from the phonetics of Maithili support, at least in part, our earlier descriptions of the Maithili diphthongs given in the second chapter as sequences of vocalic elements which form a glide within one syllable. The spectrographic measurements of our study, especially those of formant positions and overall movement, do suggest that each of the two Maithili diphthongs, /əi/ and /əu/, does have a first element which is the starting point and a second element which is the point in the direction of which the glide is made.

The description of these diphthongs as dual vocalic segments is relevant to the phonology of Maithili, too. One factor bearing out this claim is their length. As stated earlier in the second chapter, the long allophonic variants of the Maithili vowels usually occur in stressed syllables. For example, the Maithili [i:] and [a:] may phonologically be identified as dual vocalic segments, i.e. as:

/iĭ/ as in /siĭr/ 'root', and
/aă/ as in /saăr/ 'wife's brother',

the first segment of which may be regarded as 'syllabic' and the second one as 'non-syllabic'. Like the long vowels, the diphthongs /əi/ and /əu/ also occur primarily in stressed syllables because they attract stress, and their phonological length in such syllables is similar to that of the long vowels in Maithili. Each of the two diphthongs may therefore be regarded as a pair of vocalic segments (i.e. as /əĭ/ and /əŭ/), the first segment of each pair being 'syllabic' and the second one being 'non-syllabic'.

Secondly, the morphophonology of Maithili provides us with the strongest evidence as to why each of the two diphthongs /əi/ and /əu/ has to be regarded as comprising two segments rather than one. We can see the following Maithili verb forms, for example:

(1)

Verb form	Gloss
/kə'həliyə/	'(I) said (to you)'
/de'k^{h}əliyə/	'(I) saw (you)'
/li'k^{h}əliyə/	'(I) wrote (to you)'
/de'liyə/	'(I) gave (you)'

As we discuss this point at some considerable length later in the eighth chapter, the Maithili verbs are marked differently in accordance with the difference in the social status of both their grammatical subject and object. The above verb forms in (1) are used in Maithili when their grammatical object is in the *non-honorific but intimate* second person. If there is any further change in the social status of the grammatical object, then a further change is bound to occur in the above verb forms. For example, if the object is a *non-honorific and non-intimate* second person, then the suffix *-u* must be added to the above verb forms:

(2)

Stem + Suffix	Word	Gloss
/kəhəliyə + -u/	/kəhəli'yəu/	'(I) said (to you)'
/dekʰəliyə + -u/	/dekʰəli'yəu/	'(I) saw (you)'
/likʰəliyə + -u/	/likʰəli'yəu/	'(I) wrote (to you)'
/deliyə + -u/	/deli'yəu/	'(I) gave (you)'

Similarly, if the grammatical subject is either in the first person or in the honorific form of the second person, and if the grammatical object is in the *non-honorific form* of the second parson, then the suffix *-i* is added to the verb forms given earlier in (1):

(3)

Stem + Suffix	Word	Gloss
/kəhəliyə + -i/	/kəhəli'yəi/	'(I/you) said (to him)'
/dəkʰəliyə + -i/	/dekʰəli'yəi/	'(I/you) saw (him)'
/likʰəliyə + -i/	/likʰəli'yəi/	'(I/you) wrote (to him)'
/deliyə + -i/	/deli'yəi/	'(I/you) gave (him)'

Thus, the examples given in (2) and (3) show that whenever the suffix *-i* or *-u* is added to the verb forms given in (1), then in the final syllables of the resultant words the diphthongs /əi/ and /əu/, i.e.

ə + i ⟶ əi

ə + u ⟶ əu,

are realised at the surface level. This clearly means that each of the two Maithili diphthongs has to be regarded as containing two vocalic segments, the first of which is a syllabic ə, while the second segment is either a non-syllabic i or a non-syllabic u.

4.3 Summary of Conclusions

The acoustical measurements displayed in this chapter, together with close inspection of formant amplitudes and the relative intensity of the first three formants of all the oral and nasal vowels and of the two oral diphthongs in Maithili, lead to the following main observations.

First, all the oral and nasal vowels in Maithili, whether spoken in isolation or in words, are clearly differentiated from one another in terms of their formant frequencies. The results show a good deal of similarity between the overall frequency-patterns of the Maithili oral and nasal vowels. Yet, on the whole, when compared with their oral counterparts, the nasal vowels occupy relatively more extreme positions in the formant charts than the oral vowels.

Second, the results support the observations of most previous investigators of nasal vowels (e.g. House and Stevens, 1956: 225; Fant, 1960: 148-49; Kongsdal, 1967: 59-66; Dave, 1977: 62-68; R. Yadav, 1984: 107) that the major attributes for these vowels lie in the region of F_1. This study reveals that the major attribute for nasal vowels in the F_1 region is F_1 frequency. The results of F_1 frequency-measurements show that, on average, all the nasal vowels in Maithili maintain relatively higher frequency values, and therefore relatively lower 'vowel height', than their oral counterparts. It was also observed that in the nasal vowels, when compared with their oral counterparts, the F_1 loses much of its intensity in favour of the F_2. In addition, the F_1 amplitude for the nasal vowels remains relatively lower than that of their oral couterparts.

Third, almost all spectrograms investigated in this study show that the relative intensity of F_3 is much weaker in the Maithili nasal vowels than in their oral counterparts.

Fourth, the appearance of nasal formants has been reported to be an important attribute of nasal vowels (e.g. Joos, 1948; Fant, 1960: Delattre, 1969; Cagliari, 1977; Dave, 1977; Ladefoged, 1982). According to Smith (1951), nasal formants usually occur in nasal vowels at around 1000 Hz. The Fn measurements presented in this study support Smith's claim, but only partly. Although it does not always seem easy to determine the exact Fn frequency of nasal vowels, the results show that the average Fn frequency region for the Maithili nasal vowels has a range between 952 and 1722 Hz. This range should not be taken as surprising because Ladefoged (1982: 173), too, reports the presence of "pseudoformants" for some American English vowels at around 1700 Hz "due to a slight degree of nasalization", and Dave (1977: 67) also reports the presence of "extra formants" for some Gujarati nasal vowels "in the region of 1000 to 2500 cps".

Fifth, in general, the results also confirm that, other things being equal, in Maithili open vowels remain longer in duration than close vowels.

Finally, from our findings and from what the literature has to say about diphthongs, it may be concluded that the phonetic features emerging from the consideration of diphthongs in a particular language are not necessarily sufficient or optimal to characterise the phenomenon in general. Hence, for example, in Spanish (e.g. Manrique, 1979) the prevalence of one steady-state over the other depends on the position of the open vowels; in English (e.g. Lehiste and Peterson, 1961; Gay, 1968; Gerber, 1972) it is the onset steady-state which is always most relevant; while our results suggest that the most significant attributes of the Maithili diphthongs are two: (1) their onset frequency position and (2) their second-formant rate of change, which is always very stable in these diphthongs across changes in duration conditions. This stability is a fact of the production. It seems that the speaker maintains the stability here because he believes this section of the diphthong to be that most relevant for diphthong-perception.

Chapter 5

ELECTROGLOTTOGRAPHIC STUDY OF VOWEL DURATION IN MAITHILI

5.0 Introduction

This chapter gives a detailed account of the duration of the Maithili vowels in various phonetic contexts. In the past there have been quite a few studies on vowel duration in various languages of the world—for instance, in German (e.g. Meyer, 1904), in French (e.g. Gregorie, 1911; Belasco, 1953; Chen, 1970), in Italian (e.g. Metz, 1914), in English (e.g. House and Fairbanks, 1953; Peterson and Lehiste, 1960; House, 1961), in Spanish (e.g. Tomas, 1916; Zimmerman and Sapon, 1958), in Dutch (e.g. Slis and Cohen, 1969), in Russian and Korean (e.g. Chen, 1970), in Bengali (e.g. Kostic and Das, 1972), in Tamil (e.g. Balasubramanian, 1981b), and so on.

One of the major findings of most of these studies has been that, other things being equal, vowels are longer before voiced consonants than before voiceless ones. This phenomenon has usually been considered (e.g. Hollien, 1974; Hardcastle, 1976; Laver, 1980) to be due to an inherent property of the speech production mechanism. A number of different proposals have so far been made as to what precise mechanism is responsible for this lengthening of vowels. Some proposals (e.g. Chomsky and Halle, 1968; Chen, 1970) aim only to account for the lengthening of vowels before voiced and voiceless consonants, while others also aim to account for such factors as: the degree of opening of the vowel (e.g. House and Fairbanks, 1953; Peterson and Lehiste, 1960; House, 1961); place, manner and force of articulation (e.g. Belasco, 1953; Fischer-Jørgensen, 1964; Mohr, 1971) of the following consonants; the structure of the syllable in which the vowel occurs (e.g. Balasubramanian, 1981b), the nature of the phonemic contrasts employed by the language in question (e.g. Zimmerman and Sapon, 1958), and the degree of glottal opening (e.g. Chen, 1970; Ingemann and Yadav, 1978) as well as the airflow rate of the following consonants (e.g. Kim, 1965; Nihalani, 1975a).

It has to be admitted that comparatively little has been published so far on the effect of syllable structure and of aspiration on vowel duration. Relatively recently, Balasubramanian (1981b) has studied the effect of different syllable structures on vowel duration in Tamil, a Dravidian language spoken in South India. Maddieson and Gandour (1976) studied the effect of aspiration on the duration of the Hindi vowel /a/—as spoken in Delhi—and found some interaction between aspiration and vowel duration. In a later study, Maddieson (1977) investigated five languages—i.e. Assamese, Bengali, Hindi, Marathi and Eastern American—and came to the conclusion that vowel lengthening before aspirated consonants is not universal.

The present study reports the results of an electroglottographic study on the relative duration of the Maithili vowels in various phonetic contexts. To present the report systematically, the chapter is divided into three main sections: the first section outlines the experimental methods used to carry out this study; the second section deals with the duration of the major allophonic variants of the Maithili vowels, both oral and nasal; and the third section discusses the influence of aspiration on vowel duration.

5.1 Experimental Method

5.1.1 *Test Utterances*

For the purpose of the present study, appropriate test utterances—as given in Tables 5.1, 5.2 and 5.3—were prepared. Table 5.1 lists test utterances containing the Maithili oral vowels and their major allophonic variants in words of up to four syllable-structure types: V, VC. CV and CVC; Table 5.2 lists test utterances containing the Maithili nasal vowels and their major allophonic variants again in words of up to four syllable-structure types: ṽ̱, ṽ̱C, Cṽ̱ and Cṽ̱C. Both Tables 5.1 and 5.2 contain monosyllabic words as well as words of two syllables and even those of more than two syllables. A blank against a particular column in these first two tables as well as in the tables and figures that follow indicates that no samples could be found in that category.

Table 5.3 lists 24 monosyllabic test utterances containing the following six Maithili oral vowels, /i e a ə o u/, each followed by phonologically

Table 5.1: Test utterances containing the major allophonic variants of the Maithili oral vowels in words of up to 4 syllable-structure types: V, VC, CV and CVC.

Position of vowels in words containing 4 syllable structures: V, VC, CV and CVC				
Vowels	V	VC	CV	CVC
[i:]	[i:] 'this'	[i:š] 'God'	['gi:tə] 'song'	[si:r] 'root'
[i]	[i'nã:m] 'prize'	[iǰ'la:s] 'court'	['ra:ti} 'night'	[sir'ki:] 'tent'
[e:]	['e:kə] 'one'	[e:h] 'oh'	['pe:ṭə] 'stomach'	[se:r] 'kilogramme'
[e]	[e'nã:] 'like this'	[ek'sə: r] 'alone'	[be 'sa:h] 'purchase (n)'	[čel'ha:] 'a fish'
[æ:]	['æ: : bə] 'defect'	[æ:l] 'came'	[mæ:] 'mother'	[sæ:r] 'walking'
[æ]	[æ'la:] '(he) came'	- - -	- - -	- - -
[a:]	['a:rə] 'more; and'	[a:s] 'hope'	['ta:rə] 'wire'	[sa:r] 'wife's brother'
[a]	[a'ka:rə] 'shape'	- - -	[ba'ča:lə] 'eloquent'	- - -
[ə:]	['ə:čʰi] 'has/have'	[ə:ṛ] 'get stuck'	['gʰə:rə] 'house/home'	[sə:r] 'arrow'; 'sir'
[ə]	[ə'mə: rə] 'immortal'	[əs'tʰi:] 'bone'	[sə'ra:p] 'curse'	[ǰən'ta:] 'citizen'
[ɔ:]	['ɔ: ṛʰə] 'hidden'	[ɔ:t] 'will come'	[sɔ:] 'hundred'	[sɔ:r] 'sky'
[ɔ]	[ɔ'ta:] '(he) will come'	- - -	[sunɔ'ti:] '(she) will narrate'	- - -
[o:]	[o:] 'he/she'	[o:s] 'dew'	['čo:rə] 'thief'	[so:r] 'noise'
[o]	[o'sa:rə] 'corridor'	[oǰʰ 'ra:eb] 'disorder'	[kʰo'nã:ṭʰə] 'hot ashes'	[gor'ki:] 'a fair woman'
[u:]	['u:kə] 'a torch'	[u:ṭʰ] 'get up (imp.)'	['mu:lə] 'root; main'	[su:r] 'brave'
[u]	[u'sa:sə] 'consolation'	[ul'ǰʰə̃:n] 'trouble'	[pu'rã:n] 'old'	[sur'ba:l] 'trousers'

Table 5.2: Test utterances containing the major allophonic variants of the Maithili nasal vowels in words of up to four syllable-structure types: ṽ̲, ṽ̲C, Cṽ̲ and Cṽ̲C.

Vowels	Position of vowels in words containing four syllable structures: ṽ̲, ṽ̲C, Cṽ̲ and Cṽ̲C			
	ṽ	ṽC	Cṽ	CṽC
[ĩ:]	['ĩ:ṭa:]'brick'	[ĩ: k^h] 'sugar-cane'	[tõ'hĩ:] 'just you'	[č^{h}ĩṭ] 'garment dyed with spots'
[ĩ]	[ĩ'ǰo:t] 'light'	[ĩjori'ya:] 'moonlight'	['bã:hĩ] 'arm'	- - -
[ẽ:]	[ẽ:ṛə] 'heel'	[ə̃:h] 'a groaning sound'	['gẽ: ṭ^{h}ə] 'knot'	[bẽ:ṭ] 'a ratten'
[æ̃:]	[æ̃:] 'what'	- - -	[sæ̃:] 'husband; lover'	[b^{h}æ̃:t] 'type; kind'
[ã:]	['ã:k^{h}i] 'eye'	[ã:t] 'intestine'	[kə̃'hã:] 'where'	[bã:s] 'bamboo'
[ə̃:]	['ə̃:ṭə] 'get placed'	[ə̃:h] 'no'; 'oh'	[hə̃:] 'yes'	[hə̃:s] 'laugh (imp.)'
[ə]	[ə̃'hĩ:] 'only you'	- - -	[kə̃'ṭa:h] 'thorny'	- - -
[ɔ̃:]	['ɔ̃:ṭə] 'boil (imp.)'	- - -	[su'k^{h}ɔ̃:tə] 'dried vegetable'	[gɔ̃:t] '(cattle) urine'
[õ:]	- - -	- - -	['k^{h}õ: čə] 'slightly torn'	- - -
[õ]	- - -	- - -	[ṭõṭi'æ̃: l] 'seedling becoming apparent'	- - -
[ũ:]	['ũ:ṭə] 'camel'	[ũ:č] 'high'	[kə̃'hũ:] 'somewhere'; 'in case'	[sũṛ^h] 'trunk'
[ũ]	- - -	[ũčka:] 'the one on height'	[sũṛi'yã:nĩ:] 'a hamlet of brewers'	- - -

Table 5.3: Test words containing six Maithili oral vowels followed by voiced and voiceless, aspirated and unaspirated consonants.

Vowels	Words with glosses	Vowels	Words with glosses
/i/	[bi:č] 'centre' [bi:č^h] 'pick up (imp.)' [bi:ǰ] 'seed' [bi: ǰ^h] 'rust'	/ə/	[gə:p] 'talk' *[gə:p^h] (a nonsense word) [gə:b] 'seedings made ready for transplantation (e.g. of paddy crops)' [gə:b^h] 'pregnancy (e.g. of paddy crops)— a metaphorical use'
/e/	[se:p] 'saliva' [se:p^h] 'safe (n)' [se:b] 'to serve' [se:b^h] 'shave'	/o/	[so:k] 'sorrow' [so:k^h] 'swallow' [so:g] 'distress' *[so:g^h] (a nonsense word)
/a/	[sa:t] 'seven' [sa:t^h] 'together' [sa:d] 'longing' [sa:d^h] 'capacity'	/u/	[ku:t] 'amount of grain given by tenants to landlords' [ku:t^h] 'push (e.g. breath out of lungs)' [ku:d] 'jump' *[ku:d^h] (a nonsense word)

contrasting series of four stop or affricate consonants—i.e. voiceless unaspirated, voiceless aspirated, voiced unaspirated and voiced aspirated. Where a complete series of words containing all the stops with differing phonation types in a given place of articulation did not exist, phonologically well-formed nonsense utterances were added to fill the gaps in distribution. Only three such nonsense items were required for the purposes of this study: i.e. *[gɘ:pʰ], *[so:gʰ] and *[ku:dʰ], as given in Table 5.3.

5.1.2 *Equipment*

Each test utterance was afterwards put in a normal conversational sentence context, the frame of the sentence being [ˈpʰe:ro . . . ˈuččaːɽɘ̃ṇ kɘˈru:] 'please . . . pronounce again'. Each test utterance was said in the same frame so as to make sure that the differences are not due to variation in the rate of utterance. The sentences were first randomized and then spoken in a relaxed informal style at a normal conversational speed, without putting any contrastive stress on the test utterances. Sixteen tokens of each test utterance, each token embedded in the above sentence frame, were recorded in a soundproof studio of Essex University with the author as the speaker. These recordings were made on a Revox B 77 tape-recorder. The glottal signal was obtained using an Electroglottograph F-J Electronics Type EG 830. Oscillomink tracings of waveform and amplitude produced from the recorded readings were obtained using a Mingograf Type EM 34T, No. 105. Calculations relating to the 'mean', the 'standard deviation' (SD) and the 'coefficient of variation' (v) of all tokens of each test utterance were made using a Tektronix 31 calculator.

5.1.3 *Duration Measurements*

Of the sixteen tokens of each test utterance, the first two as well as the last two tokens were ignored. All the remaining twelve tokens were used to obtain the duration measurements of the vowels investigated in this study. The first measurements of vowel duration were made from the start of the vowel in question to the closure of the following consonant. In the case of words beginning with voiced stops or affricates and even voiceless unaspirated stops or affricates, the measurement was begun at the release of the initial stop or affricate. After voiceless aspirated stops or affricates, the onset of voicing was used as the starting point.

Afterwards, a simple arithmetic mean of the values of all the twelve tokens of each test utterance and their SD's was worked out. To relate the variation between the different sets of data presented in this chapter, the duration values of all test utterances were normalised by obtaining a coefficient of variation of each test utterance, the equation used being:

$$v = \frac{SD}{Mean} \times 100.$$

5.2 Duration of the Major Allophonic Variants of the Maithili Vowels

Length is a term used in phonetics to refer to the physical duration of a sound or utterance. In phonology this term refers to the abstract relative duration of sounds and syllables. Sometimes the term is restricted to phonological contexts, the phonetic dimension being referred to as 'duration'. Phonologically 'long' and 'short' values are conventionally recognised, both for vowels and consonants. Languages often have one degree of phonological length, and they may have more than one.

Maithili has instances of long and short vowels, although variations in vowel length are completely allophonic in this language. Long vowels occur primarily in stressed contexts, whereas short ones usually occur in unstressed contexts. Length is shown in this study by [:] placed after the concerned symbol. It is used to designate a segment which has relatively greater duration than its shorter variant otherwise phonetically identical. We shall deal with the durations of all the major allophonic variants of the Maithili oral and nasal vowels separately.

5.2.1 ***Duration of the Oral Vowels***

As stated earlier in the second chapter, the oral vowels in Maithili have two (i.e. long and short) major allophonic variants each. The earlier Table 5.1 lists utterances containing both long and short allophonic variants of the Maithili oral vowels. Impressionistically it is felt that in each of these utterances the short allophonic variant is comparatively lax, lower and slightly more centralised than its corresponding long variant. It is also felt that the long allophonic variants of these vowels are at least twice as long as their corresponding short variants.

Table 5.4 gives the mean duration values (in ms) of the major allophonic variants of the Maithili oral vowels as spoken in words of up to four syllable-structure types: V, VC, CV, and CVC, together with their standard deviation and coefficient of variation. The table clearly shows that in words of identical syllable structure the long allophonic variants of

Table 5.4: The mean duration values, the standard deviation and the coefficient of variation (in ms) of the major allophonic variants of the Maithili oral vowels as spoken in words of up to four syllable-structure types: V, VC, CV and CVC.

Vowel	Allophonic variant	Word	Syllable structure	Mean	SD	v
/i/	[i:]	[i:]	V	280	6	2
	[i]	[i'nã:m]	V	71	5	7
	[i:]	[i:š]	VC	230	4	2
	[i]	[iǰ'la:s]	VC	40	4	9
	[i:]	['gi:ṭə]	CV	200	4	2
	[i]	['ra:ti]	CV	45	4	9
	[i:]	[si:r]	CVC	184	5	3
	[i]	[sir'ki:]	CVC	60	4	6
/e/	[e:]	['e:kə]	V	250	6	2
	[e]	[e'nã:]	V	78	5	6
	[e:]	[e:h]	VC	200	6	3
	[e]	[ek'sə:r]	VC	50	4	7
	[e:]	['pe:ṭə]	CV	215	5	2
	[e]	[be'sa:h]	CV	67	5	7
	[e:]	[se:r]	CVC	200	7	3
	[e]	[čel'ha:]	CVC	85	4	5
/æ/	[æ:]	['æ:bə]	V	279	5	2
	[æ]	[æ'la:]	V	120	4	3
	[æ:]	[æ:l]	VC	245	4	2
	[æ]	---	VC	----	-	-
	[æ:]	[mæ:]	CV	254	6	2
	[æ]	- - -	CV	----	-	-
	[æ:]	[sæ:r]	CVC	220	5	2
	[æ]	---	CVC	----	-	-
/a/	[a:]	['a:rə]	V	290	6	2
	[a]	[a'ka:rə]	V	130	5	4
	[a:]	[a:s]	VC	253	5	2
	[a]	----	VC	----	-	-
	[a:]	['ta:rə]	CV	249	4	2

(Contd.)

Vowel	Allophonic variant	Word	Syllable structure	Mean	SD	v
	[a]	[ba’ča:l]	CV	101	4	4
	[a:]	[sa:r]	CVC	234	4	2
	[a]	---	CVC	---	-	-
/ə/	[ə:]	[‘ə:č^{h}i]	V	150	5	3
	[ə]	[ə’mə:rə]	V	50	5	10
	[ə:]	[ə:ṛ]	VC	165	5	3
	[ə]	[əs’t^{h}i:]	VC	49	5	10
	[ə:]	[‘g^{h}ə:rə]	CV	141	5	3
	[ə]	[sə’ra:p]	CV	40	5	13
	[ə:]	[sə:r]	CVC	104	4	3
	[ə]	[ǰən’ta:]	CVC	45	4	9
/ɔ/	[ɔ:]	[‘ɔ:ṛ^{h}ə]	V	260	4	2
	[ɔ]	[ɔ’ta:]	V	105	4	4
	[ɔ:]	[ɔ:t]	VC	249	4	2
	[ɔ]	---	VC	---	-	-
	[ɔ:]	[sɔ:]	CV	270	4	2
	[ɔ]	[sunɔ’ti:]	CV	120	4	3
	[ɔ:]	[sɔ:r]	CVC	221	8	3
	[ɔ]	---	CVC	---	-	-
/o/	[o:]	[o:]	V	281	6	2
	[o]	[o‘sa:rə]	V	80	4	5
	[o:]	[o:s]	VC	229	6	2
	[o]	[oǰ^{h}‘ra:eb]	VC	75	4	5
	[o:]	[’čo:rə]	CV	248	5	2
	[o]	[k^{h}o’nã:ṭ^{h}ə]	CV	70	4	6
	[o:]	[so:r]	CVC	205	5	2
	[o]	[gor’ki:]	CVC	65	5	7
/u/	[u:]	[’u:kə]	V	242	5	2
	[u]	[u’sa:sə]	V	70	5	6
	[u:]	[u:ṭ^{h}]	VC	211	5	2
	[u]	[ul’ǰ^{h}ə:n]	VC	72	5	7
	[u:]	[’mu:lə]	CV	215	5	2
	[u]	[pu’rã:n]	CV	60	5	9
	[u:]	[su:r]	CVC	184	4	2
	[u]	[sur’ba:l]	CVC	69	4	6

these oral vowels have more than twice the duration that their short counterparts have. That is why in Maithili quantity is very important in distinguishing between the major allophonic variants of its vowels.

The table also shows that, other things being equal, open vowels are longer than close vowels. The standard deviation of the allophonic variants given in this table shows a spread of duration values ranging between ±4 and ±8 from the mean values of all the utterances of this table. The coefficient of variation of the long allophonic variants has values ranging between 2 and 3; the coefficient of variation of the short allophonic variants has values ranging between 3 and 13. The range of spread in our data can therefore be regarded as fairly consistent. In each subsequent utterance we can therefore confidently expect the duration of its oral vowels to have either the same score as its mean or somewhere very close to that number.

Table 5.4 also shows that, in general, the more syllables there are in an utterance the lower the duration and the higher the coefficient of variation of the particular vowel studied in that utterance. On the basis of the results of some previous studies (e.g. Lashley, 1951; Peterson and Shoup, 1966), it appears highly likely that articulatory movements are indeed programmed as sequences, and that the time patterns of these articulatory sequences are correlated with linguistic units. As it has been observed in many other languages (e.g. Jones, 1948), Maithili also confirms that an important factor influencing the duration of a speech sound is its position within a higher level phonological unit. It appears that Maithili is one of those languages in which the word as a whole has a certain duration that tends to remain relatively constant, and if the word contains a greater number of segmental sounds, the duration of the segmental sounds decreases as their number in the word increases. The average durations given above in Table 5.4 show that the longer the word, the shorter the actual duration of the vowels. It also seems very likely that the Maithili listener interprets the duration of a particular allophonic variant of the Maithili vowel by relating it to the duration of the word as a whole.

5.2.2 *Duration of the Nasal Vowels*

As stated earlier in the second chapter, there are eight nasal vowels in Maithili: /ĩ ẽ æ̃ ã ə̃ ɔ̃ õ ũ/. Of these, /ẽ æ̃ ã ɔ̃/ are the ones which occur in stressed syllables only, and they therefore have only one variant each.

Table 5.5: The mean duration values, the standard deviation and the coefficient of variation (in ms) of the major allophonic variants of the Maithili nasal vowels as spoken in words of up to four syllable-structure types: ṽ, ṽC,, Cṽ and CṽC.

Vowels	Allophonic variant	word	Syllable structure	Mean	SD	v
/ĩ/	[ĩ:]	['ĩ:ṭa:]	ṽ	170	6	3
	[ĩ]	[ĩ'ǰo:t]	ṽ	80	6	8
	[ĩ:]	[ĩ:kʰ]	ṽC	181	6	3
	[ĩ]	[ĩǰori'ya:]	ṽC	50	4	8
	[ĩ:]	[tõ'hĩ:]	Cṽ	150	5	3
	[ĩ]	['bã:hĩ]	Cṽ	65	5	7
	[ĩ:]	[čʰĩ:ṭ]	CṽC	140	5	4
	[ĩ]	---	CṽC	---	-	-
/ẽ/	[ẽ:]	['ẽ:ṛə]	ṽ	196	5	3
	[ẽ:]	[ẽ:h]	ṽC	245	5	2
	[ẽ:]	['gẽ:ṭʰə]	Cṽ	180	5	3
	[ẽ:]	[bẽ:ṭ]	CṽC	175	3	2
/æ̃/	[æ̃:]	[æ̃:]	ṽ	293	5	2
	[æ̃:]	---	ṽC	---	-	-
	[æ̃:]	[sæ̃:]	Cṽ	250	5	2
	[æ̃:]	[bʰæ̃:t]	CṽC	206	5	2
/ã/	[ã:]	['ã:kʰi]	ṽ	245	6	2
	[ã:]	[ã:t]	ṽC	249	5	2
	[ã:]	[kə̃'hã:]	Cṽ	211	5	2
	[ã:]	[bã:s]	CṽC	237	6	2
/ə̃/	[ə̃:]	['ə̃:ṭə]	ṽ	140	5	4
	[ə̃]	[ə̃'hĩ:]	ṽ	65	4	6
	[ə̃:]	[ə̃:h]	ṽC	150	4	3
	[ə̃]	---	ṽC	---	-	-
	[ə̃:]	[hə̃:]	Cṽ	164	4	2
	[ə̃]	[kə̃'ṭa:h]	Cṽ	50	5	10

(Contd.)

	[ə̃:]	[hə̃:s]	Cṽ̲C	130	5	3
	[ə̃]	---	Cṽ̲C	---	-	-
/ɔ̃/	[ɔ̃:]	['ɔ̃:ṭə]	ṽ̲	232	4	2
	[ɔ̃:]	---	ṽ̲C	---	-	-
	[ɔ̃:]	[su'kʰɔ̃:tə]	Cṽ̲	184	6	3
	[ɔ̃:]	[gɔ̃:t]	Cṽ̲C	195	5	2
/õ/	[õ:]	---	ṽ̲	---	-	-
	[õ]	---	ṽ̲	---	-	-
	[õ:]	---	ṽ̲C	---	-	-
	[õ]	---	ṽ̲C	---	-	-
	[õ:]	['kʰõ:čə]	Cṽ̲	176	6	-
	[õ]	[ṭõṭi'æ:l]	Cṽ̲	74	6	8
	[õ:]	---	Cṽ̲C	---	-	-
	[õ]	---	Cṽ̲C	---	-	-
/ũ/	[ũ:]	['ũ:ṭə]	ṽ̲	195	4	2
	[u]	---	ṽ̲	---	-	-
	[ũ:]	[ũ:č]	ṽ̲C	205	4	2
	[ũ]	[ũčka:]	ṽ̲C	50	4	9
	[ũ:]	[kə̃'hũ:]	Cṽ̲	165	4	2
	[ũ]	[sũri'ya:nĩ:]	Cṽ̲	65	6	9
	[ũ:]	[sũ:rʰ]	Cṽ̲C	178	7	4
	[ũ]	---	Cṽ̲C	---	-	-

The remaining four nasal vowels /ĩ ə̃ õ ũ/ occur in both stressed and unstressed syllables, and they therefore have both long and short allophonic variants. As in the case of the oral vowels, impressionistically it is felt that the short allophonic variants of the Maithili nasal vowels are also comparatively lax, lower and more centralised than their corresponding long variants. It is also felt that the duration of the long allophonic variants of /ĩ ə̃ ɔ̃ ũ/, too, is more than twice that of their short variants.

Table 5.5 presents the mean duration values (in ms) of all the major allophonic variants of the Maithili nasal vowels as spoken in words of up to four syllable-structure types: ṽ̲, ṽ̲C, Cṽ̲ and Cṽ̲C, together with their standard deviation and coefficient of variation. This table also shows that in words of identical syllable structure the duration of the long allophonic variants of /ĩ ə̃ õ ũ/, too, is more than twice that of their short variants. The table further shows that, other things being equal, in syllables of identical structure the open nasal vowels are longer in duration than the close ones.

As in the case of the oral vowels, quantity is again seen to be very important in distinguishing between the major allophonic variants of the Maithili nasal vowels. The standard deviation of all the allophonic variants given in Table 5.5 shows a spread of duration values ranging between ±3 and ±7 from the mean values of all the utterances given in this table. The coefficient of variation of all the long allophonic variants of the nasal vowels has values ranging between 2 and 4; the coefficient of variation of the short allophonic variants of these nasal vowels has values ranging between 4 and 7. Thus, the range of spread in our data can, once again, be regarded as quite consistent, and in each subsequent utterance we can therefore confidently expect the duration of the nasal vowel under investigation to have either the same score as its mean given in Table 5.5 or somewhere very close to that number.

Once again, it is found that, in general, the more syllables there are in an utterance the lower the duration and the higher the coefficient of variation of the nasal vowel under investigation in that utterance. In other words, the data given in Table 5.5 clearly show that the position of the speech sound within a higher level phonological unit is one of the most important factors influencing the duration of that speech sound. These data, too, strengthen the observation that Maithili is one of those languages in which the word as a whole has a certain duration that tends to remain relatively constant, and if the word contains a greater number of segmental sounds, the duration of the segmental sounds decreases as their number in the word increases. The average durations given in Table 5.5 show that the longer the word, the shorter the actual duration of the vowels. It seems very probable that the Maithili listener interprets the duration of a particular vowel, whether oral or nasal, by relating it to the duration of the word as a whole.

5.3. The Influence of Aspiration on Vowel Duration in Maithili

Since from a preliminary survey of some published sources (e.g. House and Fairbanks, 1953; Zimmerman and Sapon, 1958; Peterson and Lehiste, 1960; House, 1961; Delattre, 1962; Fischer-Jørgensen, 1964) preceding consonants exhibit no readily discernible patterns of environmental influence on the duration of the following vowels, we have restricted ourselves in the present study to the influence of the following consonants on the duration of preceding vowels. As stated earlier in the third chapter, Maithili has four phonologically contrasting series of stop and affricate consonants—i.e. voiceless unaspirated, voiceless aspirated, voiced unaspirated and voiced aspirated. The present study looks into the influence of these four contrasting series of postvocalic consonants on the duration of vowels in Maithili.

Table 5.6: The mean duration values, the standard deviation, the coefficient of variation and the duration-ratio of the six Maithili oral vowels followed by voiced and voiceless, aspirated and unaspirated consonants.

Vowel	Word	Mean	SD	v	Ratio
/i/	[bi:č]	165	5	3	1.00
	[bi:čʰ]	183	5	3	1.15
	[bi:ǰ]	210	5	3	1.27
	[bi:ǰʰ]	224	5	2	1.35
/e/	[se:p]	174	5	3	1.00
	[se:pʰ]	195	5	3	1.12
	[se:b]	218	4	2	1.25
	[se:bʰ]	240	5	2	1.37
/a/	[sa:t]	202	6	3	1.00
	[sa:tʰ]	226	7	3	1.11
	[sa:d]	240	5	2	1.18
	[sa:dʰ]	275	6	2	1.36
/ə/	[gə:p]	104	4	4	1.00
	*[gə:pʰ]	120	5	4	1.15
	[gə:b]	134	6	5	1.28
	[gə:bʰ]	159	4	3	1.52
/o/	[so:k]	166	5	3	1.00
	[so:kʰ]	180	8	4	1.08
	[so:g]	204	8	4	1.22
	*[so:gʰ]	239	6	3	1.43
/u/	[ku:t]	155	5	3	1.00
	[ku:tʰ]	175	4	2	1.12
	[ku:d]	220	5	2	1.41
	*[ku:dʰ]	240	5	2	1.54

As mentioned earlier (5.1.1), twenty-four monosyllabic test utterances—three of which are in fact *nonsense* but phonogically *possible* in Maithili—containing the Maithili oral vowels /i e a ə o u/ were chosen for this study. As listed earlier in Table 5.3, each of these six vowels occurs in four minimal word pairs, and each word of these pairs differs only in the final consonant. The experimental method used to record these minimal word pairs, and the procedure used to measure vowel duration in these words were the same as outlined earlier in the first section (5.1) of this chapter.

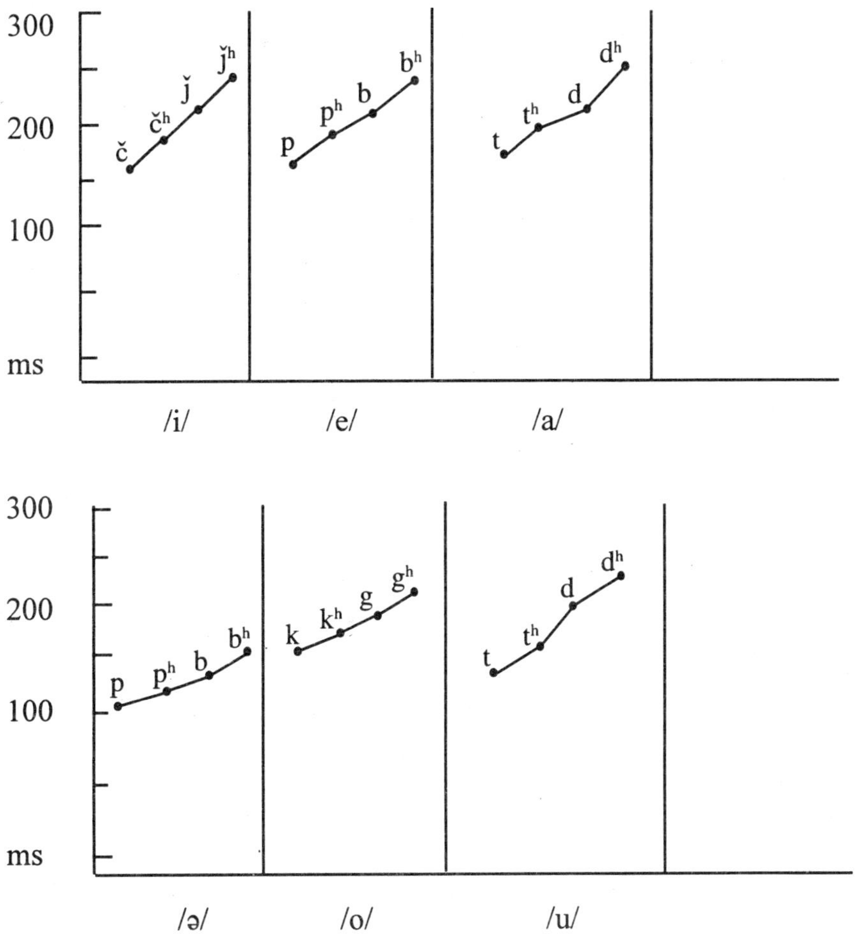

Figure 5.1: The mean duration of the Maithili oral vowels as spoken in monosyllabic minimal word pairs, each word of the pair differing only in the final cosonant.

Table 5.6 presents the results of this study. It shows the mean duration values of the six oral vowels as obtained form the twelve tokens of each test utterance, the standard deviation of the twelve tokens of each utterance, the coefficient of variation of every utterance as well as the ratio of the duration of vowels preceding voiced and aspirated consonants to the duration of vowels preceding voiceless unaspirated consonants. A representation of the mean duration values of this table is given in Figure 5.1. This figure shows postvocalic stop and affricate consonants of various places of articulation, against the duration of the six oral vowels in milliseconds (ms).

Both Table 5.6 and Figure 5.1 clearly show that all six vowels investigated in this study have longer mean durations before voiced and aspirated stop as well as affricate consonants than before their voiceless unaspirated counterparts. All the mean duration-measurements and their illustrations given in Table 5.6 and in Figure 5.1, respectively, amply show that the aspiration of the following consonant does affect vowel duration in Maithili. The present data sufficiently reveal that the overall pattern found between the relative durations of the six Maithili oral vowels—each vowel preceding consonants of four different phonation types—is very similar, and that in this language:

(i) vowels are relatively longer in duration before voiceless aspirated consonants than before voiceless unaspirated consonants;
(ii) vowels preceding voiced unaspirated consonants are relatively longer in duration than those preceding either voiceless unaspirated or voiceless aspirated consonants;
(iii) vowels are relatively longer in duration before voiced aspirated consonants than before voiced unaspirated consonants; and
(iv) in general, other things being equal, open vowels are relatively longer than close vowels.

The results of the present study suggest that two rules, perhaps 'low-level phonetic rules', operate in Maithili. They may be written as in (1) below:

(1)

a. vowel adds 1 increment of length before aspirates; and
b. vowel adds 2 increments of length before voicing.

Applying these rules gives the results shown in (2) below:

(2)

vowel before voiceless unaspirates:	0 increment
vowel before voiceless aspirates:	1 increment
vowel before voiced unaspirates:	2 increments
vowel before voiced aspirates:	3 increments

These findings offer support for the traditional grouping of the Maithili consonants—like perhaps the consonants of most other Indo-Aryan languages—not only into voiced and voiceless categories but also into aspirated and unaspirated. In other words, we may say with confidence that in Maithili the features of both voice and aspiration do independently lend increments of length to the preceding vowel. From a diachronic perspective it would seem possible that a 'phonologization' of the rule that lengthens vowels before aspirated consonants could result in long vowels being the historical reflection of aspiration.

While these questions of diachronic and synchronic phonology are of interest, the most interesting aspect of our results is the challenge presented to the various proposed 'explanations' (e.g. Belasco, 1953; Delattre, 1962; Halle and Stevens, 1967; Chomsky and Halle, 1968; Slis and Cohen, 1969; Chen, 1970; Lehiste, 1970b; Mohr, 1971) of the cause of the intrinsic length of vowels before consonants of different phonation types. Four main theories appear to be represented in the literature on this subject. We shall first briefly state each one of them and then we shall see how each one of them fits in with our data from Maithili.

One theory (e.g. Belasco, 1953; Delattre, 1962) proposes that the duration of a vowel varies inversely with the force of articulation required for the following consonant. This theory assumes that, other things being equal, the 'force' used for each syllable is kept constant. As voiceless stops and affricates are usually considered (e.g.. Belasco, 1953; Delattre, 1962; Gimson, 1970) to be more 'fortis' than voiced ones, this theory predicts that less forceful, and hence 'shorter', vowels will occur before voiceless consonants. But, as discussed in detail in the next chapter (6.2.7), relatively recent experimental evidence—as obtained from cineradiographic studies (e.g. Kim, 1970) as well as from fiberoptic studies (e.g. Kagaya, 1974; Kagaya and Hirose, 1975; Ingemann and Yadav, 1978)—do not suggest that aspirated stops are articulated with less force than unaspirated ones. This theory therefore fails to predict that vowels are longer before aspirated consonants.

A second theory (e.g. Kozhevnikov and Chistovich, 1965; Slis, 1968; Slis and Cohen, 1969; Lehiste, 1970b) posits a relatively constant duration for the syllable. This duration is said to be maintained by adjusting the duration of segments. In the case of vowels before voiced and voiceless consonants, it is the length of the vowel that is assumed to be adjusted. A further assumption that this theory makes is that voiced consonants are inherently shorter than voiceless ones, and for that reason longer vowels are predicted to appear before the voiced consonants to compensate for their shorter duration.

If this theory is to make the correct predictions about our data, we should find that the duration of, for example, /t/ is longer than the durations of /t^h/ and /d/, and that the duration of /d^h/ is the shortest of all. Although there was some difficulty in measuring the duration of the consonants as it was not always easy to identify the moment of release for the dental stops in all tokens, nevertheless the durations of the final consonants of four Maithili words were measured with a fair amount of accuracy. The results of these measurements are given in Table 5.7:

Table 5.7: The mean duration of the postvocalic / t t^h d d^h/ as spoken in four Maithili minimal word pairs (in ms).

Consonants	Words with glosses	Duration
/t/	[sa:t] 'seven'	75
/t^h/	[sa:t^h] 'together'	85
/d/	[sa:d] 'longing; wish'	90
/d^h/	[sa:d^h] 'capacity'	100

As the table shows, both the unaspirated and aspirated stops of the words measured are distinguished by marked differences in duration. That is to say, both the aspirated dental consonants of the table are markedly longer in duration than their unaspirated counterparts. Yet the vowels before / t^h/ and /d^h/ are longer than the ones before /t/ and /d/, respectively. Therefore a theory of compensatory temporal adjustment cannot fully explain the pattern of vowel length found in our Maithili data.

A third theory (e.g. Peterson and Lehiste, 1960; Elert, 1965; Halle and Stevens, 1967; Chomsky and Halle, 1968; Mohr, 1971) posits that vowels before voiced consonants are longer because it requires a complex, and therefore *slow* adjustment to move from the glottal configuration for voicing in a vowel ('spontaneous voicing') to that for voicing in an obstruent ('non-spontaneous voicing', due to a reduced pressure drop across the glottis). The movement from the glottal configuration for voicing in a vowel to the open glottal configuration for a voiceless consonant is a rather simple, and hence more rapidly executed, adjustment. This theory predicts a long vowel before an aspirated consonant *only if* the adjustment of the glottis required is a complex one similar to that required in moving a voiced obstruent.

But—as we discuss and illustrate this point at some considerable length in the sixth chapter (6.2.7)—voiceless aspirated stops *are* produced with a glottis widely open—in fact, with more open a glottis than that required for the production of voiceless unaspirated stops. Yet the Maithili vowel preceding voiceless aspirated stops is regularly longer in duration than the one preceding voiceless unaspirated stops. Similarly, the glottal opening for the voiced aspirates is always much wider than it is for the voiced unaspirates, and yet the Maithili vowels preceding voiced aspirates *are* invariably longer in duration than those preceding voiced unaspirates.. Therefore, the greater length of vowels before aspirated consonants cannot be explained by 'slow' adjustment in the positioning of the vocal folds. Further problems with this laryngeal adjustment theory have also been pointed out by other researchers (e.g. Chen, 1970; Wang, 1972).

A fourth theory (e.g. Chen, 1970) suggests that shorter vowels are due to the wider glottal opening and stronger airflow for voiceless consonants. According to this theory, a more energetic closure is required to overcome the stronger airflow, and such an energetic closure is achieved more rapidly than the closure for the articulators in production of a voiced stop. Chen (1970) presents data from English and shows that the closure for a final /p/ in English is carried out within a shorter period of time than the closure for /b/. If the rate of closure is determined by airflow and if durational differences are the result of faster or slower rates of closure, then the length of vowels before aspirated consonants must also be determined by the airflow rates for these consonants. Thus, as both voiceless and voiced aspirates (e.g. /p^h/ and /b^h/) have higher airflow rates than their voiceless and voiced unaspirated counterparts (e.g. /p/ and / b/), this theory predicts a shorter vowel before voiceless and voiced aspirates (e.g. before /p^h/ and /b^h/) than before voiceless and voiced unaspirates (e.g. before /p/ and /b/), respectively. But our data from Maithili have shown the opposite results.

5.4 Summary of Conclusions

Thus, the results of the present electroglottographic study on the duration of vowels in various phonetic environments in Maithili lead to the following main observations.

First, variations in vowel length are completely allophonic in Maithili: the long allophonic variants of its vowels occur primarily in stressed syllables; the short variants occur mainly in unstressed syllables. The oral vowels have both long and short variants each; the four nasal vowels / ĩ ə̃ õ ũ/, too, have both long and short variants each, while the remaining four nasal vowels /ẽ æ̃ ã ɔ̃/ occur in stressed syllables only and they therefore have only one variant each. In general, other things being equal, the average duration of the stressed long vowels is more than twice the duration of their unstressed short counterparts.

Second, the duration of the Maithili vowels, whether oral or nasal, seems to be correlated with tongue height. That is to say, in general, other things being equal, open vowels in Maithili are longer in duration than close vowels.

Third, Maithili shows that an important factor influencing the duration of a speech segment is its position within a higher level phonological unit. The results of our study have shown that the Maithili vowels are longest in duration in syllables of the structure V/ṽ̲ and shortest in syllables of the structure CVC/Cṽ̲C. It also appears from our results that Maithili is one of those languages in which the word as a whole has a certain duration that tends to remain relatively constant, and if the word contains a greater number of segmental sounds, the duration of the segmental sounds decreases as their number in the word increases. Hence, the longer the word, the shorter the actual duration of the vowels in it.

Finally, the results of the present study clearly show that phonation types other than voicelessness and voicing also affect the relative duration of the vowel preceding a consonant. We have found that the features of both voice and aspiration independently lend increments of length to the preceding vowels in Maithili. This clearly means that the 'explanations' proposed in the literature so far (e.g. Belasco, 1953; Delattre, 1962; Halle and Stevens, 1967; Chomsky and Halle, 1968; Slis, 1968; Slis and Cohen, 1969; Lehiste, 1970b; Chen, 1970; Mohr, 1971) to account for vowel lengthening before voiced and voiceless stops cannot be extended to account also for vowel lengthening before both voiceless and voiced aspirated obstruents. We therefore hope that the results of our study will promote a rethinking of recent and current explanations of the interaction of phonation type and vowel duration, and will assist in the formation of new theories predicting the influence of the following aspirated/unaspirated consonants on the relative duration of preceding vowels.

Chapter 6

DISTINCTIVE FEATURES AND REDUNDANCY CONDITIONS OF THE MAITHILI PHONEMES

6.0 Introduction

This chapter has three main sections. In the first, we present a brief account of the theory of distinctive features. In the second, we propose a set of sixteen distinctive features to characterise both the individual sound segments in Maithili and the natural classes of segments which undergo similar phonological processes in this and other Indic languages. Of these sixteen features, fifteen are in fact the Chomsky-Halle features which we only briefly outline. But our 16th feature is: [aspirated]. Our treatment of this feature is very different from that of Chomsky and Halle's (1968: 326) 'heightened subglottal pressure'. We therefore put forward a detailed discussion on aspiration and present a more realistic description of it, recommending that the feature [aspirated] be included in the Chomsky-Halle theory of distinctive features. In the third section of this chapter, we outline some of the main segmental redundancy conditions in Maithili. Our conclusions are summarised at the end of the chapter.

6.1 Distinctive Feature Theory in Brief

The relationship between segment and sound is a central concern of phonology. A framework for the definition of this relationship is that of distinctive features. Distinctive features may be seen either as part of the definition of phonemes, or as an alternative to the notion of the phoneme. The first of these views is found in the approach of the Prague School (e.g. see Trubetzkoy, 1939/1969), where the phoneme is seen as a bundle of phonetic distinctive features. The traditional system of articulatory phonetics is basic and necessary to an understanding of the phonological literature. But in formulating phonological rules, it is sometimes helpful to have another way of talking about speech sounds. Instead of treating sound segments as indivisible or atomic entities, as the symbols of the phonetic alphabet would suggest they are, linguists (e.g. Jakobson, Fant, and Halle, 1952; Jakobson and Halle, 1956; Chomsky and Halle, 1968) prefer to describe speech sounds as complexes of properties called distinctive features. It is now widely held (e.g. see Chomsky and Halle, 1968; Schane, 1973; Hyman, 1975; Sommerstein, 1977) that it is the features which are the minimal units of phonological analysis, not the phonemes. It is argued that by substituting features for phonemes in this way, generalisations can be made about the relationships between speech sounds in a language, which would otherwise be missed. Moreover, because features are usually phonetic units, it would be possible to make inter-language and cross-language comparisons, and eventually statements about phonological universals, more readily than by using a phonemic model of phonology.

The distinctive features of Chomsky and Halle (1968) are based to a great extent on the work of Jakobson, Fant and Halle (1952) and Jakobson and Halle (1956). But the Chomsky-Halle distinctive features do reveal a number of modifications. These modifications are to be found both in the specific set of distinctive features used to capture contrasts and in the conceptualisation of these features. While the emphasis in the Jakobson and Halle (1956) approach is firmly on the nature of the oppositions between the *underlying* features involved, rather than on the description of the range of phonetic realisations each feature represents, in the Chomsky-Halle (1968) approach more attention is paid to the phonetic realisations of the underlying features recognised, and a different system of feature classification is set up.

One of the most important questions in connection with distinctive feature theories is whether features should be defined in articulatory, acoustic or auditory terms. Since the earliest phonetic studies, speech segments have been classified according to their *articulatory* properties. While this is the most common and oldest way of classifying speech sounds, it is also possible with technological advances to group speech sounds according to their acoustic properties. That is, phonetic features such as the one distinguishing [p] from [b] can be stated either in terms of what is involved in the production of such speech sounds in the vocal tract or in terms of the characteristics of the acoustic signal which results from the different articulatory gestures. In other words, segments can be similar or dissimilar either in the way they are made or in the way they sound—both aspects are of course related, and there is a need for both articulatory and acoustic features in phonology.

While Jakobson and his associates attempted to combine articulatory, acoustic and auditory features, they do not give auditory definitions. As Jakobson (1962: 489) himself says, "the distinctive features have been portrayed only on the motor and on the acoustic level, because these are the only two aspects for which we so far possess detailed information". While Jakobson favours the approach to define features mainly in acoustic terms, Chomsky and Halle favour articulatory definitions of their features. Although it is true to say that perception and historical linguistics cannot get by without the use of articulatory features alongside acoustic ones, the higher levels of phonology (i.e. the ones before phonetic interpretation) may well need only articulatory features, as Chomsky and Halle (1968) tacitly assumed.

The present author has found no cases where acoustic features are demonstrably superior to articulatory features for synchronic phonological analyses. The present study therefore maintains that a feature theory, in so far as it seeks to account for independently controllable aspects of speech events, must be articulatorily based; for the control is control over muscular movements, not over their acoustic effects. Although not entirely conclusive, the evidence (cf. Stevens, 1972) nonetheless does suggest that we perceive speech not directly in terms of sound waves, but in terms of the articulations that we would have to make to generate those sound waves. This study therefore regards that, from the point of view of the requirement of phonetic specifiability, an articulatorily based feature system is not only justifiable but also necessary.

6.2 Distinctive Features of the Maithili Phonemes

The set of distinctive features put forth by Chomsky and Halle (1968) is a significant reformulation of the distinctive feature theory. Although not ideal, their set does nevertheless represent a considerable improvement over earlier work. The discussion of the distinctive features which follows is based primarily on their work, with only two modifications which seemed necessary in this study. The two areas affected here concern: (1) the phonological characterisation of the Maithili [h], and (2) the treatment of aspiration in this language. As stated earlier (6.0), sixteen distinctive features are used in this study for the description and classification of the Maithili phonemes. All these features are mainly articulatorily based, like the Chomsky-Halle features, as they all describe the Maithili phonemes from the point of view of the requirement of phonetic specifiability. Since fifteen of these features have already been described in detail by Chomsky and Halle (1968: 301-29), the present study gives mainly the articulatory correlates of these features and comments briefly on some of them. The main bulk of our discussion lies in our sixteenth feature, [aspirated], which is not at all included even in the Chomsky-Halle set of distinctive features.

6.2.1 *Some Basic Concepts*

Before we embark upon the description of the distinctive features in Maithili, we must first say a few words in connection with the following three fundamental concepts: binarity, the neutral position, and vocal cord vibration—spontaneous and otherwise.

One of the main contributions of Jakobson and his associates was the idea to convert all phonological features into binary ones. Binary features are properties which can be used to classify linguistic units in terms of two mutually exclusive possibilities—e.g. in phonology the presence versus the absence of vocal cord vibration. Binary features are a major organisational principle of distinctive feature theories of phonology, where it is conventional to mark the opposition using +/- in square brackets. In this study it is maintained that the binary notation is ideal for all features indicating opposite qualities. The simplicity of the binary system allows us to inquire whether all features—including those which at first are not obviously binary, such as the height features for vowels or the place of articulation features for consonants—are capable of a binary interpretation. The principle of binarity is maintained in this study only at the phonological level, whereas scales are permitted at the phonetic level. In the phonological matrix only we will use a + or - to indicate that the particular phoneme belongs to one of two opposite categories.

Since Chomsky and Halle define their features primarily from an articulatory point of view, they make an important attempt to clarify the notion of the 'neutral position'. According to them (Chomsky and Halle, 1968: 300), it can readily be observed that just prior to speaking speakers position their vocal tracts in a certain characteristic manner. They call this configuration the 'neutral position', and describe four main ways in which this configuration differs from the configuration of the vocal tract during quiet breathing. We shall present the description of the distinctive features of the Maithili phonemes accepting, on the whole, the Chomsky-Halle's notion of the neutral position.

Chomsky and Halle (1968: 300-301) point out that there are two major factors controlling vocal cord vibration: (1) the difference in air pressure below and above the glottis, and (2) the configuration of the vocal cords themselves—i.e. their tension, shape, relative position, and so on. They postulate that in the neutral position the positioning of the vocal cords remains such that they can vibrate spontaneously in response to the unimpeded air flow—as it happens in the articulation of sonorants. However, it is also well-established (e.g. see Halle and Stevens, 1967; Laver, 1980) that vocal cord vibrations also occur when there is a radical constriction, or even total closure, in the oral cavity—as it happens in the articulation of some obstruents. Chomsky and Halle hold that obstruents require different mechanisms for voice from those used for sonorants: they call the voicing of obstruents to be "non-spontaneous", while that of sonorants to be "spontaneous", Relatively recent studies (e.g. Nihalani, 1975a and 1975b; Laver, 1980) seem to support the theoretical conclusion that the air flow in voiced obstruents is noticeably faster than in sonorants. This fact can readily be explained on the ground (e.g. see Ingemann and Yadav, 1978) that the average glottal opening is larger in obstruents than in vowels. Moreover, lengthening of vowels before voiced obstruents (e.g. see R. Yadav, 1984; S.K. Jha, 1990) also strengthens the Chomsky-Halle stand. Therefore, for the purpose of our description of the distinctive features of the Maithili phonemes, we take the Chomsky-Halle view of vocal cord vibration ("spontaneous"/"non-spontaeous") as unarguable.

6.2.2 *Major Class Features*

As in the case of other languages, three features—i.e. [sonorant], [syllabic] and [consonantal]—interact to yield the major speech sound classes in Maithili. Each of these features focuses on a different aspect of the open-versus-closed phase of the vocal tract in speech. These features define the distinctions between vowels, consonants, liquids and nasals, as well as glides. Since all languages distinguish between these classes of speech sounds, the major class features define a much more basic opposition than some of the other features that will be discussed later.

The feature [sonorant] refers to the resonant quality of a speech sound. That is, it is used to classify all those speech sounds that are made by shaping the vocal tract so that the airstream passes essentially unimpeded through either the oral or nasal cavity, with a vocal cord position such that spontaneous voicing is possible. The Maithili vowels, nasals and approximants are all therefore classified as [+ sonorant], whereas stops, fricatives and affricates are all classified as [- sonorant].

Since both vowels and glides are classified as [+ sonorant], a second feature is therefore necessary to distinguish between these two classes. The feature [syllabic] is used for this purpose. This feature characterises the speech segments with the greatest prominence in a syllable. That is, [syllabic] designates those speech sounds that form the nucleus of the syllable. Since the syllable has not yet been defined satisfactorily in phonetic terms, the phonetic correlates of this feature are unclear. Like all other languages, the Maithili vowels usually constitute the nucleus of the syllable and are hence [+ syllabic], while glides, liquids and nasals, as well as obstruents are normally [-syllabic].

The feature [consonantal] is used to designate those speech sounds that are produced either with contact between articulator and point of articulation, or with a degree of closure severe enough to produce frication. Therefore, the feature [consonantal] groups together liquids, nasals, and obstruents and opposes these speech sounds to vowels and glides, which are [- consonantal].

It should be made clear here that in the present study the phonological characterisation of /h/—at least in terms of the above-mentioned three 'major class features'—is done rather differently from that of Chomsky and Halle. They specify (Chomsky and Halle, 1968: 303) /h/ as: [+ sonorant,- syllabic (vocalic), - consonantal]; our specification of the Maithili /ɦ/, on the other hand, is as: [-sonorant, -syllabic, +consonantal]. A few words must therefore be said as to why we specify the Maithili /ɦ/ as [- sonorant, + consonantal], and not as [+ sonorant, - consonantal].

The 'standard' characterisation of [h] is "an oblique challenge" (Lass, 1976: 145) to the traditional term: 'glottal fricative'. Chomsky and Halle assign [h], with hardly any discussion, to the category 'glide', with [?] and [y w]. Their interpretation of [h] appears to derive from Jakobson, Fant and Halle (1952: 19):

> The so called glides . . . like the English *h* and the "glottal catch", are distinguished from vowels in that they have either a non-harmonic source as in the case of [h] or a transient onset of the source as in [?]. They are distinct from consonants in that they have no significant zeroes in their spectra.

In the present study it is held that the physiological correlates, phonological behaviour, and historical sources of the Maithili phoneme /h/ (e.g. see S. Jha, 1958: 190-92, for the historical details of this speech segment) do not support the above acoustic definition of [h] as given by Jakobson, Fant and Halle (1952: 19).

The Maithili /h/ is a non-oral segment. The present study classifies it as a voiceless glottal fricative, since in its articulation there does occur a glottal stricture impeding the flow of air through the mouth—although /h/ seems to have a smaller area of occlusion than the fricative, say, /s/. It should be recalled that Chomsky and Halle (1968: 302) define sonorant articulations as those where 'spontaneous voicing' can occur—that is, where a low rate of transglottal air-flow is sufficient to produce a pressure-drop. The Maithili /h/ certainly does not permit this 'spontaneous voicing' and it cannot therefore be classified as [+ sonorant].

If we turn to the phonology of Maithili, we find a phenomenon related to the phoneme /h/ itself: i.e. the common dropping of $\underline{h}$ in different phonological contexts, as put in informal terms below:

$$h \longrightarrow Ø / V \text{———} V \ \#$$

Synchronic evidence for this elision of h is discussed at some considerable length in the eighth chapter of this study. We have not come across any significant evidence where /h/ can be said to undergo any common phonological process with the Maithili glides /y/ and /w/. [h] is perceptually less distinct than other segments, because of its lack of a locational gesture in the oral cavity. This accounts for the ease with which [h] is influenced by the cavity shapes of surrounding vowels. And this in turn may suggest why it is so eminently deletable: perceptually it is in fact a voiceless anticipation of a vowel, and as such can easily merge with one if the voicing is simply extended back a little.

6.2.3 *Place of Articulation Features*

Chomsky and Halle (1968: 303-304) classify four principal places for consonantal articulation—labial, dental, palatoalveolar and velar—using two features: [anterior] and [coronal]. This classification is based on two main points: (1) whether the constriction is at the extreme forward region of the oral cavity or it is more retracted; and (2) whether the articulator is the blade of the tongue or some other articulator.

Speech sounds articulated at or in front of the alveolar ridge are anterior; those that are articulated farther back than the alveolar ridge are non-anterior. Thus, labials, dentals and alveolars are [+ anterior], while palato-alveolars, palatals and velars are all [- anterior]. The feature [coronal] is used to characterise those speech sounds that are made by raising the apex or front of the tongue to form a partial or total obstruction. Since these parts of the tongue can be used only in articulations involving the teeth, alveolar ridge or palate, the dentals, alveolars, retroflexes and palatoalveolars in Maithili are therefore classified as [+ coronal], whereas its labials, glides and velars are all classified as [- coronal].

6.2.4 *Body of Tongue Features*

Three features relate to the position of the body of the tongue: [high], [low] and [back]. Chomsky and Halle (1968: 304-308) define these features with respect to a reference point, which is the position of the tongue when it is in the 'neutral position'. High vowels are articulated by raising the tongue body above this point, low vowels by lowering the tongue body below this point, and back vowels by retraction from this point.

Chomsky and Halle's definitions of the features [high] and [low] prohibit a speech sound from being simultaneously [+ high] and [+ low], because the articulation underlying this configuration is impossible on account of the fact that the tongue cannot simultaneously be raised and lowered. Therefore, in the Chomsky-Halle system vowels have to be classified in terms of not more than three possible degrees of vowel height: i.e. 'high', 'mid', and 'low', specified as [+ high], [- high, - low] and [+ low], respectively. Since Maithili distinguishes three degrees of vowel height, the features [high] and [low] are therefore adequate to define those phonological rules in Maithili (as discussed in the next chapter) that depend on vowel height. As for the feature [back], the Maithili vowels can be classified in terms of the binary values [+ back] and [- back]. But the process of the 'breaking' of vowels in Maithili, which we discuss at some length in the next chapter, suggests that it can sometimes be convenient to use the phonological possibilities [front], [central] and [back].

6.2.5 *Lip Shape Feature*

The feature [round] distinguishes speech sounds with lip rounding from those without. According to Chomsky and Halle (1968: 309), "Rounded sounds are produced with a narrowing of the lip orifice; non-rounded sounds are produced without such a narrowing". The Maithili vowels /ɔ ɔ̃ o õ u ũ/ and the bilabial glide /w/ are [+ round], while the remaining speech sounds are [- round].

6.2.6 *Manner of Articulation Features*

As mentioned earlier (6.2.2), the features [sonorant] and [consonantal] enable us to distinguish obstruents from sonorants, and glides from other consonants. But among obstruents we still need to distinguish stops, fricatives and affricates. Similarly, among sonorant consonants, we still have to differentiate nasals from liquids, and, for the latter, laterals from non-laterals. We use the following five Chomsky-Halle features—i.e. [continuant], [delayed release], [strident], [nasal] and [lateral]—in order to distinguish all these speech sounds in Maithili on the basis of the manner of their articulation.

The stops, affricates and fricatives in Maithili are distinguished by the features [continuant] and [delayed release]. The stops and affricates have a stricture that impedes air flow and hence are classified as [-continuant], while the fricatives permit air to flow through their stricture and hence are classified as [+ continuant]. The feature [delayed release] distinguishes the two types of consonants produced with closure. In affricates the release of the closure is gradual and hence there is a period after the release when the articulators assume the position of the cognate fricative. Since stops are abruptly released, no such fricative phase occurs during their production. The Maithili affricates are therefore classified as [+ delayed release], while its stops are classified as [- delayed release].

The feature [strident] is used to handle variations in the sibilance of a speech sound. Strident speech sounds are defined articulatorily and acoustically, as those sounds produced by a relatively complex stricture, and marked by relatively high frequency and intensity. This manner of articulation creates a large amount of frication resulting in the hissing sound characteristic of strident segments. The Maithili fricative /s/ and its affricates /č č^h ǰ ǰ^h/ are all articulated in this way and hence they are specified as [+ strident], while the remaining consonants in Maithili are specified as [- strident].

The features [nasal] and [lateral] have the same definition in both distinctive feature theory and traditional phonetics. Speech sounds produced with the velum lowered so that some or all of the airstream passes out through the nose are classified as [+ nasal]; those that are made by diverting the airstream laterally around the tongue are classified as [+ lateral].

6.2.7 *Source Features*

The two source features, i.e. [voice] and [aspirated], are also very essential in order to classify the Maithili speech sounds. The feature [voice] characterises those speech sounds whose articulations include periodic vibrations of the vocal cords. The Maithili vowels, glides, and liquids are specified as [+ voice], and so are the obstruents /b b^h d d^h ḍ ḍ^h g g^h ǰ ǰ^h/.

The feature [aspirated] is regarded in the present study as quite essential to distinguish between the stops and affricates in Maithili. Chomsky and Halle (1968: 326) talk simply about "heightened subglottal pressure", but not at all about the feature [aspirated]. We must therefore make an attempt to discuss and describe this feature at some length here.

Aspiration is a term used in traditional phonetics for the audible breath which may accompany a sound's articulation. It is usually symbolised by a raised [^{h}] following the main symbol. In some languages, as in English, for example, aspiration is said (e.g. Hyman, 1975: 6) to be redundant, but in Maithili it is phonologically distinctive. Figure 6.1

Class	Voiceless/ voiced	Unaspirated	Aspirated
Obstruents	Voiceless	p t ṭ k č	p^h t^h ṭ^h k^h č^h
	Voiced	b d ḍ g ǰ	b^h d^h ḍ^h g^h ǰ^h

Figure 6.1: The unaspirated and aspirated obstruents in Maithili.

presents a summary of all the unaspirated obstruents in Maithili along with their aspirated counterparts. The matrix in the above figure is quite symmetrical. To distinguish between these speech sounds as well as to describe some phonological processes occurring in Maithili, here we put forward the feature [aspirated].

But the question is: How do we describe 'aspiration'? There has been considerable confusion regarding the description of aspiration in general and voiced aspirated consonants in particular. Opinions of linguists have been very much divided. According to Ladefoged (1975: 261), aspiration "specifies when the voicing starts with respect to the timing of the articulation". He further held (*ibid.*) that "if it were not for the convenience of retaining the traditional term aspiration, this feature might have been called Voice Onset Time". Ladefoged preferred to use the feature [voice onset time] for two main purposes: (1) to distinguish voiced, voiceless unaspirated and voiceless aspirated consonants; and (2) to use phonation types (i.e. 'voice' and 'murmur') to distinguish voiced unaspirated from voiced aspirated consonants. Put Ladefoged's way, the Maithili obstruent categories would be represented in a matrix given below in Figure 6.2, which is quite asymmetrical:

VOICE ONSET TIME

	Before release	At release	Delayed
Normal voice	b d ḍ g ǰ	p t ṭ k č	p^h t^h ṭ^h k^h č^h
Murmur	b̤^{h} d̤^{h} ḍ̤^{h} g̤^{h} ǰ̤^{h}		

Figure 6.2: The Maithili obstruents categorised according to Ladefoged's analysis (1975: 124/1982: 131).

In his treatment, Ladefoged seems to have been influenced by Lisker and Abramson's (1964) work, who hold that voicing commonly occurs during the period of oral closure. Since Lisker and Abramson (1964) regard all vibrations of the vocal cords as voicing, voice onset time does not distinguish voiced aspirated from voiced unaspirated consonants.

Catford (1977: 113), on the other hand, is of the view that voice onset time can be used for the voiced aspirates as well provided it is redefined as:

> delayed onset of *normal* voicing: the fact is that in such sounds as [bh] there is *whispery voice* rather than voice during the stop and for a certain period after its release. Just as with voiceless aspirated stops, there is thus a delay in the onset of normal voice.

In addition to these, some other descriptions of aspiration have also been put forward in the literature. For example, aspiration has been called a 'puff of air'. In an article on Igbo, Ladefoged (1976: 162) speculated that "a better solution might be to revert to an older phonetic tradition, and define aspiration in terms of the rate of airflow". Some researchers have shown (e. .g. Nihalani, 1975a) that there is usually greater airflow for aspirated speech sounds than for unaspirated ones. However, Kim's findings were rather different in his study of the Korean stops; he found greater airflow for the Korean voiceless tense stops (Kim, 1965)—which are never considered aspirated—than for the voiceless "slightly aspirated" stops. As such, greater airflow alone cannot be accepted as a sufficient condition for aspiration.

Some researchers (e.g. Chomsky and Halle, 1968: 326) have also attributed aspiration to greater subglottal air-pressure. But Ohala and Ohala (1972) and Ohala (1983) have demonstrated that in Hindi aspiration is not always accompanied by increased subglottal pressure. Similarly, Nihalani (1974a) has also shown that in Sindhi aspiration is not necessarily accompanied by heightened subglottal pressure. This means that increased subglottal pressure cannot be regarded as a sufficient condition for aspiration.

Some researchers (Kim, 1970) have also attributed aspiration to the size of the glottal opening. In his study of the glottal opening phenomenon of the Korean stops, Kim (1970) found that in Korean the glottal width at the moment of the articulatory release was much greater for aspirated than for non-aspirated stops. Although Kim's study was based on cineradiographic evidences alone, a later fiberoptic study of Korean done by Kagaya (1974) confirms Kim's earlier description. According to Kim (1970: 112), "what is controlled by the laryngeal muscles in the case of aspiration is not the timing of the glottal opening (Lisker and Abramson's view) but the size of the glottal opening". Kim holds that the voicing lag observed by Lisker and Abramson (1964) is caused by the fact that it takes longer to close a wide glottis than a relatively narrow one.

Although each of the above-mentioned studies does point out some of the important attributes of aspiration, for the description of aspiration as it is used in Maithili and other Indo-Aryan languages, Kim's (1970: 112) view seems to be more appropriate. But it must be remembered that since Kim's investigation concerned simply Korean, which has only voiceless stops, he did not therefore pay any attention to voiced aspirates. Hence, if we accept Kim's definition of aspiration without any modification, we will still be left with the dilemma of the description of voiced aspirates since the vocal cords cannot simultaneously be widely abducted and vibrating.

The discussions that have gone on so far motivate us to direct our attention to the mode of vocal cord vibrations for voiced aspirates. With the development of fiberoptics, it is now possible to observe and film the vocal cords during connected speech and thus see exactly what is happening throughout the period of the production of speech sounds, whether aspirated or unaspirated. Kagaya and Hirose (1975) made a fiberoptic study of the stops in Hindi. Figure 6.3 shows their findings concerning typical openings for intervocalic [p pʰ bʰ] and [t tʰ dʰ]:

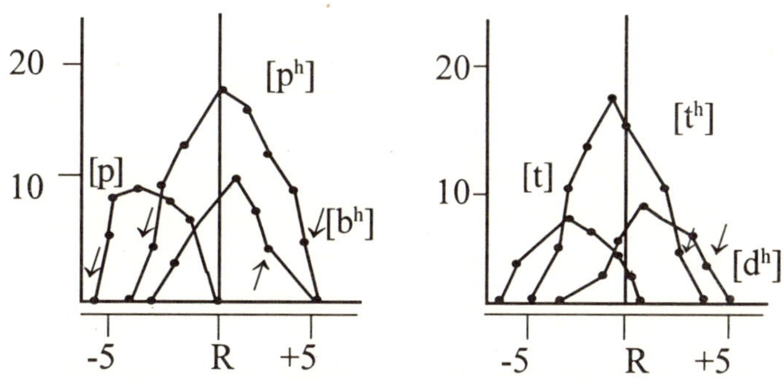

Figure 6.3: Typical glottal width contours for intervocalic [p pʰ bʰ] and [t tʰ dʰ] in Hidni, as shown in Kagaya and Hirose (1975).

In the above figure time is represented by frames on the horizontal axis (50 frames per second), glottal width is shown on an arbitrary scale on the vertical axis, and R is used to indicate the moment of articulatory release. As the figure shows, the glottis opens much wider for the voiceless aspirated [pʰ] than it does for the voiceless unaspirated [p]. Very similar difference can be observed between [tʰ] and [t]. The figure also shows that the glottal opening for the voiced aspirated [bʰ] is only slightly wider than that of [p] but the glottal width for [bʰ] still remains much less than that of [pʰ]. Similarly, the glottal width for the voiced aspirated [dʰ] is only slightly more than that of [t] but much less than what it is for the voiceless aspirated [tʰ].

Ingemann and Yadav (1978) also made a fiberoptic study of voicing and aspiration in Maithili. Their findings—as displayed in Figure 6.4—show curves similar to those of Kagaya and Hirose (1975) shown earlier in Figure 6.3. Filmed 60 frames per second, Ingemann and Yadav's (1978) fiberoptic data plotted in Figure 6.4 show typical glottal width contours for intervocalic [t tʰ dʰ] as pronounced in the Maithili utterances: [itir], [itʰik], and [idʰia], respectively.

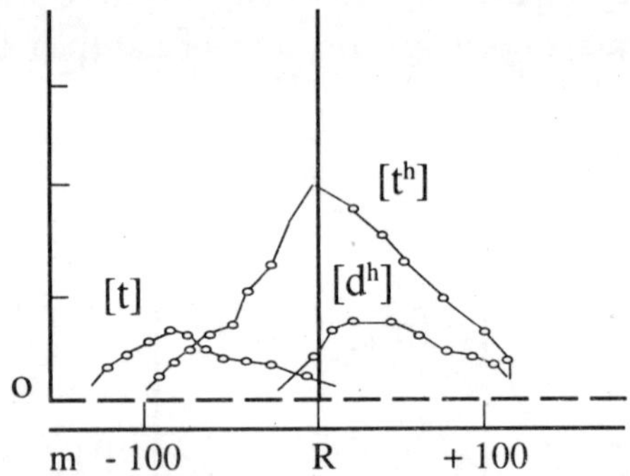

Figure 6.4: Typical glottal width contours for the intervocalic [t tʰ dʰ] in Maithili, as reported in Ingemann and Yadav (1978: 340).

A vexing problem for those supporting the voice onset time proposal has been how to deal with the aspirated and unaspirated distinctions in word-final position which can clearly be differentiated by the listeners of such Indo-Aryan languages as, for example, Bhojpuri (e.g. Prasad, 1950), Hindi (e.g. Ahmed and Agrawal, 1969; Bhatia, 1976) and Maithili (e.g. S. Jha, 1941 and 1958; G. Jha, 1974 and 1979; Yadav, 1984). Since there is no voicing following these stops, voice onset criteria cannot strictly be applied for them. Kagaya and Hirose (1975) did not include any word-final stops in their study of Hindi. But Ingemann and Yadav (1978) did include the Maithili stops even word-finally. Their data, as plotted in Figure 6.5, show the typical glottal contours for word-final [k k^h g g^h] as spoken in the Maithili words: [bik], [bik^h], [bag] and [bag^h], respectively.

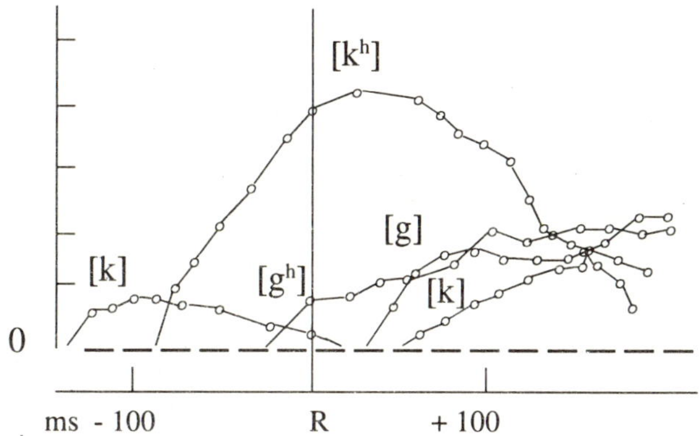

Figure 6.5: Typical glottal width contours for word-final [k k^h g g^h] in Maithili, as reported in Ingemann and Yadav (1978: 340).

As Figure 6.5 shows, just prior to the release of both the word-final voiceless aspirated [k^h] and the voiced aspirated [g^h], the glottis quickly opens widely. In fact, the glottal width contour for the voiceless aspirated [k^h] near its release is much greater than what it is near the release of the voiced aspirated [g^h]. For the voiceless unaspirated [k], on the contrary, the glottis is narrow and in the token of the above figure it actually appears to close near the release of [k]. This therefore clearly means that the critical factor for voiceless stops in word-final position is the glottal width. Ingemann and Yadav's (1978: 341) observation that

> Since there is no following gesture other than widening for respiration, the narrowed glottis of the unaspirated stops can only be attributed to the lack of aspiration. Because glottal width differences are also observable in other positions, width would seem to be a better characterization of aspiration than voice onset time, which is only sometimes applicable.

does seem to lead us toward a better description of aspiration, especially with regard to voiceless stops.

Turning our attention to voiced stops, both aspirated and unaspirated, Kagaya and Hirose (1975: 42) summarise their findings concerning the glottal width contours for the voiced aspirates in Hindi—as displayed earlier in Figure 6.3—in the following terms:

> The voiced aspirated type is characterized by the closed glottis mostly during the articulatory closure period and by the open glottis immediately before and after the release.

Ingemann and Yadav's Maithili data—as displayed earlier in Figures 6.4 and 6.5—also strengthen the above claim. In Figure 6.4 the glottal opening for the voiced aspirate [d^h] begins at the release. In Figure 6.5 the glottal opening for the voiced aspirate [g^h] begins earlier than for the voiced unaspirated [g]. The glottal opening in fact remains narrow until approximately the point at which the glottis begins to open after the voiced stop—for both [g] and [g^h], that is—and then it widens rapidly.

The above-mentioned data make it clear that glottal width is the major factor for aspiration of voiced stops. A modification of Kim's (1970: 112) earlier definition of aspiration as glottal width will enable us to include both types of aspiraton (i.e. aspiration with or without voice) in the same phonetic category. Such a modified definition of aspiration would be: aspiration is greater glottal width than there would otherwise be for the corresponding voiced and voiceless consonants. This approach would be in agreement with Halle and Stevens' (1971) proposed feature "spread glottis"; and , indeed, this approach would also be similar to the one taken by Catford (1977: 115).

In addition to the glottal width factor, there is also a second key factor for aspiration: i.e. timing of the glottal width. As can be noted from Figures 6.3 and 6.4, the greatest glottal width for aspirated stops, whether voiced or voiceless, is neither the onset nor the midpoint of the stop, but at or very close to the moment of the articulatory release. The same timing relationship holds not only for stops but also for other voiced aspirated consonants. Figure 6.6 shows Ingemann and Yadav's (1978: 341-42) results for the glottal openings for intervocalic [r^h l^h n^h] as spoken in the Maithili words: [pir^hi], [pil^hi] and [bin^hi], respectively. These data amply demonstrate that the timing which is important to production of

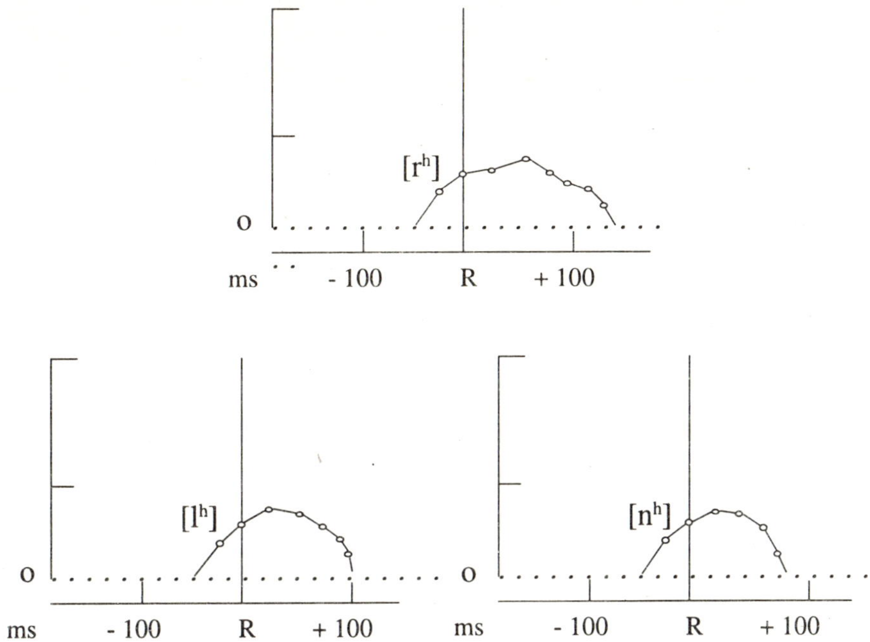

Figure 6.6: Typical glottal width contours for intervocalic [rʰ lʰ nʰ] in the Maithili words, as reported in Ingemann and Yadav (1978: 342).

aspiration is not voice onset but the moment of maximum glottal width, and that the voicing lag is a natural result of this timing. This aspect of timing has therefore to be regarded as an integral part of the description of aspiration.

Thus, the findings discussed above amply demonstrate that aspiration in both voice and voiceless speech sounds consists of glottal width and a timing factor locating the peak of the width near the consonant release. Since we have defined aspiration in phonetic terms, we can use the feature [aspirated] with confidence. This feature, like every other feature that we have chosen to use in this study, has its foundation in phonetics, and this feature is regarded as very essential and useful because it allows us to characterise not only the individual sound segments in Maithili but also the natural classes of segments which undergo similar phonological processes.

6.3 Redundancy Conditions of the Maithili Phonemes

In the previous section we included a set of sixteen distinctive features to characterise the Maithili phonemes. These features accommodate all the necessary phonological contrasts available in Maithili. The analysis of the Maithili phonemes at the systematic phonemic level into distinctive features results in the matrix as presented in Table 6.1, the columns of which stand for the phonemes and the rows for their features. A+ or - entry in a particular cell indicates whether that phoneme possesses the property or feature in question. In the matrix of Table 6.1 no two phonemes have identical specifications for all the features; there is at least one feature for which the value between phonemes differs.

In the classical Prague theory a distinction was drawn between 'relevant' and 'irrelevant' properties (e.g. see Fischer-JØrgensen, 1975). Jakobson, Fant and Halle (1952) correspondingly distinguish between distinctive and redundant features; this terminology is more suitable since non-distinctive features may be important for perception, for example, and therefore cannot be said to be irrelevant. Unlike distinctive features, however, redundant features are not independent but rather concomitant phenomena. That is, some features depend on other features in the same phoneme. If the value for a certain feature always implies a particular value for another feature, it would be redundant to specify both. The matrix of Table 6.1 is fully specified. But some of the values for some phonemes in the matrix can certainly be predicted on the basis of the values that the same phonemes have for some other features. The matrix in Table 6.1 therefore contains a certain amount of redundancy. In the present section we shall state some of the main segment redundancy conditions in Maithili, following Stanley's (1967: 426) if-then condition format.

1. If: [+ sonorant]

$$\downarrow$$

Then: [+ voice]

The above condition states that in Maithili there are no voiceless vowels (whether oral or nasal), glides, nasals or liquids at the systematic phonemic level. A [+ sonorant] segment is therefore always [+ voice] in this language.

Table 6.1: The classification of the Maithili phonemes in terms of their distinctive feature values.

Features \ Phonemes	i	e	æ	a	ə	ɔ	o	u	ĩ	ẽ	æ̃	ã	ə̃	ɔ̃	õ	ũ	p	pʰ	b	bʰ	t	tʰ	d	dʰ	ṭ	ṭʰ	ḍ	ḍʰ	k	kʰ	g	gʰ	č	čʰ	ǰ	ǰʰ	s	h	w	y	m	n	ŋ	r	ṛ	l
Sonorant	+	+	+	+	+	+	+	+	+	+	+	+	+	+	+	+	-	-	-	-	-	-	-	-	-	-	-	-	-	-	-	-	-	-	-	-	-	-	+	+	+	+	+	+	+	+
Syllabic	+	+	+	+	+	+	+	+	+	+	+	+	+	+	+	+	-	-	-	-	-	-	-	-	-	-	-	-	-	-	-	-	-	-	-	-	-	-	-	-	-	-	-	-	-	-
consonantal	-	-	-	-	-	-	-	-	-	-	-	-	-	-	-	-	+	+	+	+	+	+	+	+	+	+	+	+	+	+	+	+	+	+	+	+	+	+	-	-	+	+	+	+	+	+
anterior																	+	+	+	+	+	+	+	+	-	-	-	-	-	-	-	-	-	-	-	-	-	-	+	-	+	+	-	+	-	+
coronal	-	-	-	-	-	-	-	-	-	-	-	-	-	-	-	-	-	-	-	-	+	+	+	+	+	+	+	+	-	-	-	-	-	+	+	+	+	+	-	-	-	+	-	+	+	+
high	+	-	-	-	-	-	-	+	+	-	-	-	-	-	-	+	-	-	-	-	-	-	-	-	+	+	+	+	+	+	+	+	+	+	+	+	-	-	+	+	-	-	+	-	+	-
low	-	-	+	+	-	+	-	-	-	-	+	+	-	+	-	-	-	-	-	-	-	-	-	-	-	-	-	-	-	-	-	-	-	-	-	-	-	+	-	-	-	-	-	-	-	-
back	-	-	-	+	+	+	+	+	-	-	-	+	+	+	+	+	-	-	-	-	-	-	-	-+	+	+	+	+	+	+	+	-	-	-	-	-	-	+	-	-	-	-	+	-	+	-
rounded	-	-	-	-	-	+	+	+	-	-	-	-	-	+	+	+	-	-	-	-	-	-	-	-	-	-	-	-	-	-	-	-	-	-	-	-	-	-	+	-	-	-	-	-	-	-
continuant																	-	-	-	-	-	-	-	-	-	-	-	-	-	-	-	-	-	-	-	-	+	+	+	+	-	-	-	+	+	+
delayed release																		-	-	-	-	-	-	-	-	-	-	-	-	-	-	-	-	+	+	+	+	-	-	-	-	-	-	-	-	-
strident																	-	-	-	-	-	-	-	-	-	-	-	-	-	-	-	-	+	+	+	+	+	-	-	-	-	-	-	-	-	-
nasal	-	-	-	-	-	-	-	-	+	+	+	+	+	+	+	+	-	-	-	-	-	-	-	-	-	-	-	-	-	-	-	-	-	-	-	-	-	-	-	-	+	+	+	-	-	-
lateral																	-	-	-	-	-	-	-	-	-	-	-	-	-	-	-	-	-	-	-	-	-	-	-	-	-	-	-	-	-	+
voiced	+	+	+	+	+	+	+	+	+	+	+	+	+	+	+	+	-	-	+	+	-	-	+	+	-	-	+	+	-	-	+	+	-	-	+	+	-	-	+	+	+	+	+	+	+	+
aspirated	-	-	-	-	-	-	-	-	-	-	-	-	-	-	-	-	-	+	-	+	-	+	-	+	-	+	-	+	-	+	-	+	-	+	-	+	-	-	-	-	-	-	-	-	-	-

2. If: [+ syllabic]

$$\downarrow$$

Then: $\begin{bmatrix} - & \text{coronal} \\ + & \text{sonorant} \\ - & \text{consonantal} \\ - & \text{aspirated} \end{bmatrix}$

The above segment structure condition states that at the systematic phonemic level in Maithli if a segment is [+ syll], then it is always [+ son, - cor]. It also states that this language does not have any syllabic glides or consonants, nor does it have any aspirated syllabic segments at the systematic phonemic level.

3. If: a. [+ high] b. [+ low]

$$\downarrow \qquad \downarrow$$

Then: [- low] [- high]

The above segment structure conditions state that in Maithili: (a) a segment which is [+ high] is always [- low]; and (b) a segment which is [+ low] is always [- high].

4. If: a. [- back] b. [+ round]

$$\downarrow \qquad \downarrow$$

Then: [- round] [+ back]

These segment structure conditions state that at the systematic phonemic level in Maithili: (a) a segment which is [- back] is always [- round]; and (b) a segment which is [+ round] is always [+ back].

5. If: [- sonorant]

$$\downarrow$$

Then: $\begin{bmatrix} - \text{nasal} \\ - \text{lateral} \end{bmatrix}$

The above segment structure condition states that at the systematic phonemic level all the stop, fricative and affricate consonants in Maithili are always [- nasal] and [- lateral].

6.

$$\text{If:} \quad \begin{bmatrix} + & \text{consonantal} \\ + & \text{nasal} \end{bmatrix}$$

$$\downarrow$$

$$\text{Then:} \quad \begin{bmatrix} - & \text{continuant} \\ - & \text{delayed release} \\ - & \text{strident} \\ - & \text{lateral} \end{bmatrix}$$

This segment structure condition states that all the Maithili nasal consonants are always [- cont, - del rel, - strid, - lateral] at the systematic phonemic level.

7.

$$\text{If:} \quad [-\ \text{delayed release}]$$

$$\downarrow$$

$$\text{Then:} \quad \begin{bmatrix} - & \text{continuant} \\ - & \text{strident} \\ - & \text{lateral} \end{bmatrix}$$

The above segment structure condition states that all the Maithili stop and nasal consonants are always [- cont, - del rel, - strid, - lateral] at the systematic phonemic level.

8.

$$\text{If:} \quad \begin{bmatrix} - & \text{sonorant} \\ + & \text{consonantal} \\ + & \text{continuant} \end{bmatrix}$$

$$\downarrow$$

$$\text{Then:} \quad \begin{bmatrix} + & \text{anterior} \\ + & \text{coronal} \\ - & \text{voice} \end{bmatrix}$$

The above condition states that Maithili has only two consonantal fricatives: /s/ and /h/.

9.

$$\text{If:} \quad \begin{bmatrix} -\ \text{syllabic} \\ -\ \text{consonantal} \\ -\ \text{low} \end{bmatrix}$$

$$\downarrow$$

$$\text{Then:} \quad \begin{bmatrix} -\ \text{anterior} \\ -\ \text{coronal} \\ -\ \text{strident} \\ -\ \text{nasal} \\ -\ \text{lateral} \\ -\ \text{aspirated} \end{bmatrix}$$

The above segment structure condition states that at the systematic phonemic level the Maithili glides, /w/ and /y/, are always [- ant, - cor, - strid, - nasal, - lateral, - asp].

Table 6.2 presents a modified matrix in which the redundant feature-values for the Maithili phonemes are marked by + or - as appropriate, but all of them are kept within small brackets. Although the bracketed features in the matrix are redundant, this does not mean that we are not interested in their values, or that these values are not significant, but only that they are predictable from other values. Redundant values may in fact be important whenever we need to make reference to a natural class comprising several segments.

Moreover, not all the sixteen features included in this study are relevant for characterising all classes of phonemes in Maithili. For example, the features [anterior], [continuant], [delayed release], [strident] and [lateral] do not differentiate vowels. Following the arguments put forward by Henderson (1976: 321-25), we have not specified any values for these features for the Maithili vowels in the matrix of Table 6.2.

6.4 Summary

To summarise, in generative phonology the description of the phonological and phonetic levels as well as of the rules connecting these levels is formulated by means of distinctive features. In this chapter we have included a set of sixteen features to characterise all the phonologically contrasting segments in Maithili. The feature system used here is that of Chomsky and Halle (1968) modified in the ways as seemed essential for the appropriate description and classification of the Maithili

Table 6.2: Distinctive and redundant feature values for the Maithili phonemes.

Features \ Phonemes	i	e	ae	a	ə	ɔ	o	u	ĩ	ẽ	æ̃	ã	ə̃	ɔ̃	õ	ũ
Sonorant	(+	+	+	+	+	+	+	+	+	+	+	+	+	+	+	+)
Syllabic	+	+	+	+	+	+	+	+	+	+	+	+	+	+	+	+
consonantal	-	-	-	-	-	-	-	-	-	-	-	-	-	-	-	-)
anterior																
coronal	(-	-	-	-	-	-	-	-	-	-	-	-	-	-	-	-)
high	+	-	(-	-)	-	(-)	-	+	+	-	(-	-)	-	(-)	-	+
low	(-)	-	+	+	-	+	-	(-	-)	-	+	+	-	+	-	(-)
back	-	-	-	+	+	(+	+	+)	-	-	-	+	+	(+	+	+)
rounded	(-	-	-)	-	-	+	+	+	(-	-	-)	-	-	+	+	+
continuant																
delayed release																
strident																
nasal	-	-	-	-	-	-	-	-	+	+	+	+	+	+	+	+
lateral																
voiced	(+	+	+	+	+	+	+	+	+	+	+	+	+	+	+	+)
aspirated	(-	-	-	-	-	-	-	-	-	-	-	-	-	-	-	-)

Features \ Phonemes	p	pʰ	b	bʰ	t	tʰ	d	dʰ	ṭ	ṭʰ	ḍ	ḍʰ	k	kʰ	g	gʰ	č	čʰ	ǰ	ǰʰ	s	h	w	y	m	n	ŋ	r	r	l
Sonorant	-	-	-	-	-	-	-	-	-	-	-	-	-	-	-	-	-	-	-	-	-	-	+	+	+	+	+	+	+	+
Syllabic	-	-	-	-	-	-	-	-	-	-	-	-	-	-	-	-	-	-	-	-	-	-	-	-	-	-	-	-	-	-
consonantal	+	+	+	+	+	+	+	+	+	+	+	+	+	+	+	+	+	+	+	+	+	+	-	-	+	+	+	+	+	+
anterior	+	+	+	+	+	+	+	+	-	-	-	-	-	-	-	-	-	-	-	-	(+)	-	(-	-)	+	+	-	+	-	+
coronal	-	-	-	-	+	+	+	+	+	+	+	+	-	-	-	-	-	+	+	+	(+)	-	(-	-)	-	+	-	+	+	+
high	-	-	-	-	-	-	-	-	+	+	+	+	+	+	+	+	+	+	+	+	-	(-)	+	+	-	-	+	-	+	-
low	-	-	-	-	-	-	-	-	(-	-	-	-	-	-	-	-	-	-	-	-)	-	+	(-	-)	-	-	(-)	-	(-)	-
back	-	-	-	-	-	-	-	-+	+	+	+	+	+	+	+	-	-	-	-	-	-	-	(+)	-	-	-	+	-	+	-
rounded	(-	-	-	-	-	-	-	-)	-	-	-	-	-	-	-	-	(-	-	-	-	-	-)	+	(-	-	-)	-	(-)	-	(-)
continuant	(-	-	-	-	-	-	-	-	-	-	-	-	-	-	-	-)	-	-	-	-	+	+	+	+	(-	-	-)	+	+	+
delayed release		-	-	-	-	-	-	-	-	-	-	-	-	-	-	-	-	+	+	+	+	-	-	-	(-	-	-)	-	-	-
strident	(-	-	-	-	-	-	-	-	-	-	-	-	-	-	-	-)	+	+	+	+	+	-	(-	-)	(-	-	-)	-	-	-
nasal	(-	-	-	-	-	-	-	-	-	-	-	-	-	-	-	-	-	-	-	-	-)	-	(-	-)	+	+	+	-	-	-
lateral	(-	-	-	-	-	-	-	-	-	-	-	-	-	-	-	-	-	-	-	-	-)	-	(-	-)	(-	-	-)	-	-	+
voiced	-	-	+	+	-	-	+	+	-	-	+	+	-	-	+	+	-	-	+	+	(-)	-	(+	+	+	+	+	+	+	+)
aspirated	-	+	-	+	-	+	-	+	-	+	-	+	-	+	-	+	-	+	-	+	-	-	(-	-)	-	-	-	-	-	-

phonemes. We have differed from Chomsky and Halle in two main areas: (1) in our specifications of the Maithili /h/, and (2) in our treatment of aspiration. Chomsky and Halle regard /h/ as a glide and specify it as: [+ son, - syll, -cons]; we regard the Maithili /h/ as a glottal fricative and our specifications of it in terms of the major class features are: [- son, - syll, + cons]. Some major phonological processes shown in the following two chapters of this book back up our feature specifications of /h/. Like the distinctive features of Chomsky and Halle, our feature [aspirated] has its foundation in phonetics. We hold that there are two major factors for aspiration: (1) glottal width, and (2) timing of the glottal width. We believe that the timing which is important to production of aspiration is not voice onset but the moment of maximum glottal width, and that the voicing lag is a natural result of this timing. Since we have defined aspiration in phonetic terms, we can use the feature [aspirated] with confidence, and we recommend that this feature be included in the destinctive feature theory of Chomsky and Halle.

The description of the sixteen features included in this study is given in articulatory terms. In Table 6.1 each speech segment of Maithili is represented as a matrix of phonetic features. The main segmental redundancy conditions in Maithili are outlined in the third section of this chapter. A final summary of the distinctive and redundant feature values of the Maithili phonemes is presented in the matrix of Table 6.2. Although there have been various attacks on the Chomsky-Halle feature system (e.g. see Foley, 1970 and 1977; Ladefoged, 1971 and 1975/82; Vennemann, 1972; Henderson, 1976) and there is still much that remains to be resolved in the distinctive feature theory (e.g. see Hyman, 1975: 52-58; Sommerstein, 1977: 114-169, for more details), the Chomsky-Halle model, with some necessary modifications, has nevertheless been found satisfactory in characterising not only the individual sound segments in Maithili but also the natural classes of segments which undergo similar phonological processes in this language.

Chapter 7

SOME NATURAL PROCESSES IN MAITHILI PHONOLOGY

7.0 Introduction

Like the consonants and vowels of many other languages, the Maithili consonants and vowels are also subject to strengthening and weakening processes relative to their position within syllables and words. This chapter looks into some major strengthening and weakening processes of both consonants and vowels in Maithili, and investigates some major assimilatory and non-assimilatory processes in the phonology of this language. Our conclusions are summarised at the end of this chapter.

7.1 Gemination of Consonants in Maithili

In this section we shall first make a brief survey of previous studies done on the consonant gemination of various languages of the world, including the Indo-Aryan languages. We shall also distinguish between 'long' and 'geminate' consonants, and shall then concentrate on the system of consonant gemination in Maithili.

7.1.1 *Consonant Gemination and Previous Studies on It*

For more than a hundred years phoneticians have been debating on the question whether or not there exists any difference between long consonants and geminates. Two opposing views are found in the literature on this topic. According to one (e.g. Sievers, 1876; Stetson, 1951; Delattre, 1971; Lehiste, Morton and Tatham, 1973; Catford, 1977), geminate consonants differ from long consonants primarily because the former's production involves a rearticulation of the consonant in question. This view holds that each sequence of geminate consonants contains a syllable boundary word-internally, and that each such sequence therefore consists of two phases: the first phase constitutes a syllable-final occurrence of the consonant, while the second, rearticulated phase begins the next syllable and thus constitutes a syllable-initial occurrence of the consonant. The opposing view (e.g. Rousselot, 1891; Hegedüs, 1959) denies the existence of the above-mentioned two phases and refuses to recognise any difference between long consonants and geminates.

Basing his claim on auditory and kinesthetic perception, it was Sievers (1876) who proposed for the first time this two-phase theory of geminate sequences. Later on other phoneticians went ahead with some intensive experimental investigation in this area. For example, Rousselot (1891) made a kymographic study of the Gallo-Roman dialect of Cellefrouin and found no double articulation of long consonants in that dialect. Stetson (1951), on the contrary, found clear evidence for double articulation in his study of abutting consonants in English phrases, such as: 'up puppy', 'top pick', and so on. Hegedüs' (1959) studied single and geminate consonants in Hungarian but his measurements of acoustic intensity did not give him any significant evidence in the intensity of curves for rearticulation of the Hungarian geminates. Delattre (1971) studied consonant geminates in English, German, Spanish and French, employing x-ray motion pictures and spectrography, as well as speech synthesis. He found that geminates were distinguished from single consonants in that the former showed two phases in their articulation: one with the features of final consonants, the other with the features of initial consonants.

It should be mentioned that Hegedüs' (1959) negative results were obtained in a study of intervocalic geminates within a word, while the positive results of Stetson (1951) and Delattre (1971) were obtained in studies of consonants abutting at word boundary. It seems interesting to study both types of situation within the framework of a single experimental investigation. Lehiste, Morton and Tatham (1973) did in fact do just that type of investigation, concentrating on two languages, English and Estonian. They made electromyographic (emg) recordings, associated with lip closure in bilabial stops, and took intraoral air pressure (Pi) measurements of items containing single and geminate consonants in word-internal intervocalic position and at word boundaries, with the aim of investigating differences between single and geminate consonants. They assumed that the emg signal would indicate the duration and extent of the electro-chemical activity within the muscle consequent upon in-

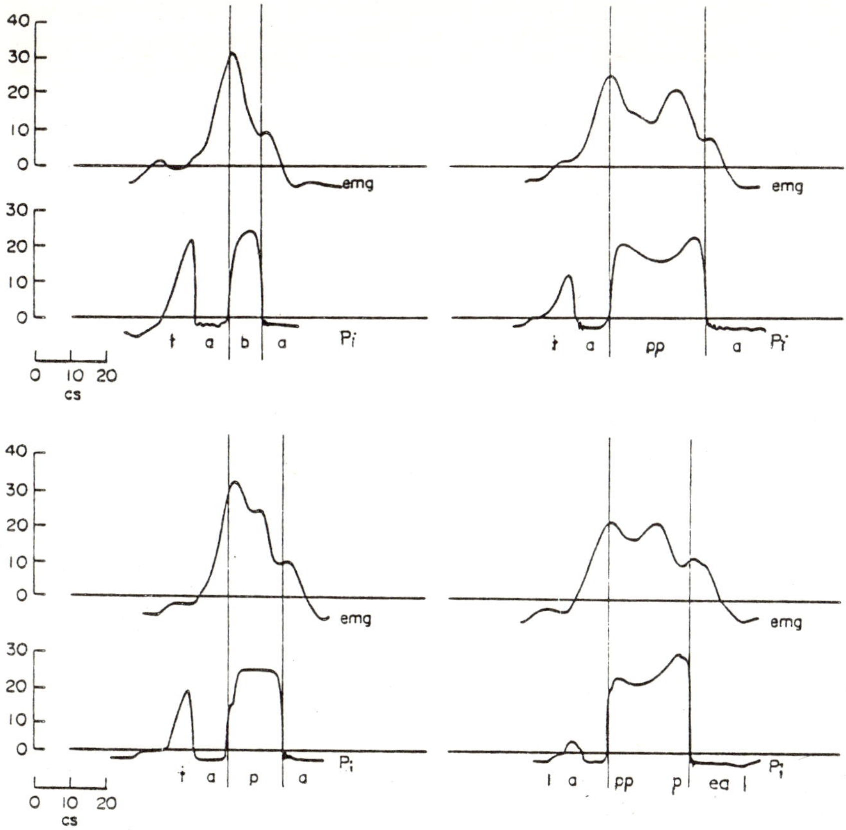

Figure 7.1: The emg and intraoral air pressure measurements (Pi) of four Estonian utterances, as reported in Lehiste, Morton and Tatham (1973: 133).

nervation of that muscle. They sampled the intraoral air pressure to detect accurately the movements of closure and opening of the lips—i.e. the stop phase of the bilabials [p] and [b]. Figure 7.1 shows some of their results concerning four Estonian utterances—i.e. *taba*, *tapa*, *tappa* and *lap peal*—as spoken by a native speaker (Ilse Lehiste). This figure does show, as they claim, enough "evidence for rearticulation, i.e. for the production of true geminates, in productions of Estonian intervocalic long and overlong consonants as well as junctural C+C sequences" (Lehiste, Morton and Tatham, 1973: 148).

Studies, such as the above-mentioned ones, have amply shown enough reasons to distinguish between 'long' consonants and geminates. The term 'geminate' is now widely used in phonetics and phonology for a sequence of two identical adjacent segments of a sound in a single word containing at least two syllables. As sequences of two identical articulations, geminate consonants—e.g. [pp], [kk], [jj], [mm] and so on—do involve continuity of articulation, as the closure or obstruction is held momentarily before release. And, since in the pronunciation of each geminate sequence there is a prolongation of the articulatory posture, one might therefore term such a sequence as a 'long' consonant, rather than as a geminate sequence of two identical segments. As most of the above-mentioned studies have now fairly clearly established, the term 'geminate' is most commonly used when, in spite of the continuity of articulation, the bi-segmental nature of the sequence is made clear by the presence of a syllable division within the period of maintained articulation. That is to say, the production of geminate consonants involves a rearticulation of the consonant in question, which thus consists of two phases: the first phase constitutes a syllable-final occurrence of the consonant; the second, rearticulated phase starts the next syllable and thus constitutes a syllable-initial occurrence of the consonant.

For this reason, an utterance like, for example, [rə-' ssa:] with a syllable division before the lengthened [s]-articulation would be regarded in the present study as containing a long [s] and be transcribed as [rə's:a]. On the other hand, an utterance like ['rəs-sa:], with a syllable division right in the middle of the lengthened [s]-articulation would be considered here as containing a geminate sequence, and be transcribed as ['rəssa:]. On account of this sort of syllable division, or two-phase articulation, a geminate sequence cannot be regarded as simply a long consonant, and transcriptional differences must indicate this—e.g. the above-mentioned [-s:-] is long but [-ss-] is geminate.

In addition to the above-mentioned phonetic studies on consonant gemination, there is also a growing literature on the phonology of geminates. For example, Foley (1970) studied the consonant geminates of some languages, including Italian, Danish and Spanish. Similarly, Skousen (1972) studied the geminates of some Savo dialects of Finnish; Kenstowicz and Pyle (1973) present their findings on the phonological integrity of geminate clusters. Other researchers (e.g. Schein and Steriade, 1986; MacCarthy, 1986) have also taken up the phonological study of geminates and have presented their accounts on them. A summary of the findings on gemination is included in Hayes' (1986) phonological study.

But it has to be accepted that studies on the consonant gemination of Indo-Aryan languages have unfortunately been few and far between. Most published materials on geminates are rather sketchy and they make only a few tentative observations on the topic (e.g. Chatterji, 1926/1970: 447-48; Varma, 1929/reprint 1961: 99-125; Allen, 1953: 79; Arun, 1961: 6 and 26-27; Goswami, 1966: 65; Pattanayak, 1966: 61; Mehrotra, 1980: 164-69).

As for the consonant geminates in Maithili, both S. Jha (1958: 193-194) and G. Jha (1974: 89-90) only list a few Maithili words containing geminate consonants. Similarly, R. Yadav (1984: 25-26) also lists a few Maithili words, presents "only a tentative account" (*ibid.*, p. 26) of them, and suggests (*ibid.*) that "further investigation needs to be undertaken" in this area. The present study attempts to investigate the system of consonant gemination in Maithili at some length.

7.1.2 *General Remarks on Consonant Gemination in Maithili*

Gemination is one of the important characteristics of the Maithili consonant system. But in this language geminate consonants never occur either word-initially or word-finally, because in such environments sequences of two identical articulations would indeed be physiologically impossible on account of the fact that each consonant could be articulated only due to its reliance on a vowel. There are, however, a few loan words—borrowed especially from Sanskrit and Persian sources—in which their word-final consonants are usually lengthened in speech. For example:

[rə:d:] "cancelled"
[kʰə:n:] "the sound made by the fall of a coin"
[ṭə:r:] "croaking of frogs"
[hə:ǰ:] "a pilgrimage to Mecca"

Each word of the above examples contains only one syllable, and in each case the syllable-final consonant is just lengthened in pronunciation, as the closure or obstruction is held momentarily before release.

Like most other Indo-Aryan languages, it is in fact only in the word-internal intervocalic position that geminate consonants occur in Maithili. Moreover, in this language geminate sequences do not occur in monomorphemes, and there is no phonological contrast available between geminate consonants and single consonants. In other words, geminate consonants do not occur in Maithili underlyingly; it is simply at the surface level that geminate sequences occur in this language.

7.1.3 *Gemination of Consonants in Maithili and Its Rules*

In Maithili consonants are divided into five main categories in accordance with their manners of articulation: i.e. stops, affricates, fricatives, nasals and approximants. The unaspirated stops in Maithili are eight in number: /p b t d ṭ ḍ k g/. All these stops occur in word-internal geminate sequences. For example:

(1)		*Stem*	*Suffix*	*Word*	*Gloss*
	-pp-	/gəp +	-i/	['gəppi:]	"a talkative person"
	-bb-	/həb +	-ər/	['həbbə:r]	"extreme haste"
	-tt-	/pət +	-i/	['pətti:]	"blade"
	-dd-	/rəd +	-i/	['rəddi:]	"useless"
	-ṭṭ-	/gəṭ +	-a/	['gəṭṭa:]	"wrist"
	-ḍḍ-	/guḍ +	-i/	['guḍḍi:]	"kite"
	-kk-	/pək +	a/	['pəkka:]	"firm; solid"
	-gg-	/ləg +	-a/	['ləgga:]	"(thin) pole"

All these unaspirated stops in Maithili have their aspirated counterparts and they, too, occur in word-internal geminate sequences. For example:

(2)		*Stem*	*Suffix*	*Word*	*Gloss*
	-pp^h-	/gəp^h +	-a/	['gəpp^{h}a:]	"the space between the fingers"
	-bb^h-	/bəb^h +	-ən/	['bəbb^{h}ə̃n]	"related to the Brahmins"
	-tt^h-	/hət^h +	-a/	['hətt^{h}a:]	"bunch of banana"
	-dd^h-	/sid^h +	-i/	['sidd^{h}i:]	"success"
	-ṭṭ^h-	/b^{h}əṭ^h +	-a/	['b^{h}əṭṭ^{h}a:]	"brick chimney"
	-ḍḍ^h-	/gəḍ^h +	-a/	['gəḍḍ^{h}a:]	"ditch"
	-kk^h-	/suk^h +	-a/	['sukk^{h}a:]	"dry; draught"
	-gg^h-	/məg^h +	-a/	['məgg^{h}a:]	"a lunar mansion"

Similarly, the two unaspirated affricates in Maithili—i.e. /č/ and /ǰ/—also occur in word-interior geminate sequences. For example:

(3)		*Stem*	*Suffix*	*Word*	*Gloss*
	-čč-	/bəč +	-a/	['bečča:]	"child"
	-ǰǰ-	/uǰ +	-ər/	['uǰǰə:r]	"white"

These unaspirated affricates in Maithili have also their aspirated counterparts, and they, too, occur in word-internal geminate sequences. For example:

(4)

	Stem	*Suffix*	*Word*	*Gloss*
-čč^{h}-	/mə̃č^{h} +	-əṛ/	[ʻmə̃čč^{h}ə:ṛ]	"mosquito"
-ǰǰ^{h}-	/mĩǰ^{h} + -əṛ/		[ʻmĩ ǰ ǰ^{h}ə:ṛ]	"mingled"

But of the two fricatives in Maithili—i.e. /s/ and /h/—only the former occurs in geminate sequences. For example.

(5)

	Stem	*Suffix*	*Word*	*Gloss*
-ss-	/his +	-a/	[ʻhissa:]	"share"

Likewise, of the three nasal consonants in Maithili, i.e. /m n ŋ/, only /m/ and /n/ occur in geminate sequences. For example:

(6)

	Stem		*Suffix*	*Word*	*Gloss*
-mm-	/ǰəm	+	-ã/	[ʻǰə̃mmã:]	"total"
-nn-	/sun	+	-ã/	[ʻsũnnã:]	"zero"

In the same way, the five approximant consonants in Maithili, i.e. /w y r ṛ l/, only /r/ and /l/ occur in geminate sequences. For example:

(7)

	Stem		*Suffix*	*Word*	*Gloss*
-rr-	/kər	+	-a/	[ʻkərra:]	"swan"
-ll-	/həl	+	-a/	[ʻhəlla:]	"noise"

All the above examples of the Maithili word-internal geminate sequences of both unaspirated and aspirated stops and affricates, as well as the geminate sequences of the Maithili fricatives, nasals and approximants reveal three main regularities: (1) that all the above-mentioned consonants in Maithili occur in geminate sequences only intervocalically; (2) that in each example the vowel preceding the geminate sequence is always short and stressed; and (3) that the vowel following each geminate sequence is always long and unstressed. To account for these data, two crucial questions need to be answered: (1) What causes stress on the vowel preceding the geminate sequences?; and (2) What causes length on the vowel following the geminate sequences?

We shall take up the first question first: i.e. What causes stress on the vowel preceding the geminate sequences? Since gemination has been interpreted in this study as the rearticulation of identical adjacent segments of a sound, this calls for the syllabification rules. Syllabification is the term which refers to the division of a word into syllables. Providing precise definition of the syllable is not an easy matter, and there are several theories in both phonetics and phonology which have tried to clarify matters. From a phonetic viewpoint, attempts have been made to define the syllables of a language on the basis of the articulatory effort needed in order to produce them. A combination of factors is probably involved, including sonority, stress, length, pitch, and certain phonetic features characteristic of the beginnings and endings of syllables. Phonological views of the syllable, on the other hand, focus on the ways sounds combine in individual languages to produce typical sequences. For the purpose of the present study, phonological views of the syllable are extremely important because in our view a phonological analysis using the syllable as a hierarchical unit can provide an insightful account of gemination in Maithili.

A consonant-vowel (CV) sequence—often called an *open syllable* type—is a very natural pattern commonly used in Maithili. Consonant-vowel-consonant (CVC) and vowel-consonant (VC) patterns—often called *closed syllable* types—are also very common in this language. In a CVC pattern, the opening segment of the syllable is called the *onset,* its closing segment is called the *coda,* while the central segment is called the *centre* or *nucleus.* A useful collective term for the opening and closing segments is the *margins* of the syllable. Depending upon the composition of its core, a syllable may be said to be weak or strong (e.g. see for more details, Sloat *et al.,* 1978; Hyman, 1975). The syllable onset has no bearing on this matter at all. The core of a weak syllable contains a short vowel followed by no more than one short consonant. A strong syllable occupies more than one mora. Its core is composed of one of the following:

(a) a long vowel, with or without a coda of any length;

(b) a short vowel followed by two or more consonants;
(c) a short vowel followed by at least one long consonant.

Like Latin, English and some such Indo-Aryan languages as Gujarati, Marathi and Hindi, in Maithili the distinction between strong and weak syllables is important in stress placement. A number of researchers (e.g. Chomsky and Halle, 1968; Ross, 1973; Hoard and Sloat, 1973; Sloat, 1974) assume that syllable structure is also relevant to stress placement in the words of languages like English. Like most other Indo-Aryan languages, syllabification rules in Maithili automatically predict stress on the heavy syllable—i.e. the syllable preceding the intervocalic cluster, including geminates. Stress in all the instantiated cases of our study as presented in (1)-(7) is on account of the penult syllable being heavy, as the first member of the geminate goes with the preceding vowel—as, for example, in [ˈgəp-pi:] "a talkative person". Normally schwa, [ə], is the weakest vowel and it rebuffs the stress. But due to the consonantal frame, as shown in all our data presented thus far, it becomes obligatory even for the vowel [ə] to take the stress. This means that stress in the preceding vowel of all Maithili words containing geminates is derived by rule. That is to say, stress in such environments is neither underlying, nor does it take place before gemination. Indeed, it is the consonantal frame which makes each penult syllable heavy, as the first member of the geminate goes with the preceding vowel, and this therefore makes it obligatory for all such preceding vowels to take the stress. This answers the first question we posed earlier: i.e. What causes stress in the vowel preceding the geminate sequences?

To answer the second question: i.e. What causes length on the vowel following the geminate sequences?, we need to turn to the phonology and morphology of Maithili. But before we embark upon the phonological and morphological discussions relevant to our study here, it has to be made clear that Maithili has plenty of words where their intervocalic consonants are preceded by short unstressed vowels and followed by long stressed ones. And in all such words none of the intervocalic consonants is ever geminated. Moreover, Maithili simply does not have such words where their intervocalic single consonants can be found preceded by short stressed vowels and followed by long unstressed ones. The examples given below emphasise the above statements:

(8) [nə̃ˈpa:] "cause to measure (imp.)"

*[nə̃p'pa:], *['nə̃pa:]

[mə̃'ta:] "cause to intoxicate (imp.)"
*[mə̃t'ta:], *['mə̃ta:]

[lə'da:] "cause to load (imp.)"
*[ləd'da:], *['ləda:]

[pə'ka:] "cause to ripen or roast (imp.)"
*[pək'ka:], *['pəka:]

[lə'ga:] "put on; grow (imp.)"
*[ləg'ga:], *['ləga:]

In all the above examples of (8) gemination of intervocalic consonants does not occur because the morphological rules of Maithili do not allow it. In Maithili the suffix *-a*, for example, is added to its root morphemes to form verbs—as the examples in (8) show, e.g. /pək + a/. This suffix *-a* is always realised in the resulting words as a long *and* stressed vowel—i.e. /pək + a/ is realised as [pə'ka:]. But when the same suffix *-a* is added to the root morphemes to form nouns or agent nouns, then in the resulting words the length of the vowel is retained but the stress is lost. In fact, the stress in such cases shifts back to the penult syllable on account of the intervocalic non-geminate [k] becoming geminate [kk]—i.e. /pək +a/ becoming ['pəkka:]. So if we recall our second question: What causes length on the vowel following the geminate sequences?, we may say that the duration of a Maithili vowel, like the vowels of other languages, is usually determined by the nature of the vowel itself, that is, by its point and manner of articulation. Typically, in Maithili, too, tense vowels take longer to produce than their lax counterparts, low vowels take longer than higher ones, and diphthongs take longer than simple vowels. As in Maithili words containing geminates the second, rearticulated member of the geminate is always followed by either a 'tense' or a 'low' vowel and the second syllable of such a word usually remains as an 'open' syllable, the vowel following the geminate sequences is therefore bound to remain long. That is to say, the length of the vowel of the second syllable of such a word is always retained even when its preceding nongeminate becomes geminate.

Thus, to account for all our Maithili data presented so far, this language has four general rules:

(9) Whenever such suffixes as *-a*, *-ã*, *-i*, *-ər*, *-əṛ*, *əl*, *-ət* and so on are added to the Maithili root morphemes in order to form verbs, then it is only the long allophonic variants of the vowels in these suffixes that are realised at the surface level in the resulting words and all these long vowels are always stressed in such contexts.

(10) Whenever such suffixes as *-a*, *-ã*, *-i*, *-ər*, *-əṛ*, *-əl*, *-ət* and so on are added to the Maithili root morphemes in order to form nouns or agent nouns, then it is only the long allophonic variants of the vowels in these suffixes that are realised at the surface level in the resulting words and all these long vowels always lose their stress.

(11) The long stressed Maithili vowels of the environments mentioned in Rule (9) lose their stress on account of the fact that the intervocalic non-geminate of each word instantiated in our data, (1)-(7), becomes geminate as a result of the reasons mentioned in Rule (10).

(12) The stress of the long stressed Maithili vowels—as mentioned in Rule (9)—always shifts back to the heavy penult syllable, as the first member of the geminate goes with the preceding vowel.

In addition to these four general rules, there is also a phonetic rule in Maithili which drops off the aspiration of the first member of the geminate and retains the aspiration of its second member:

(13) Whenever occurring in the word-internal intervocalic contexts as stated in Rule (11), the Maithili aspirated consonants occur in geminate sequences, and in all such sequences the aspiration of the first segment is always dropped off while the aspiration of the second segment is retained at the surface level.

To obtain at the surface level a Maithili word, such as ['pəkka:], for example, the above rules apply as follows:

The word at the underlying level:	/pək +a/
	↓
The word after the application of Rule (9):	pə'ka:
	↓

The word after the application of the Rule (10): pəka:

↓

The word after the application of Rule (11): pəkka:

↓

The word after the application of Rule (12): 'pəkka:

↓

The word at the surface level: ['pəkka:]

Similarly, to obtain at the surface level a Maithili word, such as ['sidd^{h}i:], for example, the above-mentioned rules apply as follows:

The word at the underlying level: /sid^h + i/

↓

The word after the application of Rule (9): si'd^{h}i:

↓

The word after the application of Rule (10): sid^{h}i:

↓

The word after the application of Rule (11): sid^{h}d^{h}i:

↓

The word after the application of Rule (12): 'sid^{h}d^{h}i:

↓

The word after the application of Rule (13): 'sidd^{h}i:

↓

The word at the surface level: ['sidd^{h}i:]

7.1.4 *Conclusion*

To conclude, gemination is one of the important characteristics of the Maithili consonant system. In this language two identical adjacent consonant segments occur in an environment where the segments in question are preceded by short stressed vowels and followed by long unstressed ones. We hold that stress in the preceding vowel of each Maithili word containing geminates is derived by rule. We believe that it is the consonantal frame which makes each penult syllable heavy, as the first member of the geminate always goes with the preceding vowel. This makes it obligatory for all such preceding vowels to take the stress. In our view, the length of the vowel following geminates is morphologically governed. As stated earlier in Rules (10) and (12), the length of the vowel following geminates is always retained but the stress of that vowel always shifts back to the heavy penult syllable on account of the fact that the intervocalic non-geminate becomes geminate. In addition, like other languages having aspiration, the Maithili aspirated consonants occur in geminate sequences, but in all such sequences the aspiration of the first member is always dropped off while the aspiration of only its second member is retained at the surface level.

7.2 Some Assimilatory Processes in Maithili

'Assimilation' is a general term in phonetics which refers to the influence exercised by one sound segment upon the articulation of another, so that the sounds become more alike, or identical. To put it another way, in assimilatory processes a segment takes on features from a neighbouring segment—for example, a consonant may pick up features from a vowel, a vowel may take on features of a consonant, one consonant may influence another, or one vowel may have an effect on another. The study of assimilation has been an important part of linguistic study, especially historical linguistic study. Relatively recently, particularly in the second half of the twentieth century, several researchers (e.g. Schachter, 1969; Cairns, 1969; Miller, 1972; Schane, 1972; Chen, 1973; Morton and Tatham, 1980) have also made synchronic speech analysis by using different experimental methods. These and similar other experimental investigations to analyse passages of natural conversation also emphasise the fact that the most common way a speech segment may change is to assimilate to another speech segment.

Several types of assimilation can be recognised. One classification is in terms of whether the change of the speech sound involved is the result of the influence of an adjacent speech sound, or of one further away. Another classification is in terms of the direction in which the assimilation works: there are three possibilities—(1) *regressive* or *anticipatory* assimilation, i.e. a process in which a speech sound becomes more like a following speech sound; (2) *progressive* assimilation, i.e. a process in which a speech sound becomes more like a preceding speech sound; and (3) *coalescent* or *reciprocal* assimilation, i.e. a process in which there is mutual influence (even fusion) of the speech sounds upon each other. In this section we shall look into the main regressive and coalescent assimilatory processes in Maithili.

7.2.1 *Regressive Assimilatory Processes in Maithili*

As stated earlier, the individual sound segments within a word or phrase have an effect on one another. However, not all the changes sound segments undergo when in conjunction with one another are equally likely to occur. In fact, certain processes of sound change are extremely widespread in the languages of the world, whereas others are relatively rare. For example, the most common way a speech sound may change is to assimilate to another speech sound. One of the most common types of assimilation is the nasalisation of vowels which are adjacent to a nasal consonant.

As in the case of various other languages of the world, nasalisation is especially common in the Maithili vowels preceding nasal consonants. For example:

/tam/	[tã:m] 'copper'	/čam/	[čã:m] 'leather'
/dam/	[dã:m] 'price'	/dan/	[dã:n] 'charity'
/tan/	[tã:n] 'pull (imp.)'	/rəŋ/	[rə̃:ŋ] 'colour'

The nasalisation of vowels in these examples is only phonetic—i.e. at the underlying level of the phonology these vowels remain [- nasal]. Like English and many other languages, in Maithili a derived level [- nasal] vowel is phonetically nasalised at the surface level, whenever the vowel is followed by a nasal consonant. This fact can be stated by a descriptive phonetic rule:

(14)

$$\begin{bmatrix} \text{V} \\ \text{- nasal} \end{bmatrix} \longrightarrow \begin{bmatrix} \text{V} \\ \text{+ nasal} \end{bmatrix} / \longrightarrow \begin{bmatrix} \text{C} \\ \text{+ nasal} \end{bmatrix}$$

This rule describes a universal effect manifested as a partial (or delayed) stopping off of the nasal passage by the velum in environments like the above ones.

Like many other languages, a second important assimilatory process in Maithili is the devoicing of its obstruents. That is to say, at times the Maithili voiced obstruent /d/ loses its voicing when it is followed by a voiceless obstruent. For example:

	Stem		*Stem*	*Word*	*Gloss*
d > t	/təd	+	kal/	[tət'ka:l]	'immediately'
	/bəd	+	tər/	['bəttə:r]	'worse'

The obstruent devoicing assimilatory processes that the above examples show can be stated in terms of the following rule:

(15)
$$\begin{bmatrix} +\text{ cons} \\ -\text{ son} \\ +\text{ ant} \\ +\text{ cor} \\ -\text{ cont} \\ -\text{ asp} \\ +\text{ voice} \end{bmatrix} \rightarrow [\text{-voice}] \; / \; \text{——} + \begin{bmatrix} +\text{ cons} \\ -\text{ son} \\ -\text{ cont} \\ -\text{ voice} \end{bmatrix}$$

The above rule says that a stem-final /d/ in Maithili is realised as /t/ whenever it is followed by any stem-initial voiceless consonants like /k/, /t/, and so on.

A third most widespread assimilatory process occurring in various languages of the world, including Maithili, is intervocalic voicing. This process assimilates voiceless segments to the voicing of the neighbouring sound segments. For example, Maithili uses such words as:

	Stem		*Stem*	*Word*	*Gloss*
t > d	/ǰəgət	+	iš/	[ǰəgə'di:š]	'God—the Master of the world'
ṭ >ḍ	/ṣəṭ	+	anən/	[ṣəḍa: nə̃n]	'six-headed'
č >ǰ	/əč	+	ənt/	[ə'ǰə:nt]	'unborn'

where the voiceless obstruents /t ṭ č/ are realised as [d ḍ ǰ], respectively, in intervocalic contexts. This intervocalic voicing of obstruents can be stated by means of a rule given in (16) below:

(16)
$$\begin{bmatrix} +\text{ cons} \\ -\text{ son} \\ -\text{ cont} \\ -\text{ asp} \\ -\text{ voice} \end{bmatrix} \rightarrow [\,+\text{ voice}] \; / \; \text{V ------ V}$$

However, intervocalic voicing is not always limited to the environment V——V. It is true that assimilatory voicing of obstruents in environments other than sonorants is rather rare in many languages of the world (e.g. see Sloat *et al.*, 1978: 115-16). But Maithili does have plenty of words, primarily of Sanskrit origin, which show obstruent voicing in such environments. That is to say, in spoken Maithili voiceless obstruents become voiced in assimilating to a voiced obstruent, although in written Maithili the graphemes corresponding to the voiceless segments are usually retained. For example:

	Prefix		*Stem*	*Word*	*Gloss*
p > b	/əp	+	bʰəkčʰək/	[ʻəbbʰə: kčʰək]	ʻone who eats uneatable things'
	/up	+	bas/	[ʻubba:s]	ʻfasting'
	/up	+	bʰog/	[ʻubbʰo:g]	ʻconsumption'

	Stem		*Stem*	*Word*	*Gloss*
t > d	/sat	+	din/	[ʻsaddĩ:n]	ʻseven days'
	/bəhut	+	din/	[bə'huddĩ:n]	ʻmany days'
ṭ >ḍ	/pəṭ	+	bari/	[pəd'ba:ri:]	ʻa village accountant'
č > ǰ	/pãč	+	ǰən/	[ʻpãǰǰə:n]	ʻfive persons'
k > g	/dik	+	gəǰ/	[ʻdiggə:ǰ]	ʻgreat'; ʻprofound'
	/ḍak	+	gʰər/	[ʻdaggʰə:r]	ʻpost office'
	/ḍak	+	gaṛi/	[ʻḍagga:ṛi:]	ʻmail train'

The assimilation of the above voiceless obstruents into their voiced counterparts can be stated in terms of the following rule given in (17) below:

(17)

$$\begin{bmatrix} +\text{cons} \\ -\text{son} \\ -\text{cont} \\ -\text{asp} \\ -\text{voice} \end{bmatrix} \rightarrow [+\text{voice}] \;/\; \underline{\quad\quad} + \begin{bmatrix} +\text{cons} \\ -\text{son} \\ -\text{cont} \\ +\text{voice} \end{bmatrix}$$

The above rule says that the Maithili voiceless obstruents /p t ṭ č k/ are realised as /b d ḍ ǰ g/ whenever they are followed by their voiced, whether aspirated or unaspirated, counterparts.

Maithili also has, in addition, various examples of regressive assimilation where features of one consonant segment are totally anticipated in the articulation of the preceding consonant segment. For example:

	Stem		*Stem*	*Word*	*Gloss*
t > č	/ut	+	čarəṇ/	[ˈuččaːrə̃ṇ]	'pronunciation'
	/ut	+	čʰed/	[ˈuččʰeːd]	'unheeded'
t > ǰ	/sət	+	ǰən/	[ˈsəǰǰə̃ːn]	'gentleman'
	/ut	+	ǰwəl/	[ˈuǰǰwəːl]	'bright'
t > l	/ut	+	las/	[ˈullaːs]	'courage'
	/ut	+	lekʰ/	[ˈulleːkʰ]	'reference'
	/tət	+	lin/	[ˈtəllĩːn]	'extremely busy'
t > ṭ	/sat	+	ṭa/	[ˈsaṭṭaː]	'seven pieces'

In the above example—i.e. /ut+čʰed/ [uččʰeːd]—aspiration of the consonant in question is never assimilated because in Maithili, like all other languages, there is a general constraint within words of *cʰ cʰ sequences.

7.2.2 *Coalescent Assimilatory Processes in Maithili*

As mentioned earlier, in coalescent assimilation each of the two adjacent articulations influence the other. Some frequent examples of vowel coalescence in Maithili include:

Stem		*Stem*	*Word*	*Gloss*
/məha	+	indrə/	[məˈhẽːndrə]	'Indra the Great'
/məha	+	iš/	[məˈheːš]	'the Hindu God—Shiva'

Examples like these show that whenever the Maithili central vowel /a/ occurs before /i/ in morphemes like the above ones, then the words which surface eventually contain the long allophonic variant of the vowel /e/ instead of the /a/ or /i/ of the original morphemes. This means that the resultant vowel /e/ assimilates the feature [- high] from the original vowel /a/ , and the feature [- back] from the original vowel /i/.

Similarly, whenever the Maithili /a/ occurs before /u/, as in the following morphemes:

Stem		*Stem*	*Word*	*Gloss*
/məha	+	udəyə/	[məˈhoːdəyə]	'sir'
/məha	+	utsəb/	[məˈhoːtsəb]	'big festival

then the vowel which surfaces eventually in the resulting words is neither the original /a/ nor /u/, but the vowel /o/ instead. That is to say, the resultant vowel /o/ assimilates the feature[- high] from the original vowel /a/ and the feature [+ back] from the original vowel /u/.

7.3 Some Non-assimilatory Processes in Maithili

Although by far the largest number of natural phonological processes are assimilatory, there are some rather common processes which do not seem to be cases of assimilation. The exact causes of some of these processes are not known, but they do occur in many languages of the world, including Maithili. In this section we shall look into three such non-assimilatory processes in Maithili: i.e. (1) breaking of vowels, (2) vowel reduction, and (3) deletion of vowel segments.

7.3.1 *Breaking of Vowels in Maithili*

One of the non-assimilatory processes that occurs in various languages of the world, including Maithili, is the breaking of long vowels. The term 'breaking' is used to refer to a process by which long vowels become diphthongs. Researchers (e.g. Labov, Yaeger, and Steiner, 1972; Miller, 1972 and 1973; Stampe, 1972) working in this area have amply shown how breaking occurs in many dialects of English, both British and American. Maithili, too, shows breaking of several lengthened vowels—for example, the lengthened /æ/ in Maithili is diphthongised as [əe], [ai] or [æ] in different contexts.

		/æ/ as [əe]		
/æs/	[əes] 'luxury'		/bæs/	[bəes] 'age'
/pær/	[pəer] 'leg'		/bær/	[bəer] 'jujube'
		/æ/ as [ai]		
/bʰæ/	[bʰai] 'brother'		/gæ/	[gai] 'cow'
		/æ/ as [ae]		
	/mæ/		[mae]	'mother'

To describe the above variations, an informal phonetic rule can be stated as follows:

$$(18)\qquad [\text{æ}] \left\{ \begin{array}{ll} [\text{əe}]\ / & \text{———}[c] \\ [\text{ai}]\ / & \left[\begin{array}{c} C \\ -\ \text{nasal------} \end{array}\right] \text{——} \\ [\text{ae}]\ / & \left[\begin{array}{c} C \\ +\ \text{nasal -----} \end{array}\right] \text{——} \end{array} \right\}$$

Similarly, the lengthened /ɔ/ in Maithili is also diphthongised as [ao] or [əo]. The diphthongisation of the lengthened /ɔ/ to [ao] occurs in those verb stems which are used to show future tense, provided that such verb stems do not have any inflectional suffixes to reveal the gender of their agent/s. For example:

/ɔ/ as [ao]

/ɔt/ [aot] 'will come' /gɔt/ [gaot] 'will sing'
/su'nɔt/ [su'naot] 'will tell' /gər'mɔt/ [gər'maot] 'will warm'

But when the suffix <u>-ah</u> (denoting masculine gender) or <u>-ih</u> (denoting feminine gender) is added to the above verb stems, then the lengthened [ɔ] is usually realised at the surface phonetic level as [əo]. For example:

Stem	*Stem with -ah suffix*	*Stem with -ih suffix*
/ɔt/	[əo'ta:h] '(he) will come'	[əo'ti:h] '(she) will come'
/gɔt/	[gəo'ta:h] '(he) 'will sing'	[gəo'ti:h] '(she) will sing'
/su'nɔt/	[sunəo'ta:h] '(he) will tell'	[sunəo'ti:h]'(she) will tell'
/gər'mɔt/	[gərməo'ta:h] '(he) will warm'	[gərməo' ti:h] '(she) will warm'

7.3.2 *Vowel Reduction in Maithili*

Vowel reduction involves the weakening of unstressed vowels, which is regarded (e.g. Fry, 1955 and 1958; Lindblom, 1963) as one of the most common processes to occur in languages with heavy stress—such as, for example, English, Swedish and Maithili. There can also be degrees, and even progressive degrees, of weakening in some languages—e.g. Russian (Jones, 1959). Like the British and American varieties of English (e.g. Fry, 1955; Lieberman, 1960), Maithili also displays morphological alternations between a stressed full vowel [a:] and an unstressed reduced vowel [ə]. For example, in the following common nouns in Maithili:

(7.3.2.1)

Stem	*Word*	*Gloss*
/bi'laṛ/	[bi'la:ṛ]	'(male) cat'
/lo'har/	[lo'ha:r]	'ironsmith'
/so'nar/	[sõ'na:r]	'goldsmith'
/kə'mar/	[kə̃'ma:r]	'blacksmith'
/hu'ṛaṛ/	[hu'ṛa:ṛ]	'wolf'
/kə'nah/	[kə̃'na:h]	'(male} one-eyed creature'
/bə'tah/	[bə'ta:h]	'(male) mad creature'

the stressed syllable in each word contains the vowel /a/. But when a derivational suffix -a is added to these words in order to change their subclassification from common nouns to agent nouns, then in the resultant words there is always a shift of stress from the final syllables of each of the common nouns given in (7.3.2.1) to the final syllable of each of the newly-formed agent nouns, as given in (7.3.2.2) below:

(7.3.2.2)

Stem		*Suffix*	*Word*	*Gloss*
/bi'laṛ	+	-a/	[bilə'ṛa:]	'a particular male cat'
/lo'har	+	-a/	[lohə'ra:]	'a particular ironsmith'
/so'nar	+	-a/	[sõnə'ra:]	'a particular goldsmith'
/kə'mar	+	-a/	[kə̃mə'ra:]	'a particular blacksmith'
/hu'ṛaṛ	+	-a/	[huṛə'ṛa:]	'a particular wolf'
/kə'nah	+	-a/	[kə̃nə'ha:]	'a particular one-eyed male'
/bə'tah	+	-a/	[bətə'ha:]	'a particular mad male'

And the stressed vowel /a/ of each common noun in (7.3.2.1) is then reduced to an unstressed [ə] in each agent noun, as the examples given earlier in (7.3.2.2) show.

To add further emphasis to the above agent nouns, a further suffix -ba is again added to the earlier words of (7.3.2.2). Then in the resultant words, as shown in (7.3.2.3),

(7.3.2.3)

Stem		*Suffix*	*Word*	*Gloss*
/bilə'ṛa	+	-ba/	[biləṛə'ba:]	'the same male cat'
/lohə'ra	+	-ba/	[lohərə'ba:]	'the same ironsmith'
/sonə'ra	+	-ba/	[sõnərə'ba:]	'the same goldsmith'

/kəmə'ṛa +	-ba/	[kə̃mərə'ba:]	'the same blacksmith'
/huṛə'ṛa +	-ba/	[huṛəṛə'ba:]	'the same wolf'
/kənə'ha +	-ba/	[kə̃nəhə'ba:]	'the same one-eyed male creature'
/bətə'ha +	-ba/	[bətəhə'ba:]	'the same mad male creature'

stress again shifts from the previous position to the final syllable of each of the newly-formed words—once again, reducing the stressed vowel /a/ of the words of (7.3.2.2) to the unstresssed short [ə] in each resultant word given above in (7.3.2.3). In each of the above examples the following vowel reduction rule in Maithili:

(19)

> Whenever a derivational or inflectional suffix— such as, -a, -ã or -ba— is added to any (noun) root or stem in Maithili to form compound/complex words, then it is only in the word-final syllable of each resultant word that the stressed full vowel [a:] or [ã:] is retained, while in the earlier syllables of all such words the [a:] or [ã:] is always reduced to the unstressed [ə] or [ə̃].

operates and, consequently, only the stressed vowel /a/ of the final syllable of each word remains, while the /a/ of each earlier syllable is always reduced to the short unstressed [ə].

7.3.3 *Elision and Deletion of Vowel Segments in Maithili*

'Elision' is a term used in phonetics and phonology to refer to the omission of sound segments in connected speech. Both consonants and vowels may be affected, and sometimes whole syllables may be elided. In Maithili, like many other Indo-Aryan languages, it happens quite often that if some particular vowel or consonant is dropped from a given item, the item is still considered to be the same as far as its meaning is concerned. As a result, several items in Maithili have two forms, which may be termed as 'contracted' and 'full' forms. Although the two forms are in free variation, the contracted form is unquestionably more common, especially in spoken Maithili, than the full form.

In the next chapter we discuss at length the elision of the Maithili consonants /t/, /k/ and /h/, as well as the shortening of /n^h/ into /n/ in various environments. In the present section we shall deal with examples of vowel deletion—of syncope, that is. Syncope is the loss of a vowel segment from some part of the word other than the end. Maithili exhibits syncope in words which are primarily of Sanskrit origin. For example:

Root	*Root*	*Word*	*Gloss*
/pustəkə	+ aləyə/	[pustə'ka:ləyə]	'library'
/debə	+ aləyə/	[de'ba:ləyə]	'temple'
/b^{h}ǒjənə	+ aləyə/	[b^{h}ǒjə'na:ləyə]	'hotel'
/himə	+ aləyə/	[hĩ'ma:ləyə]	'the house of snow'; 'the Himalayas'
/tət^{h}a	+ əpi/	[tə't^{h}a:pi]	'yet'; 'nevertheless'
/bidya	+ ərt^{h}i/	[bi'dya:rt^{h}i:]	'student'
/bidya	+ əd^{h}yəyənə/	[bi'dya:d^{h}yəyə̃nə]	'the study of lerning/ knowledge'

As all these examples show, in all compound words consisting of two root morphemes the morpheme-final or morpheme-initial /ə/ in Maithili is always deleted whenever it is preceded or followed by the long stressed vowel /a/.

The phonological process occurring in the above-mentioned examples requires a type of rule called a 'mirror image' rule. As the name implies, *mirror image rules* are rules whose environments are pertinent if read either from left to right or from right to left. To capture the phonological process involved in the earlier examples, i.e. the morpheme-initial or morpheme-final /ə/ is always deleted in Maithili either before or after the long stressed vowel /a/, we can have the following mirror image rule:

(20)

$$\begin{bmatrix} \text{V} \\ -\text{low} \\ +\text{back} \\ -\text{round} \end{bmatrix} \rightarrow \emptyset \; */ \;\underline{\qquad}\; \begin{bmatrix} \text{V} \\ +\text{low} \\ +\text{back} \\ -\text{round} \\ +\text{long} \end{bmatrix}$$

The asterisk directly before the diagonal means that the environment can be read either from left to right, as stated, or from right to left. Put another way, the above rule can be stated in a transformational rule as given below:

(21)

a.

$$\begin{bmatrix} V \\ -\text{low} \\ +\text{back} \\ -\text{round} \\ 1 \end{bmatrix} \underset{2}{+} \begin{bmatrix} V \\ +\text{low} \\ +\text{back} \\ -\text{round} \\ 3 \end{bmatrix} \Rightarrow \underset{1}{\emptyset} \quad \underset{2}{\emptyset} \quad \begin{bmatrix} V \\ +\text{low} \\ +\text{back} \\ -\text{round} \\ +\text{long} \\ 3 \end{bmatrix}$$

b.

$$\underset{1}{\begin{bmatrix} V \\ +\text{low} \\ +\text{back} \\ -\text{round} \end{bmatrix}} \underset{2}{+} \underset{3}{\begin{bmatrix} V \\ -\text{low} \\ +\text{back} \\ -\text{round} \end{bmatrix}} \Rightarrow \underset{1}{\begin{bmatrix} V \\ +\text{low} \\ +\text{back} \\ -\text{round} \\ +\text{long} \end{bmatrix}} \quad \underset{2}{\emptyset} \quad \underset{3}{\emptyset}$$

Like Hindi and other Indo-Aryan languages, Maithili also uses such compound words of Sanskrit origin, as:

Root		*Root*	*Word*	*Gloss*
/kəbi	+	indrə/	[kə'bĩ:ndrə]	'the king of poets'
/giri	+	indrə/	[gi'rĩ:ndrə]	'the king of mountains'
/giri	+	išə/	[gi'ri:šə]	'the Lord of Mountains —i.e. Shiva'
/məhi	+	indrə/	[mə'hĩ:ndrə]	'the king of the earth'
/məhi	+	išə/	[mə'hi:šə]	'the God of the earth'
/təru	+	utpənnə/	[təru: 'tpə̃nnə̃:]	'stemmed from the tree'
/b^hanu	+	udəyə/	[b^ha'nũ: dəyə]	'the rise of the sun'

Each of the above words consists of two root morphemes—the first of which contains a morpheme-final [+ high] vowel, while the second one contains a morpheme-initial [+ high] vowel of the same category as the first. The words which eventually surface as a result of such combinations end up having just one long allophonic variant of the two original vowel segments. This process can be stated by means of a phonological rule, as given below:

(22)

$$\begin{bmatrix} \text{Vi} \\ +\text{ high} \\ \\ \end{bmatrix}_1 \; +_2 \; \begin{bmatrix} \text{Vi} \\ +\text{ high} \\ \\ \end{bmatrix}_3 \Rightarrow \begin{bmatrix} \text{Vi} \\ +\text{ high} \\ +\text{ long} \end{bmatrix}_1 \quad \emptyset_2 \quad \emptyset_3$$

Similarly, Maithili also has a number of words consisting of two root morphemes, such as:

Root		*Root*	*Word*	*Gloss*
/bidya	+	aləyə/	[bi'dya:ləyə]	'school'
/məha	+	ašəyə/	[mə'ha:səyə]	'sir'

where the first morpheme ends with /-a/ and the second one begins with /a-/. When the two morphemes are combined, the resultant word retains only one long allophonic variant of /a/. This process can be stated in terms of a phonological rule, as given below:

(23)

$$\begin{bmatrix} \text{V} \\ +\text{ low} \\ +\text{ back} \\ -\text{ round} \\ 1 \end{bmatrix} \; +_2 \; \begin{bmatrix} \text{V} \\ +\text{ low} \\ +\text{ back} \\ -\text{ round} \\ 3 \end{bmatrix} \Rightarrow \begin{bmatrix} \text{V} \\ +\text{ low} \\ +\text{ back} \\ -\text{ round} \\ +\text{ long} \\ 1 \end{bmatrix} \quad \emptyset_2 \quad \emptyset_3$$

7.4 Summary

To summarise, one of the important characteristics of the Maithili consonant system is gemination. The consonants of this language occur only in word-internal intervocalic geminate sequences whenever the consonant in question is preceded by short stressed vowels and followed by long unstressed ones. The stress in the preceding vowel is derived by a rule, and the length of the following vowel is morphologically governed. We believe that the consonantal frame of such a word makes each penult syllable heavy, as the first member of the geminate always goes with the preceding vowel and this makes that vowel take the stress. The vowel following the geminate sequence retains its length but its stress always shifts back to the heavy penult syllable as the intervocalic non-geminate becomes geminate.

The most natural assimilatory processes in Maithili are regressive and coalescent. Our discussions of the regressive assimilatory processes have included the ones on nasalisation, obstruent devoicing, intervocalic voicing, obstruent voicing, as well as those processes whereby the Maithili /t/ is realised as /č/, /ǰ/, /l/ or /ṭ/ in different phonological environments. With regard to coalescent assimilatory processes, we have discussed how there is mutual influence (and even 'fusion') of the vowel segments /a/ and /i/ as well as of /a/ and /u/, when different morphemes in which they occur are combined to form new words. As a result of such combinations, in the resultant Maithili words /a/ and /i/ are realised as /e/, while /a/ and /u/ are realised as /o/. In addition, we have also discussed three major non-assimilatory processes occurring in Maithili—i.e. the breaking of vowels, vowel reduction, and elision and deletion of vowel segments.

Chapter 8

THE MORPHOPHONOLOGY OF THE MAITHILI VERBS: A STUDY ON THE WEAKENING AND ELISION OF CONSONANT SEGMENTS IN MAITHILI

8.0 Introduction

Verb is a term used in the grammatical classification of words, to refer to a class traditionally defined as 'doing' or action words—a definition which has been criticised in linguistics (e.g. Lyons, 1968: Palmer, 1971; Quirk *et al.,* 1972), largely on the grounds that many verbs do not 'act' in any obvious sense as, for example, the Maithili lagəb̲ 'to seem'. The formal definition of a verb, especially of a Maithili verb, refers to an element which can display morphological contrasts of tense, aspect, mood, voice, gender, person as well as the social status of the person used in the subject and/or object of the sentence in which the particular verb occurs. Functionally, it is the element which, singly or in combination with other verbs (i.e. 'verb phrase'), is used as the minimal predicate of a sentence, co-occurring with a subject—e.g. o̲ æla 'he came'.

The first philologist who made a close study of the system of verbs in Maithili was Grierson (1881 and 1883c). But he could not manage to explain the complexity of verb-conjugation in Maithili; nor did he make any serious attempt to analyse the series of verbal suffixes in this language. He himself confessed:

> The Maithili verb delights in a redundancy of forms. Like all *partially cultivated languages,* it has few parts of which there are not two or three optional forms. These optional forms are not local peculiarities, but are all used by the same speaker *as his fancy* or *as the rhythm of the sentence dictates.* I cannot find out that they

represent any different shades of meaning (Grierson, 1881: 50, my emphasis).

Grierson is right in pointing out that there are optional forms in Maithili verb-conjugation, but the present researcher does not agree with him that such different forms are used according to the "fancy" of the speaker and "rhythm of the sentence". The present researcher also disagrees with Grierson that the peculiarity of the conjugation in question is characteristic of "partially cultivated languages". As a matter of fact, this conjugation is so systematic and free from anomaly that it can unquestionably place Maithili in the rank of fully cultivated languages.

Apart from Grierson, the other scholars who studied and published some materials on the Maithili verbs are S. Jha (1958: 443-561) and G. Jha (1958 and 1979: 48-74). But their studies are basically diachronic in nature, and their descriptions of the Maithili verbal system are based primarily on the pre-established categories of Sanskrit grammars. The present researcher is not aware of any book published on the morphophonological study of the Maithili verbs, especially of the one based on the phonological theory described by Chomsky and Halle (1968).

This study is an attempt to provide an explicit treatment of the morphological composition of transitive verbs in Maithili and the rules that best describe the alternations in verb morphology. Our basic strategy is to investigate the interaction between morphology and phonology. And, in so doing, our primary aim is to find out what light, if any, the morphological composition of the Maithili verbs throws on the phonological processes in Maithili, especially on the processes of consonant weakening and elision that we briefly discussed in the previous chapter. The phonological theory assumed here is basically the one described in Chomsky and Halle (1968).

Before we embark upon further discussions on the morphophonology of the Maithili verbs and verb forms, some general characteristics of the Maithili verbal system must be pointed out first. The verbal system of this language is basically inflectional: i.e. many of the desinence morphemes of the Maithili verbal system consist of elements like tense, aspect, mood, voice, gender, person as well as the social status of the person used in the subject/object of the sentence in which the verb occurs. This language forms its periphrastic tenses using one of the aspectual forms and a tense-mood marker. An aspect marker is attached to the main verb root, while tense and mood are marked mainly on auxiliaries. Similarly, gender, person and social status, too, are usually marked on auxiliaries. The category 'singular' or 'plural' relates only to certain parts of the noun phrase for certain classes of nouns and pronouns in Maithili—any detailed discussions of which are beyond the scope of the present study—and this category has therefore no relevance for the morphology of the Maithili verbs. In other words, the verb form in Maithili always remains the same, no matter whether the grammatical subject of the sentence is in the singular or plural number.

To present things systematically, this chapter is divided into three main sections: the first section deals with the auxiliary verb forms in Maithili and with the light that these verb forms throw on the process of elision; the second section deals with variations of the aspect markers attached to the transitive verb-roots in Maithili and with the light that such variations throw on the process of elision, especially the elision of the dentals and the labials in Maithili; the third and final section presents a summary of our main discussions and conclusions.

8.1 The Auxiliary Verb Forms in Maithili

'Auxiliary' is a term used in the grammatical description of the verb phrase, to refer to the set of verbs, subordinate to the main lexical verb. The auxiliary verbs in Maithili are used with different markers. These markers make distinctions in tense, mood, gender as well as in person, according to the social status of both the grammatical subject and the object of the sentence in which the verb in question occurs. The present section looks into various base forms of the auxiliary verbs in Maithili and ascertains how these forms are inflected for tense, gender and person (in accordance with its social status, that is) in the indicative mood and active voice. The section is divided into two main parts: the first part deals with those auxiliary verb forms which are inflected in accordance with their grammatical subjects; the second part deals with those that are inflected in accordance with both their grammatical subjects and objects.

Before embarking upon the analyses and discussions of these verb forms, a few general points with regard to the 'social status' of the person (whether the first, the second or the third) used in Maithili sentences must be clearly stated at the outset. As mentioned earlier, Maithili has a system of verbal inflection in which the verb is inflected for person and according to the social status of both the subject and the object, and not according to person and number as, for example, in Hindi (e.g. Pray, 1969). Thus, the Maithili verbs are always used either in honorific or in non-honorific forms. As the name indicates, honorific forms are used to express levels of politeness or respect, especially in relation to the compared social status of the participants; non-honorific forms, on the other hand, are used when the social status of the person in question is relatively low. The latter forms are again sub-divided into two further categories: (a) intimate, i.e. the form which is used when the person in question is intimate to the speaker; and (b) non-intimate, i.e. the form which is used when the person concerned is not intimate to the speaker. The diagram given below in Figure 8.1 indicates the binary development of the above-mentioned social status categories in Maithili:

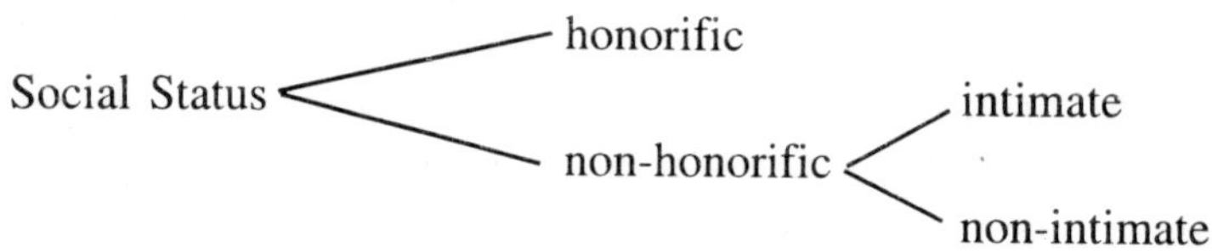

Figure 8.1: The binary development of the social status categories in Maithili.

When the grammatical subject or object of the auxiliary verb in Maithili is in the first person, the pronoun used for the subject is *həm* 'I', while the one used for the object is həmra 'to me'. Both *həm* (subject/nominative) and həmra (object/accusative) are always treated in the Maithili verbal system as having just one form each, and the social status markers attached to the auxiliary verb roots are primarily the ones that are used in the honorific forms of the second and the third persons. We shall therefore regard the verbal form of the first person in Maithili as simply 'honorific'.

But things become different when the subject or the object of the verb in Maithili is either in the second or in the third person. That is, when the subject or the object of the Maithili sentence is in the second person, the auxiliary verb can have one of the following three forms according to the social status of the subject or the object: (1) the *yəu* form, (2) the *həu* form, and (3) the *rəu* form. The *yəu* form is honorific, and the pronouns used in accordance with this form are: ãhã/əpne (subject/nominative) 'you' and ãhãkẽ/əpnekẽ (object/accusative) 'to you'; the *həu* form is at once non-honorific and intimate, and the pronouns used for this form are tõ (subject/nominative) 'you' and tora (object/accusative) 'to you'; the *rəu* form is both non-honorific and non-intimate, and the pronouns used for this form are also the same: tõ (subject/nominative) 'you' and tora (object/accusative) 'to you'.

But when the subject or the object of the sentence is in the third person, then the verb in Maithili can have either an honorific form or a non-honorific one. The third person pronouns used in the honorific form are i/o (subject/nominative) 'he/she' or 'this/that' and hinka/hunka (object/accusative) 'to him/to her', while those used in the non-honorific form are also i/o (subject/nominative) 'he/she' or 'this/that', and ekra/okra (object/accusative) 'to him/to her' or 'to this/to that'.

The first, the second and the third persons in Maithili are all now categorised in Figure 8.2 below in accordance with the forms of their respective social status (ST):

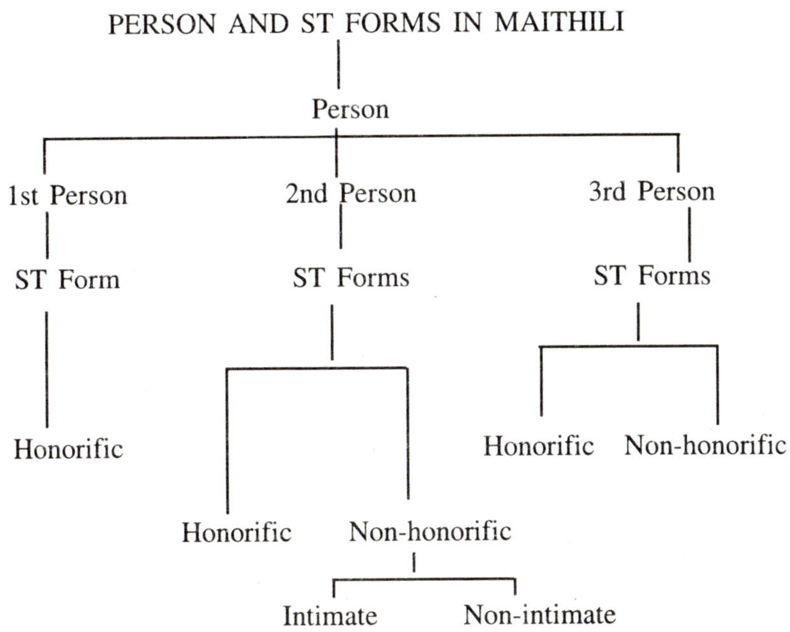

Figure 8.2: The first, the second and the third persons in Maithili categorised in accordance with the forms of their respective social status.

The above-mentioned 'person' and 'social status' categories in Maithili can be formalised in terms of four features: i.e. two features, [1st person] and [2nd person], for the categories of 'person'; and two features, [honorific] and [intimate], for the categories of 'social status'. Each of these features may be either plus or minus. And all of them may be termed inflectional features since they enter into the phonological rules which categorise both the inflection of nouns and pronouns and the phonological variation of verbal forms usually labelled 'agreement' or 'concord'. A somewhat broad specification of these features is given below in (1):

(1)

(i) V ————> [±1st person]
(ii) [- 1st Person] ————> [± 2nd person]
(iii) [+ 1st Person] ————> [+ honorific]
(iv) [+ 2nd Person] ————> [± honorific]
(v) [- 2nd Person] ————> [± honorific]
(v) [- honorific] ————> [± intimate]/ [2nd person]

8.1.1 *The Forms According to the Subject*

In this part we shall look into those auxiliary verb forms which are in accordance with the social status (ST) of their grammatical subjects. To do so systematically, we shall analyse the forms in all tenses: the present, the past and the future.

8.1.1.1 *The Forms in the Present Tense*

Table 8.1a presents six Maihili sentences containing auxiliary verb forms in the present tense. The morphological analysis of these auxiliary verb forms is done in Table 8.1b. From the study of this morphological analysis done in Table 8.1b, we can draw the following two main conclusions about the regularities with which these verb forms occur in the present tense:

First, both č^h and the suppletive əč^h are used as auxiliary verb roots in Maithili in the present tense: əč^h is used only when the grammatical subject of the sentence is in the [- honorific] form of the third person; č^h is used in all other contexts

Secondly, as present tense-cum-social status markers, Maithili uses four inflectional suffixes: -i, -ə(h), -ẽ and -ət^{h}i. The suffix -i is attached to the root č^h when the subject of the sentence is either in the first person

Table 8.1a: Six Maithili sentences containing auxiliary verb forms in the present tense.

Person	ST Form	Sentence Subject Verb	Gloss
1. 1st	honorific	həm čʰi	'I am'
2. 2nd	*yəu* form	ãhã čʰi	'You are'
3. 2nd	*həu* form	tõ čʰə (h)	'You are'
4. 2nd	*rəu* form	tõ čʰẽ	'You are'
5. 3rd	honorific	o čʰətʰi	'He/She is'
6. 3rd	non-honorific	o əčʰi	'He/she is'

Table 8.1b: The morphological analysis of the Maithili auxiliary verb forms as given in Table 8.1a.

Person	ST Form	Root		Present Tense-cum-ST Marker	Verb Form
1. 1st	honorific	čʰ	+	-i	čʰi
2. 2nd	*yəu* form	čʰ	+	-i	čʰi
3. 2nd	*həu* form	čʰ	+	-ə(h)	čʰə (h)
4. 2nd	*rəu* form	čʰ	+	-ẽ	čʰẽ
5. 3rd	honorific	čʰ	+	-ətʰi	čʰətʰi
6. 3rd	non-honorific	əčʰ	+	-i	əčʰi

or in the honorific form of the second person; -i, in addition, is also attached to the root əčʰ when the subject of the sentence is in the non-honorific form of the third person. The marker -ə(h) is attached to the root čʰ when the subject of the sentence is in the *həu* form (i.e. in [+ intimate] form) of the second person; the marker -ẽ, on the other hand, is attached to the root čʰ when the subject is in the *rəu* form (i.e. in [-intimate] form) of the second person. The suffix -ətʰi is attached to the root čʰ when the subject of the sentence is in the honorific form of the third person.

8.1.1.2 *The Forms in the Past Tense*

Given below in Table 8.2a are eight Maithili sentences containing those auxiliary verb forms that are used in the past tense:

Table 8.2a: Eight Maithili sentences containing those auxiliary verb forms that are used in the past tense.

Person	ST Form	Sentence: Subject	Sentence: Verb	Gloss
1. 1st	honorific	həm	čʰəlɔ̃(h)ũ	'I was'
2. 2nd	*yəu* form	ãhã	čʰəlɔ̃(h)ũ	'You were'
3. 2nd	*həu* form	tõ	čʰələ (h)	'You were'
4. 2nd	*rəu* form	tõ	čʰəlẽ	'You were'
5. 3rd	honorific	o	čʰələtʰi	'He/she was'
6. 3rd	honorific	o	čʰəla (h)	'He was'
7. 3rd	honorific	o	čʰəli (hi)	'She was'
8. 3rd	non-honorific	o	čʰəl	'He/she was'

The morphological analysis of these verb forms is done in Table 8.2b. From the study of the morphological analysis done in Table 8.2b, we can draw the following four main conclusions about the regularities of these verb forms:

Table 8.2b: The morphological analysis of the Maithili auxiliary verb forms as given in Table 8.2a.

Person	ST Form	Root		Aspect Marker		PT Marker		Gender/ST Marker	Verb Form
1. 1st	honorific	čʰ	+	-ə	+	-l	+	-ɔ̃(h)ũ	čʰəlɔ̃(h)ũ
2. 2nd	*yəu* form	čʰ	+	-ə	+	-l	+	-ɔ̃(h)ũ	čʰəlɔ̃(h)ũ
3. 2nd	*həu* form	čʰ	+	-ə	+	-l	+	-ə(h)	čʰələ(h)
4. 2nd	*rəu* form	čʰ	+	-ə	+	-l	+	-ẽ	čʰəlẽ
5. 3rd	honorific	čʰ	+	-ə	+	-l	+	-ətʰi	čʰələtʰi
6. 3rd	honorific	čʰ	+	-ə	+	-l	+	-a(h)	čʰəla(h)
7. 3rd	honorific	čʰ	+	-ə	+	-l	+	-i(hi)	čʰəli(hi)
8. 3rd	non-honorific	čʰ	+	-ə	+	-l	+	Ø	čʰəl

First, čʰ is always used as the root of the auxiliary verb in the past tense (PT), and -ə is used as its aspect marker.

Secondly, the morpheme -l is always used as the past tense marker. In the absence of any additional marker, the form čʰ + -ə + -l (cʰəl) always denotes the non-honorific social status of its grammatical subject.

Thirdly, -a(h) and -i(hi) are the two gender-cum-social status markers that are attached to the čʰəl form in different morphological contexts: a(h) is attached when the grammatical subject is in the masculine gender and in the honorific form of the third person; -i(hi), on the other hand, is attached wḥen the subject is in the feminine gender and in the honorific form of the third person.

Fourthly, -ətʰi, -ə̃(h)ũ, -ə(h) and -*ẽ* are the four social status markers that are attached to the čʰəl form of the auxiliary verb in different morphological contexts. Each of these social status markers remains neutral with regard to the gender of its grammatical subject. The marker -ətʰi is used when the subject is in the honorific form of the third person; -ə̃(h)ũ is used when the subject is either in the first person or in the honorific form (i.e. the *yəu* form) of the second person; ə(h) is used when the subject is in the *həu* form of the second person; and -ẽ is used when the subject is in the *rəu* form of second person.

8.1.1.3 *The Forms in the Future Tense*

Table 8.3a given below lists eight Maithili sentences containing those auxiliary verb forms that are used in the future tense:

Table 8.3a: Eight Maithili sentences containing those auxiliary verb forms that are used in the future tense.

Person	ST Form	Sentence		Gloss
		Subject	Verb	
1. 1st	honorific	həm	rəhəb	'I will be'
2. 2nd	*yəu* form	ãhã	rəhəb	'You will be'
3. 2nd	*həu* form	tõ	rəhəbə(h)	'You will be'
4. 2nd	*rəu* form	tõ	rəhəbẽ	'You will be'
5. 3rd	honorific	o	rəhətʰin$^{(h)}$ə̃	'He/she will be'
6. 3rd	honorific	o	rəhəta(h)	'He will be'
7. 3rd	honorific	o	rəhəti (hi)	'She will be'
8. 3rd	non-honorific	o	rəhət	'He/she will be'

The morphological analysis of these auxiliary verb forms is done in Table 8.3b. From the study of the morphological analysis done in Table 8.3b, we can draw the following four main conclusions about the regularities of these verb forms in the future:

First, rəh is always used as the root of the auxiliary verb forms in the future, and -ə is used as its aspect marker.

Table 8.3b: The morphological analysis of the Maithili auxiliary verb forms as given in Table 8.3a.

Person	ST Form	Root		Aspect Marker		Tense Marker		Gender/ST Marker	Verb Form
1. 1st	honorific	rəh	+	-ə	+	-b	+	Ø	rəhəb
2. 2nd	*yəu* form	rəh	+	-ə	+	-b	+	Ø	rəhəb
3. 2nd	*həu* form	rəh	+	-ə	+	-b	+	-ə(h)	rəhəbə(h)
4. 2nd	*rəu* form	rəh	+	-ə	+	-b	+	-ẽ	rəhəbẽ
5. 3rd	honorific	rəh	+	-ə	+	-t^h	+	-in$^{(h)}$ɔ̃	rəhət^hin$^{(h)}$ɔ̃
6. 3rd	honorific	rəh	+	-ə	+	-t	+	-a(h)	rəhəta(h)
7. 3rd	honorific	rəh	+	-ə	+	-t	+	-i(hi)	rəhəti(hi)
8. 3rd	non-honorific	rəh	+	-ə	+	-t	+	Ø	rəhət

Secondly, -b, -t and -t^h are the three morphemes that are used as future tense markers in Maithili. They are used in different morphological environments and they also indicate different social status of their grammatical subjects. The marker -b is attached to the auxiliary verb-root rəh, when its grammatical subject is either in the first person or in the second person. The form rəh + -ə + -b (rəhəb)—without any other social status marker attached to it—always denotes the honorific social status of its grammatical subject. The markers *-t* and -t^h, on the contrary, are attached to rəhə, when their grammatical subjects are in the third person. The form rəh + -ə + -t (rəhət), without any other social status marker attached to it, always denotes the non-honorific social status of its grammatical subject, while -t^h is attached to the form rəhə when the gender of the honorific third person remains unspecified.

Thirdly, -a(h) and -i(hi) are the two gender-cum-social status markers that are attached to the auxiliary verb form rəhət: -a(h) is attached to rəhət when its grammatical subject is in the masculine gender and in the honorific form of the third person; -i(hi), on the other hand, is attached to it when the subject is in the feminine gender and in the honorific form of the third person.

Fourthly, -ə(h) and -ẽ are the two social status markers that are attached to the auxiliary verb form rəhəb: the former is attached to rəhəb when its grammatical subject is in the *həu* form of the second person; the latter is attached to rəhəb when the subject is in the *rəu* form of the second person.

8.1.1.4 *Summary and Discussion*

To summarise, the Maithili auxiliary verb forms in the present tense consist of such elements as shown in Figure 8.3:

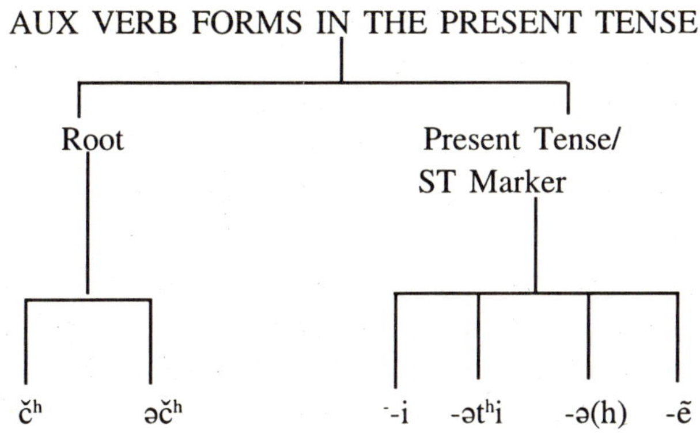

Figure 8.3: The Maithili auxiliary verb forms in the present tense.

These present tense forms of the Maithili auxiliary verb are described in Rule (1) below:

Rule (1)

(i) Aux Verb in the Present Tense ——> root + present tense/ST marker

(ii) Root ——> { čʰ / əčʰ }

(iii) present tense/ST marker ——> { -i / -ətʰi / -ə (h) / -ẽ }

The past tense forms of the Maithili auxiliary verb are summarised in Figure 8.4 below:

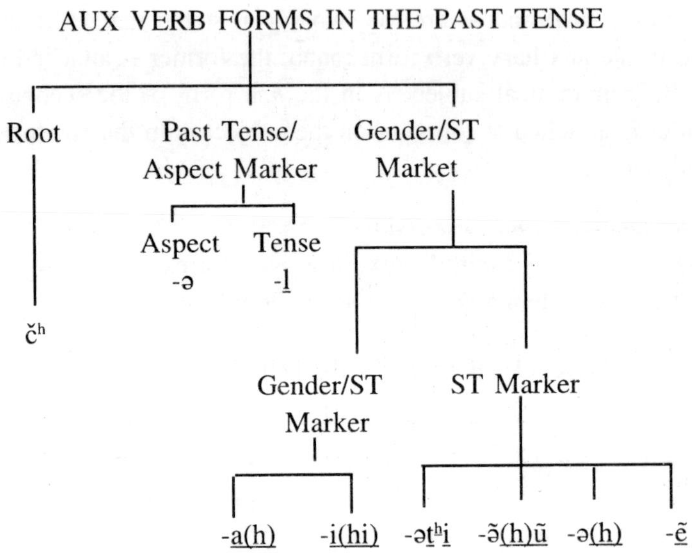

Figure 8.4: The Maithili auxiliary verb forms in the past tense.

These past tense forms of the Maithili auxiliary verb are described in Rule (2):

Rule (2)

(i) Aux Verb in the Past Tense ⟶ root + aspect marker⁺ past tense/ { a. gender/ST marker / b. ST marker }

(ii) root ⟶ cʰ

(iii) aspect marker ⟶ -ə

(iv) past tense marker ⟶ -l̲

(v) a. gender/ST marker ⟶ { -a(h) / -i(hi) }

b. ST marker ⟶ { -ət̲ʰi̲ / -ə̃(h)ũ / -ə (h) / -ẽ }

The Maithili auxiliary verb forms used in the future tense are summarised in Figure 8.5 given below:

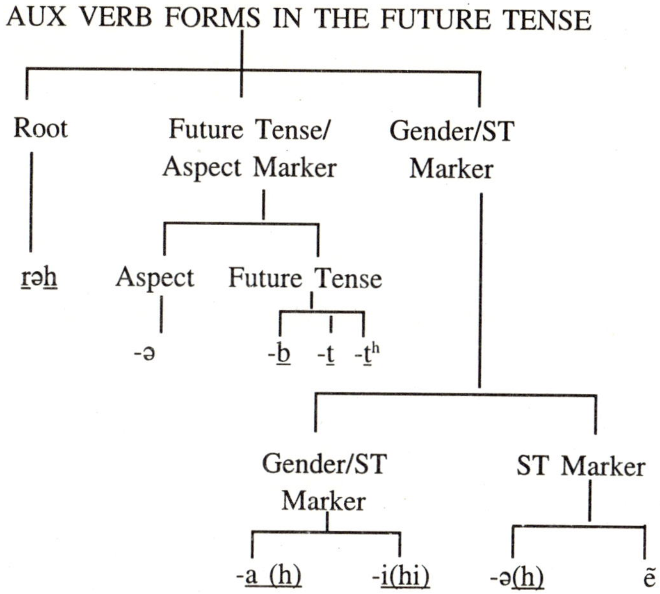

Figure 8.5: The Maithili auxiliary verb forms used in the future tense.

These forms of the Maithili auxiliary verb as used in the future tense are described in Rule (3) below:

Rule (3)

(i) Aux Verb in the future ⟶ root + future tense/aspect marker + {a. Gender/ST marker; b. ST marker}

(ii) root ⟶ rəh

(iii) aspect marker ⟶ -ə

(iv) future forms ⟶ {- *b*; - *t*; - tʰ}

(V) a. gender/ST marker ⟶ {-*a*(*h*); -*i*(*hi*)}

b. ST marker ⟶ {-ə(h); -*ẽ*}

All these studies on the auxiliary verb forms in Maithili give ample evidences of elision— i.e. the omission of sound segments in connected speech. Like many other Indo-Aryan languages (see, for example, Chatterji, 1926/1970 and 1960; Burrow, 1955; S. Jha, 1958), it has always been a feature of Mathili words that the weakly accented syllables have undergone a process of gradation, i.e. loss of phonemes or obscuration of vowels (e.g. see S. Jha, 1958). The same process of gradation, with resultant contraction, may be observed in operation in current Maithili. It is important, however, to distinguish between cases of elision which have already been established (e.g. see S. Jha, 1958) in the language for some time and those which have become current only recently, as in the case of the following Maithili auxiliary verb forms, which we already came across in earlier examples:

Present	Past	Future
č^{h}ə(h)	č^{h}ələ̃(h)ũ č^{h}ələ(h) č^{h}əla(h) č^{h}əli(hi)	rəhəbə(h) rəhət^{h}in$^{(h)}$ə̃ rəhəta(h) rəhəti(hi)

In these latter cases, the forms exhibiting the elision of a total syllable, as of (*hi*) from č^{h}əli(hi) and rəhəti(hi), or of a total phoneme, as of h from the following:

Present	Past	Future
č^{h}ə(h)	č^{h}ələ̃(h)ũ č^{h}ələ(h) č^{h}əla(h)	rəhətə(h) rəhta(h)

or of a particular distinctive feature only, as of the aspiration of n^{h} from rəhət^{h}in$^{(h)}$ə̃, are all typical of rapid, colloquial speech, whereas more formal speech tends to retain the fuller form under the preservative influence of the spelling. These examples of elided auxiliary verb forms in colloquial speech are independent of the type of reduction affecting particular words and syllables under weak accent in connected speech, as discussed in the previous chapter. In the sections that follow, we shall again have further evidences of the elision of these and other speech segments in Maithili.

8.1.2 The Forms According to Both the Subject and the Object

As stated earlier, the system of verbal inflection in Maithili is such that its verbs are inflected for person and according to the social status of both the subject and the object. In this sub-section we shall first present and analyse those auxiliary verb forms that are used in accordance with the social status of their grammatical subjects and objects in the present, past and future tenses, and then we shall summarise and discuss what light these forms throw on the process of elision in Maithili.

8.1.2.1 *The Forms in the Present, Past and Future Tenses*

To ascertain which inflectional forms are used in which cases, Table 8.4 provides a framework for all possible combinations in which the subject and the object, with their similar and/or different social status forms, can be used in the Maithili sentences. Based on this framework, later Tables 8.5a, 8.6a and 8.7a list 26 sentences each in the present, past and future tenses, respectively. The main verb of all these sentences is the same: k̲əh̲əi̲(̲t̲)̲ 'saying'; differences occur primarily in the social status forms of their subjects and objects, and consequently in their auxiliary verb forms as well.

Based on the framework outlined in Table 8.4, Table 8.5a lists 26 sentences which show how the Maithili auxiliary verb forms are inflected in the present tense in accordance with the social status of their grammatical subjects and objects. Table 8.5b presents the morphological analysis of the same auxiliary verb forms. Similarly, based on the same framework of Table 8.4, Tables 8.6a and 8.7a also list 26 sentences each and show how the Maithili auxiliary verb forms are inflected in the past tense and in the future tense, respectively. The morphological analysis of the verb forms of Table 8.6a is done in Table 8.6b, while that of Table 8.7a is done in Table 8.7b.

8.1.2.2 *Summary and Discussion*

The morphological analysis done in Tables 8.5b, 8.6b and 8.7b show a number of different markers that are quite systematically used in Maithili

Table 8.4: Possible combinations of the subject and the object that can be used in the Maithili sentences in the first, second and third persons—each person of the 'subject' and the 'object' columns is categorised in accordance with its ST forms.

Subject		Object	
Person	ST Form	Person	ST Form
1. 1st	honorific	2nd	*yəu* form
2. 1st	honorific	2nd	*həu* form
3. 1st	honorific	2nd	*rəu* form
4. 1st	honorific	3rd	honorific
5. 1st	honorific	3rd	non-honorific
6. 2nd	*yəu* form	1st	honorific
7. 2nd	*yəu* form	3rd	honorific
8. 2nd	*rəu* form	3rd	non-honorific
9. 2nd	*həu* form	1st	honorific
10. 2nd	*rəu* form	1st	honorific
11. 2nd	*həu* form	3rd	honorific
12. 2nd	*həu* form	3rd	non-honorific
13. 2nd	*rəu* form	3rd	honorific
14. 2nd	*rəu* form	3rd	non-honorific
15. 3rd	honorific	1st	honorific
16. 3rd	non-honorific	1st	honorific
17. 3rd	honorific	2nd	*yəu* form
18. 3rd	honorific	2nd	*həu* form
19. 3rd	honorific	2nd	*rəu* form
20. 3rd	non-honorific	2nd	*yəu* form
21. 3rd	non-honorific	2nd	*həu* form
22. 3rd	non-honorific	2nd	*rəu* form
23. 3rd	honorific	3rd	honorific
24. 3rd	non-honorific	3rd	honorific
25. 3rd	honorific	3rd	non-honorific
26. 3rd	non-honorific	3rd	non-honorific

Table 8.5a: Maithili sentences based on the framework outlined in Table 8.4, showing how the auxiliary verb forms are inflected in the present tense in accordance with the ST forms of their grammatical subjects and objects.

	Subject	Object	Verb: Main	Verb: Auxiliary	Gloss
1.	həm	ãhãkẽ	kəhəi(t)	čʰi	'I am saying to you'
2.	həm	tora	kəhəi(t)	čʰiyə(h)	'I am saying to you'
3.	həm	tora	kəhəi (t)	čʰiyə(h)u	'I am saying to you'
4.	həm	hunka	kəhəi (t)	čʰiyən$^{(h)}$ĩ	'I am saying to him'
5.	həm	okra	kəhəi(t)	čʰiyəi(k)	'I am saying to him'
6.	ãhã	həmra	kəhəi(t)	čʰi	'You are saying to me'
7.	ãhã	hunka	kəhəi(t)	čʰiyən$^{(h)}$ĩ	'You are saying to him'
8.	ãhã	okra	kəhəi(t)	čʰiyəi(k)	'You are saying to him'
9.	tõ	həmra	kəhəi(t)	čʰə(h)	'You are saying to me'
10.	tõ	həmra	kəhəi(t)	čʰẽ	'You are saying to me'
11.	tõ	hunka	kəhəi(t)	čʰəhun$^{(h)}$ə̃	'You are saying to him'
12.	tõ	okra	kəhəi(t)	čʰəhək	'You are saying to him'
13.	tõ	hunka	kəhəi(t)	čʰəhun$^{(h)}$ə̃	'You are saying to him'
14.	tõ	okra	kəhəi(t)	čʰəhik	'You are saying to him'
15.	o	həmra	kəhəi(t)	čʰətʰi	'He/she is saying to me'
16.	o	həmra	kəhəi(t)	əčʰi	'He/she is saying to me'
17.	o	ãhãkə̃	kəhəi(t)	čʰətʰi	'He/she is saying to you'
18.	o	tora	kəhəi(t)	čʰətʰun$^{(h)}$ə̃	'He/she is saying to you'
19.	o	tora	kəhəi(t)	čʰətʰun$^{(h)}$ə̃	'He/she is saying to you'
20.	o	ãhãkẽ	kəhəi(t)	əčʰi	'He/she is saying to you'
21.	o	tora	kəhəi(t)	čʰə (h)	'He/she is saying to you'
22.	o	tora	kəhəi(t)	čʰə(h)u	'He/she is saying to you'
23.	o	hunka	kəhəi(t)	čʰətʰin$^{(h)}$ə̃	'He/she is saying to him'
24.	o	hunka	kəhəi(t)	čʰən$^{(h)}$ĩ	'He/she is saying to him'
25.	o	okra	kəhəi(t)	čʰətʰin$^{(h)}$ə̃	'He/she is saying to him'
26.	o	okra	kəhəi(t)	čʰə(h)i	'He/she is saying to him'

Table 8.5b: The morphological analysis of the Maithili auxiliary verb forms in the present tense as given in the Maithili sentences of Table 8.5a.

	Root		Tense/ST Marker Subject		Object	Verb Form
1.	čʰ	+	-i	+	Ø	čʰi
2.	čʰ	+	-i	+	-yə(h)	čʰiyə(h)
3.	čʰ	+	-i	+	-yə(h)u	čʰiyə(h)u
4.	čʰ	+	-i	+	-yən$^{(h)}$ĩ	čʰiyən$^{(h)}$ĩ
5.	čʰ	+	-i	+	-yəi(k)	čʰiyəi(k)
6.	čʰ	+	-i	+	Ø	čʰi
7.	čʰ	+	-i	+	-yən(h)ĩ	čʰiyən$^{(h)}$ĩ
8.	čʰ	+	-i	+	-yəi(k)	čʰiyəi(k)
9.	čʰ	+	-ə$^{(h)}$	+	Ø	čʰə(h)
10.	čʰ	+	-ẽ	+	Ø	čʰẽ
11.	čʰ	+	-əh	+	-un(h)ə̃	čʰəhun$^{(h)}$ə̃
12.	čʰ	+	-əh	+	-ək	čʰəhək
13.	čʰ	+	-əh	+	-un(h)ə̃	čʰəhun$^{(h)}$ə̃
14.	čʰ	+	-əh	+	-ik	čʰəhik
15.	čʰ	+	-ətʰi	+	Ø	čʰətʰi
16.	əčʰ	+	-i	+	Ø	əčʰi
17.	čʰ	+	-ətʰi	+	Ø	čʰətʰi
18.	čʰ	+	-ətʰ	+	-un$^{(h)}$ə̃	čʰətʰun$^{(h)}$ə̃
19.	čʰ	+	-ətʰ	+	-un$^{(h)}$ə̃	čʰətʰun$^{(h)}$ə̃
20.	əčʰ	+	-i	+	Ø	əčʰi
21.	čʰ	+	Ø	+	-ə(h)	čʰə(h)
22.	čʰ	+	Ø	+	-ə(h)u	čʰə(h)u
23.	čʰ	+	-ətʰi	+	-n$^{(h)}$ə̃	čʰətʰin(h)ə̃
24.	čʰ	+	-ə	+	-n$^{(h)}$ĩ	čʰən$^{(h)}$ĩ
25.	čʰ	+	-ətʰi	+	-n$^{(h)}$ə̃	čʰətʰ in$^{(h)}$ə̃
26.	čʰ	+	-ə(h)	+	-i	čʰə(h)i

Table 8.6a: Maithili sentences based on the framework outlined in Table 8.4, showing how its auxiliary verb forms are inflected in the past tense in accordance with the ST forms of their grammatical subjects and objects.

Subject	Object	Verb: Main	Verb: Auxiliary	Gloss
1. həm	ãhãkẽ	kəhəi(t)	čʰələ̃(h)ũ	'I was saying to you'
2. həm	tora	kəhəi(t)	čʰəliyə(h)	'I was saying to you'
3. həm	tora	kəhəi(t)	čʰəliyə(h)u	'I was saying to you'
4. həm	hunka	kəhəi(t)	čʰəliyən$^{(h)}$ĩ	'I was saying to him'
5. həm	okra	kəhəi(t)	čʰəliyəi(k)	'I was saying to him'
6. ãhã	həmra	kəhəi(t)	čʰələ̃(h)ũ	'You were saying to me'
7. ãhã	hunka	kəhəi(t)	čʰəliyən$^{(h)}$ĩ	'You were saying to him'
8. ãhã	okra	kəhəi(t)	čʰəliyəi(k)	'You were saying to him'
9. tõ	həmra	kəhəi(t)	čʰələ(h)	'You were saying to me'
10. tõ	həmra	kəhəi(t)	čʰəlẽ	'You were saying to me'
11. tõ	hunka	kəhəi(t)	čʰələhun$^{(h)}$ə̃	'You were saying to him'
12. tõ	okra	kəhəi(t)	čʰələhək	'You were saying to him'
13. tõ	hunka	kəhəi(t)	čʰələhun$^{(h)}$ə̃	'You were saying to him'
14. tõ	okra	kəhəi(t)	čʰələhik	'You were saying to him'
15. o	həmra	kəhəi(t)	a. čʰələtʰi	'He/she was saying to me'
			b. čʰəla(h)	'He was saying to me'
			c. čʰəli(hi)	'She was saying to me'
16. o	həmra	kəhəi(t)	čʰəl	'He/she was saying to me'
17. o	ãhãkẽ	kəhəi(t)	a. čʰələtʰi	'He/she was saying to you'
			b. čʰəla(h)	'He was saying to you'
			c. čʰəli(hi)	'She was saying to you'
18. o	tora	kəhəi(t)	čʰələtʰun$^{(h)}$ə̃	'He/she was saying to you'
19. o	tora	kəhəi(t)	čʰələtʰun$^{(h)}$ə̃	'He/she was saying to you'
20. o	ãhãkẽ	kəhəi(t)	čʰəl	'He/she was saying to you'
21. o	tora	kəhəi(t)	čʰələ(h)	'He/she was saying to you'
22. o	tora	kəhəi(t)	čʰələ(h)u	'He/she was saying to you'
23. o	hunka	kəhəi(t)	čʰələtʰin$^{(h)}$ə̃	'He/she was saying to him'
24. o	hunka	kəhəi(t)	čʰələn$^{(h)}$ĩ	'He/she was saying to him'
25. o	okra	kəhəi(t)	čʰələtʰin$^{(h)}$ə̃	'He/she was saying to him'
26. o	okra	kəhəi(t)	čʰələ(h)i	'He/she was saying to him'

Table 8.6b: The morphological analysis of the Maithili auxiliary verbs in the past tense as given in the Maithili sentences of Table 8.6a.

						Gender/ST Marker			
	Root		Aspect Markers		Tense	Subject		Object	Verb Form
1.	č^h	+	-ə	+	-l+	-ə̃(h)ũ	+	Ø	č^{h}ələ̃(h)ũ
2.	č^h	+	-ə	+	-l+	Ø	+	-iyə(h)	č^{h}əliyə(h)
3.	č^h	+	-ə	+	-l+	Ø	+	-yə(h)u	č^{h}əliyə(h)u
4.	č^h	+	-ə	+	-l+	Ø	+	-yən$^{(h)}$ĩ	č^{h}əliyən$^{(h)}$ĩ
5.	č^h	+	-ə	+	-l+	Ø	+	-yəi(k)	č^{h}əliyəi(k)
6.	č^h	+	-ə	+	-l+	-ə̃(h)ũ	+	Ø	č^{h}ələ̃(h)ũ
7.	č^h	+	-ə	+	-l+	-i	+	-yən$^{(h)}$ĩ	č^{h}əliyən$^{(h)}$ĩ
8.	č^h	+	-ə	+	-l+	-i	+	-yəi(k)-yəi(k)	č^{h}əliyəi(k)
9.	č^h	+	-ə	+	-l+	-ə(h)	+	Ø	č^{h}ələ(h)
10.	č^h	+	-ə	+	-l+	-ẽ	+	Ø	č^{h}əlẽ
11.	č^h	+	-ə	+	-l+	-əh	+	-un$^{(h)}$ə̃	č^{h}ələhun$^{(h)}$ə̃
12.	č^h	+	-ə	+	-l+	-əh	+	-ək	č^{h}ələhək
13.	č^h	+	-ə	+	-l+	-əh	+	-un$^{(h)}$ə̃	č^{h}ələhun$^{(h)}$ə̃
14.	č^h	+	-ə	+	-l+	-əh	+	-ik	č^{h}ələhik
						a. -ət^{h}i	+	Ø	č^{h}ələt^{h}i
15.	č^h	+	-ə	+	-l+	b. -a(h)	+	Ø	č^{h}əla(h)
						c. -i(hi)	+	Ø	č^{h}əli(hi)
16.	č^h	+	-ə	+	-l+		Ø	+	Ø č^{h}əl
						a. -ət^{h}i	+	Ø	č^{h}ələt^{h}i
17.	č^h	+	-ə	+	-l+	b. -a(h)	+	Ø	c^{h}ela(h)
						c. -i(hi)	+	Ø	č^{h}əli(hi)
18.	č^h	+	-ə	+	-l+	-ət^h	+	-un$^{(h)}$ə̃	č^{h}ələt^{h}un(h)ə̃
19.	č^h	+	-ə	+	-l+	-ət^h	+	-un$^{(h)}$ə̃	č^{h}ələt^{h}un(h)ə̃
20.	č^h	+	-ə	+	-l+	Ø	+	Ø	č^{h}əl
21.	č^h	+	-ə	+	-l+	Ø	+	-ə(h)	č^{h}ələ(h)
22.	č^h	+	-ə	+	-l+	Ø	+	-ə(h)u	č^{h}ələ(h)u
23.	č^h	+	-ə	+	-l+	-ət^{h}i	+	-n(h)ə̃	č^{h}ələt^{h}in$^{(h)}$ə̃
24.	č^h	+	-ə	+	-l+	-ə	+	n$^{(h)}$ĩ	č^{h}ələn$^{(h)}$ĩ
25.	č^h	+	-ə	+	-l+	-ət^{h}i	+	n(h)ə̃	č^{h}ələt^{h}in$^{(h)}$ə̃
26.	č^h	+	-ə	+	-l+	-ə(h)	+	-i	č^{h}ələ(h)i

Table 8.7a: Maithili sentences based on the framework outlined in Table 8.4, showing how its auxiliary verb forms are inflected in the future tense in accordance with the ST forms of their grammatical subjects and objects.

			Verb		
	Subject	Object	Main	Auxiliary	Gloss
1.	həm	ãhãkẽ	kəhəit	rəhəb	'I will be saying to you'
2.	həm	tora	kəhəit	rəhəbə(h)	'I will be saying to you'
3.	həm	tora	kəhəit	rəbəbə(h)u	'I will be saying to you'
4.	həm	hunka	kəhəit	rəhəbən$^{(h)}$ĩ	'I will be saying to him'
5.	həm	okra	kəhəit	rəhəbəi(k)	'I will be saying to him'
6.	ãhã	həmra	kəhəit	rəhəb	'You will be saying to me'
7.	ãhã	hunka	kəhəit	rəhəbən$^{(h)}$ĩ	'You will be saying to him'
8.	ãhã	okra	kəhəit	rəhəbəi(k)	'You will be saying to him'
9.	tõ	həmra	kəhəit	rəhəbə(h)	'You will be saying to me'
10.	tõ	həmra	kəhəit	rəhəbẽ	'You will be saying to me'
11.	tõ	hunka	kəhəit	rəhəbəhun$^{(h)}$ə̃	'You will be saying to him'
12.	tõ	okra	kəhəit	rəhəbəhək	'You will be saying to him'
13.	tõ	hunka	kəhəit	rəhəbəhun$^{(h)}$ə̃	'You will be saying to him'
14.	tõ	okra	kəhəit	rəhəbəhik	'You will be saying to him'
15.	o	həmra	kəhəit	a. rəhəta(h)	'He will be saying to me'
				b. rəhəti(hi)	'She will be saying to me'
16.	o	həmra	kəhəit	rəhət	'He will be saying to me'
17.	o	ãhãkẽ	kəhəit	a. rəhəta(h)	'He will be saying to you'
				b. rəhəti(hi)	'She will be saying to you'
18.	o	tora	kəhəit	rəhət^{h}un$^{(h)}$ə̃	'He will be saying to you'
19.	o	tora	kəhəit	rəhət^{h}un$^{(h)}$ə̃	'He will be saying to you'
20.	o	ãhãkẽ	kəhəit	rəhət	'He will be saying to you'
21.	o	tora	kəhəit	rəhətə(h)	'He will be saying to you'
22.	o	tora	kəhəit	rəhətə(h)u	'He will be saying to you'
23.	o	hunka	kəhəit	rəhət^{h}in$^{(h)}$ə̃	'He will be saying to him'
24.	o	hunka	kəhəit	rəhətəi	'He will be saying to him'
25.	o	okra	kəhəit	rəhət^{h}in$^{(h)}$ə̃	'He will be saying to him'
26.	o	okra	kəhəit	rəhətə(h)i	'He will be saying to him'

Table 8.7b: The morphological analysis of the Maithili auxiliary verb forms in the future as given in the Maithili sentences of Table 8.7a.

							Gender/ST Marker			
	Root		Aspect Marker		Tense		Subject		Object	Verb Form
1.	rəh	+	-ə	+	-b	+	Ø	+	Ø	rəhəb
2.	rəh	+	-ə	+	-b	+	Ø	+	-ə(h)	rəhəbə(h)
3.	rəh	+	-ə	+	-b	+	Ø	+	-ə(h)u	rəhəbə(h) u
4.	rəh	+	-ə	+	-b	+	Ø	+	-ən$^{(h)}$ĩ	rəhəbən$^{(h)}$ĩ
5.	rəh	+	-ə	+	-b	+	Ø	+	-əi (k)	rəhəbi(k)
6.	rəh	+	-ə	+	-b	+	Ø	+	Ø	rəbəb
7.	rəh	+	-ə	+	-b	+	Ø	+	-ən$^{(h)}$i	rəhəbən$^{(h)}$ĩ
8.	rəh	+	-ə	+	-b	+	Ø	+	-əi (k)	rəhəbəi(k)
9.	rəh	+	-ə	+	-b	+	-ə(h)	+	Ø	rəhəbə(h)
10.	rəh	+	-ə	+	-b	+	-ẽ	+	Ø	rəhəbẽ
11.	rəh	+	-ə	+	-b	+	-əh	+	-un$^{(h)}$ə̃	rəhəbəhun$^{(h)}$ə̃
12.	rəh	+	-ə	+	-b	+	-əh	+	-ək	rəhəbəhək
13.	rəh	+	-ə	+	-b	+	-əh	+	-un$^{(h)}$ə̃	rəhəbəhun$^{(h)}$ə̃
14.	rəh	+	-ə	+	-b	+	-əh	+	-ik	rəhəbəhik
15.	rəh	+	-ə	+	-t	+	a.-a(h)	+	Ø	rəhəta(h)
							b.-i(hi)	+	Ø	rəhəti(hi)
16.	rəh	+	-ə	+	-t	+	Ø	+	Ø	rəhət
17.	rəh	+	-ə	+	-t	+	a.-a(h)	+	Ø	rəhəta(h)
							b.-i(hi)	+	Ø	rəhəti(hi)
18.	rəh	+	-ə	+	-t^{h}	+	-un $(^{h})$ə̃	+	Ø	rəhət^{h}un$^{(h)}$ə̃
19.	rəh	+	-ə	+	-t^{h}	+	-un $(^{h})$ə̃	+	Ø	rəhət^{h}un(h)ə̃
20.	rəh	+	-ə	+	-t	+	Ø	+	Ø	rəhət
21.	rəh	+	-ə	+	-t	+	Ø	+	-ə (h)	rəhətə(h)
22.	rəh	+	-ə	+	-t	+	Ø	+	-ə (h)u	rəhətə$^{(h)}$u
23.	rəh	+	-ə	+	-t^{h}	+	-i	+	-n $(^{h})$ə̃	rəhət^{h}in$^{(h)}$ə̃
24.	rəh	+	-ə	+	-t	+	-ə	+	-n $(^{h})$ĩ	rəhətən$^{(h)}$ĩ
25.	rəh	+	-ə	+	-t^{h}	+	-i	+	-n$^{(h)}$ə̃	rəhət^{h}in$^{(h)}$ə̃
26.	rəh	+	-ə	+	-t	+	-ə	+	-i	rəhətəi

to reveal the tense of each sentence as well as the gender and/or social status of the person used in its grammatical subject and/or object. Six pairs of such markers are:

(i)	-iyə(h)	(ii)	-iyə(h)u
	-ə(h)		-ə(h)u
(iii)	-iyən$^{(h)}$ĩ	(iv)	-iyəi (k)
	-ən$^{(h)}$ĩ		-əi(k)
(v)	-ət^{h}in$^{(h)}$ə̃	(vi)	-ət^{h}un$^{(h)}$ə̃
	-in$^{(h)}$ə̃		-un$^{(h)}$ə̃

In each of these pairs, the first marker is used in the present and the past tense forms with suffixes like -iy- and -ət^{h}-, while the second marker of each pair is used in future forms without using the -iy- suffix. There are, in addition, three other markers—i.e. -ək, *-ik* and -ə(h)i—and these are used in all forms: present, past and future. All these auxiliary verb forms of Tables 8.5b, 8.6b and 8.7b provide further evidences of the process of elision occurring in Maithili. That is, they provide evidences of the elision of h and k in different phonological environments, as well as evidences of the weakening of n^{h} into *n* in particular phonological contexts.

Taking instances of the elision of h first, the auxiliary verb forms shown below reveal that the elision of h from the suffix -əh occurs in three phonological environments: i.e.

Present	Past	Future
č^{h}iyə(h)	č^{h}ələ̃(h)ũ	rəhəbə(h)·
č^{h}iyə(h)u	č^{h}əliyə(h)	rəhəbə(h)u
č^{h}ə(h)	č^{h}əliyə(h)u	rəhəta(h)
č^{h}ə(h)u	č^{h}ələ(h)	rəhətə(h)
č^{h}ə(h)i	č^{h}əla(h)	rəhətə(h)u
	č^{h}ələ(h)u	rəhətə(h)i
	č^{h}ələ(h)i	

(i) when it occurs word-finally, especially when the final syllable of such words remains weakly accented;

(ii) when it occurs in the final syllable of a word, preceded and followed by oral vowels; and

(iii) when it occurs in the final syllable of a word, preceded and followed by nasal vowels.

These generalisations can be stated in terms of the following phonological rule:

Rule (4)

$$\begin{Bmatrix} + \text{cons} \\ + \text{low} \\ - \text{voice} \end{Bmatrix} \longrightarrow \emptyset \, / \, \text{v} \_\_\_ \, (\text{v}) \, \#$$

It should be emphasised that the h of the suffix -əh is elided only when it occurs in a weakly accented final syllable of a word. But if this h of -əh occurs word-medially, as in the following verb forms, for example,

Present	Past	Future
č^{h}əhun$^{(h)}$ə̃	č^{h}ələhun$^{(h)}$ə̃	rəhəbəhun(^{h})ə̃
č^{h}əhək	č^{h}ələhək	rəhəbəhək
č^{h}əhik	č^{h}ələhik	rəhəbəhik

then it simply does not elide in Mathili.

Similarly, the elision of k from the suffix -əi(k) or -ik occurs in Maithili whenever k appears word-finally, preceded by two adjacent vowels or a diphthong, as the following foms show:

Present	Past	Future
č^{h}iyəi(k)	č^{h}əliyəi(k)	rəhəbəi(k)

The elision of k can be described by means of the following phonological rule:

Rule (5)

$$\begin{bmatrix} + \text{cons} \\ - \text{ant} \\ - \text{cor} \\ + \text{back} \\ - \text{asp} \\ - \text{voice} \end{bmatrix} \longrightarrow \emptyset \, / \, \text{VV} \_\_\_ \, \#$$

But whenever the word-final k of the suffix -ək or -ik is preceded by only one vowel, as in the following verb forms, for example,

Present	Past	Future
čʰəhək	čʰələhək	rəhəbəhək
čʰəhik	čʰələhik	rəhəbəhik

then the elision of *k* never occurs in Maihtili.

Likewise, whenever such suffixes as -iyən$^{(h)}$ḭ, -ən$^{(h)}$ḭ, -ətʰin$^{(h)}$ə̰, -in$^{(h)}$ə̰, -ətʰun$^{(h)}$ə̰ and -un$^{(h)}$ə̰ are added to different auxiliary verb forms in Maithili, then the words which eventually surface contain the unaspirated nasal *n* instead of the aspirated n^h, as the following verb forms show:

Present	Past	Future
čʰiyən$^{(h)}$ḭ	čʰəliyən$^{(h)}$ḭ	rəhəbən$^{(h)}$ḭ
čʰətʰun$^{(h)}$ə̰	čʰələhun$^{(h)}$ə̰	rəhəbəhun$^{(h)}$ə̰
čʰəhun$^{(h)}$ə̰	čʰələtʰun$^{(h)}$ə̰	rəhətʰun$^{(h)}$ə̰
čʰətʰin$^{(h)}$ə̰	čʰələtʰin$^{(h)}$ə̰	rəhətʰin$^{(h)}$ə̰
	čʰələn$^{(h)}$ḭ	rəhətən$^{(h)}$ḭ

This weakening of n^h into n is phonologically conditioned: i.e. whenever n^h occurs intervocalically in the final syllable of a verb form, it loses its aspiration. This weakening process can be described in terms of the following phonological rule:

Rule (6)

$$\begin{bmatrix} +\text{ cons} \\ +\text{ nasal} \\ +\text{ ant} \\ +\text{ cor} \\ +\text{ asp} \end{bmatrix} \longrightarrow [-\text{ asp}] \;/\; V \;\underline{\qquad}\; V\ \#$$

8.2 Aspect Markers and the Elision of the Dentals and the Labials in Maithili

The category 'aspect' is used in the grammatical description of verbs, referring primarily to the way the grammar marks the duration or type of activity denoted by the verb. We divide this section into three parts:

the first part outlines the system of aspects and the elision of the dental ṯ in Maithili; the second part looks into some cases of the elision of ḇ in Maithili; and the third part presents a summary of discussions concerning the elision of the dental ṯ and the labial ḇ.

8.2.1 *The system of Aspects and the Elision of the Dental /t/ in Maithili*

A complete paradigm of finite verbs in Maithili indicates such aspectual distinctions in the indicative mood as:

1. Perfect, and
2. Non-perfect (i.e. simple, imperfect and progressive).

This system of aspects is represented in the following tree diagram:

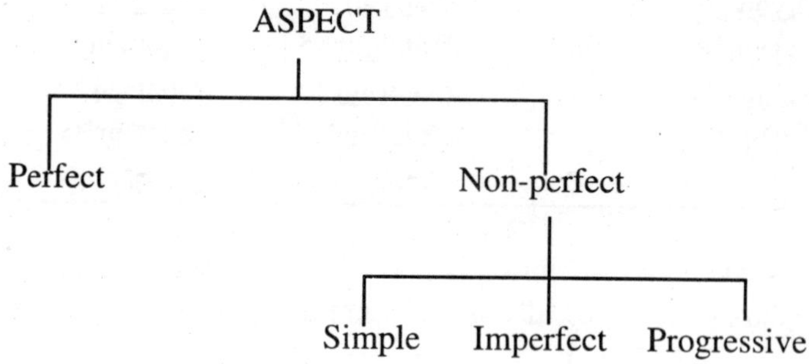

Figure 8.6: The system of aspects in Maithili.

The verb forms that each of these aspectual distinctions takes can be shown by giving a paradigm of the verb dek^h 'to see', as given in Table 8.8a.

Although each of the twelve Maithili sentences given in Table 8.8a contains only the non-honorific third person pronoun o̲ 'he/she' as its subject, it must be pointed out that the person of the subject as well as the social status of that person does not affect the choice of aspect markers in Maihili. In other words, aspect markers attached to the main verb-roots of Maithili always remain the same regardless of the person and the social status of the person given in the subject and/or object. The morphological analysis of the main verbs given in Table 8.8a is done in Table 8.8b. Relevant discussions based on the morphological analysis of Table 8.8b, especially discussions on the elision of the dental ṯ, are presented in a later sub-section (8.2.3).

Table 8.8a: A paradigm of the verb /dekʰ/, showing each of the aspectual distinctions in Maihili.

Aspect	Tense	Subject	Verb Main	Verb Aux	Gloss
Simple	Present	o	dekʰəičʰ	Ø	'He/She sees'
	Past	o	dekʰələk	Ø	'He/She saw'
	Future	o	dekʰət	Ø	'He/She will see'
Imperfect	Present	o	dekʰəi(t)	əičʰi	'He/She is seeing'
	Past	o	dekʰəi(t)	čʰəl	'He/She was seeing'
	Future	o	dekʰəit	rəhət	'He/She will be seeing'
Progressive	Present	o	dekʰ-rəhəl	əičʰi	'He/She is continuously seeing'
	Past	o	dekʰ-rəhəl	čʰəl	'He/She was continuously seeing'
	Future	o	dekʰ rəhəl	rəhət	'He/She will continuously be seeing'
Perfect	Present	o	dekʰne	əčʰi	'He/She has seen'
	Past	o	dekʰne	čʰəl	'He/She had seen'
	Future	o	dekʰne	rəhət	'He/She will have seen'

Table 8.8b: The morphological analysis of the main verbs shown in Table 8.8a.

Aspect	Root		Tense/ST Marker		Aspect Marker	Verb Form
Simple	dekʰ	+	-əičʰ	+	Ø	dekʰəičʰ
	dekʰ	+	-ələk	+	Ø	dekʰələk
	dekʰ	+	-ət	+	Ø	dekʰət
Imperfect	dekʰ	+	Ø	+	-əi (t)	dekʰəi(t)
	dekʰ	+	Ø	+	-əi (t)	dekʰəi(t)
	dekʰ	+	Ø	+	-əit	dekʰəit
Progressive	dekʰ	+	Ø	+	rəhəl	dekʰ rəhəl
	dekʰ	+	Ø	+	rəhəl	dekʰ-rəhəl
	dekʰ	+	Ø	+	rəhəl	dekʰ rəhəl
Perfect	dekʰ	+	Ø	+	-ne	dekʰne
	dekʰ	+	Ø	+	-ne	dekʰne
	dekʰ	+	Ø	+	-ne	dekʰne

8.2.2 *The Elision of the Labial /b/ in Maithili*

There are some other verb forms in Maithili which provide evidences for the elision of the bilabial stop b in different phonological environments. Table 8.9a lists a number of different main verb-roots with b as their final speech segment. Table 8.9a also shows that when these verb roots are attached with the past tense and with the honorific social status markers, then the b of the original verb-root is elided from the verb forms that eventually surface. The morphological analysis of the verb forms given in Table 8.9a is done in Table 8.9b. Relevant discussions based on the morphological analysis of Table 8.9b, especially discussions on the elision of the bilabial stop *b*, are presented in the next sub-section.

Table 8.9a: The Maithili verb forms providing evidences for the elision of the bilabial /b/.

Root	Gloss	Honorific Past Tense Form of the Verb	Gloss
pib	'to drink'	pilə̃(h)ũ	'drank'
deb	'to give'	delə̃(h)ũ	'gave'
sib	'to sew'	silə̃(h)ũ	'sewed'
č^{h}ub	'to touch'	č^{h}ulə̃(h)ũ	'touched'
leb	'to take'	lelə̃(h)ũ	'took'
d^{h}ob	'to wash'	d^{h}olə̃(h)ũ	'washed'

Table 8.9b: The morphological analysis of the verbs forms in Table 8.9a.

Root		Past Tense Marker		Honorific ST Marker	Verb Form	Gloss
pib	+	-l	+	-ə̃(h)ũ	pilə̃(h)ũ	'drank'
deb	+	-l	+	-ə̃(h)ũ	delə̃(h)ũ	'gave'
sib	+	-l	+	-ə̃(h)ũ	silə̃(h)ũ	'sewed'
č^{h}ub	+	-l	+	-ə̃(h)ũ	č^{h}ulə̃(h)ũ	'touched'
leb	+	-l	+	-ə̃(h)ũ	lelə̃(h)ũ	'took'
d^{h}ob	+	-l	+	-ə̃(h)ũ	d^{h}olə̃(h)ũ	'washed'

8.2.3 *Summary and Discussion*

From the study of the morphological analysis of aspects done in Table 8.8b, we can draw the following conclusions about their regularities:

(i) In the simple form, the main verb-roots in Maithili are not marked for aspect—they are attached with tense and/or social status markers only;

(ii) The imperfect markers in Maithili are -ai(t) and -əit and they are always affixed to the root of the preceding main verb: -əi(t) is used in the present and past tense forms, but -əit is used in the future tense only;

(iii) The progressive form in Maithili is always marked with *rəhəl*, which is a free morpheme and which always occurs after the root of the main verb; and

(iv) The perfect marker in Maithili is *-ne* and it, too, is always affixed to the root of the preceding verb.

Thus, the aspects in Maithili can be either unmarked, as in the 'simple' form, or marked in any one of the following three ways:

(i)	-əi(t)/-əit	(Imperfect)
(ii)	rəhəl	(Progressive), or
(iii)	-ne	(Perfect)

Of all these aspect markers, the imperfect marker -əi(t) is the one which is very significant for us here as it provides some important evidence for the process of elision occurring in Maithili. The marker -əi(t) has two main realisations: i.e. -əi(t) and -i(t). Table 8.10 shows the phonological contexts in which the two forms, -əi(t) and -i(t), occur in Maithili. That is, Table 8.10 clearly shows that there are two different phonological environments in which *əi(t)* and -i(t) occur: -əi(t) occurs when it is preceded by a consonant of the main verb-root; -i(t), on the other hand, occurs when it is preceded by a vowel of the main verb-root. An informal rule given in (7) describes the two different environments in which the two imperfect aspect markers occur in Maithili.

Rule (7)

Imperfect Aspect Marker ————> { -əi(t) / C ——— # ; -i(t) / V ——— # }

Table 8.10: The forms /-əi(t)/ and /-i(t)/ attached to the main verb-roots in Maithili.

The Form	Verb Root	Aspect Marker	Verb Form	Gloss
-əi(t)	dek^h +	-əi(t)	dek^{h}əi(t)	'seeing'
	sun+	-əi(t)	sunəi(t)	'hearing'
	kəh +	-əi(t)	kəhəi(t)	'saying'
	hə̃s +	-əi(t)	hə̃səi(t)	'laughing'
	sut +	əi(t)	sutəi(t)	'sleeping'
-i(t)	ǰa +	-i(t)	ǰai(t)	'going'
	k^{h}a +	-i(t)	k^{h}ai(t)	'eating'
	d^{h}o +	-i(t)	d^{h}oi(t)	'washing'
	ho +	-i(t)	hoi(t)	'happening'
	nəha +	-i(t)	nəhai(t)	'bathing'

Each of the two aspect markers, -əi(t) and -i(t), shows the elision of the dental *t* occurring in Maithili. The phonological context in which this elision takes place can be described in terms of the following phonological rule:

Rule (8)

$$\begin{bmatrix} +\ \text{cons} \\ +\ \text{ant} \\ +\ \text{cor} \\ -\ \text{asp} \\ -\ \text{voice} \end{bmatrix} \longrightarrow \text{Ø} \ / \ \text{VV}\text{———}\#$$

This rule says that the dental *t* occurring in the word-final position of the Maithili verb is elided, whenever it is preceded by two adjacent vowels.

Similarly, the verb forms presented in Table 8.9a and morphologically analysed in Table 8.9b show that the labial *b* in the Maithili verb-roots like pib, deb, leb and so on is elided, whenever the past tense marker -l̠ and the honorific social status marker -ə̃(h)ũ are attached to them. The phonological context in which this elision of the labial *b* occurs in Maithili can be stated in terms of the phonological rule given below:

Rule (9)

$$\begin{bmatrix} +\text{ cons} \\ +\text{ ant} \\ -\text{ cor} \\ -\text{ asp} \\ +\text{ voice} \end{bmatrix} \longrightarrow \text{Ø} \;/\; [\text{V}] \;\text{———}\; \begin{bmatrix} +\text{ cons} \\ +\text{ lateral} \\ -\text{ asp} \end{bmatrix}$$

8.3 Summary

To summarise, it has always been a feature of the structure of Maihili words that weakly accented syllables have undergone a process of gradation—i.e. loss of phonemes, obscuration of vowels, and so on (e.g. see S. Jha, 1958, for more details). The same process of gradation, with resultant contraction, weakening and even total elision of speech segments, may be observed in operation in current Maithili. The forms exhibiting the weakening or elision of speech segments in Maithili are very typical of rapid, colloquial speech, while more formal speech tends to retain the fuller form under the preservative influence of spelling.

The morphophonology of the Maithili verbs and verb foms provides significant evidences regarding the weakening of n^h to n and the elision of k b t and h in different phonological environments. Since elision indicates relative phonological strength (e.g. see Foley, 1977), this study shows that in Maithili velars are weaker than dentals or labials. As the dental t and the labial b are phonologically stronger than the velar k, both t and b always dominate k in the Maithili clusters: kt and kb. With regard to the dentals and labials, the dentals in Maithili are strongest as they or their reflexes remain while velars and labials weaken. Like Sanskrit and many other Indo-Aryan languages (e.g. see Beames, 1872-79/reprint 1966; Kellogg, 1876/1893; Chatterji, 1926/1970 and 1960; Burrow, 1955; S. Jha 1958), the Maithili voiced dental d shifts to its voiceless counterpart t, as in the following compounds, for example:

təd + kal = tətkal "immediately"
sənsəd + sədəsyə = sənsətsədəsyə "member of Parliament"

This consonant shift, discussed in detail in the previous chapter, must be regarded as an example of strengthening. Since according to the inertial development principle (e.g. Foley, 1977) strengthening applies preferentially to strong elements, if only one element of a velar, labial or dental group strengthens, "that element is the strongest element" (Foley, 1977: 50). Since in Maithili dentals strengthen in preference to velars and labials, dentals are stronger than velars and labials. Thus, within the group of stops, the relative phonological strength in Maithili can be shown as in Figure 8.7:

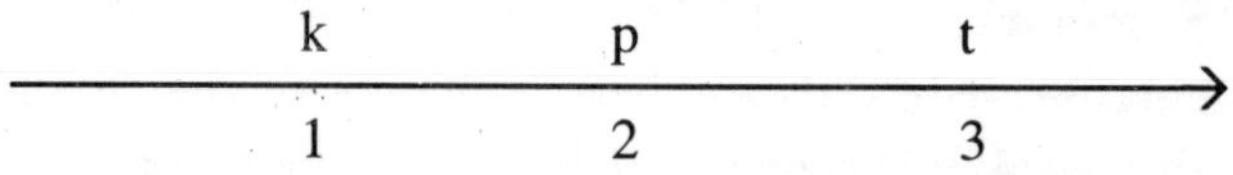

Figure 8.7: The relative phonological strength of stops in Maithili.

Even though our results concerning the relative phonological strength of stops in Maithili do not quite follow the pattern witnessed in most Romance and Germanic languages, for example, they should not be regarded as surprising. For, like Maithili, even in the group of Germanic languages, the dentals of German, too, are said (e.g. Foley, 1977: 50) to be phonologically stronger than labials. It therefore makes sense to say that for any particular language an order of relative phonological strength must be determined, as we have already done in the case of the Maithili stops, and that we may expect different languages to choose different orders. The phonological strength of stops in Maithili chooses an order which is similar to that of a language like German but not so similar to that of a language like English, for instance.

BIBLIOGRAPHY

Abercrombie, D. 1967. *Elements of General Phonetics.* Edinburgh: Edinburgh University Press.

Ahmed, R., and Agrawal, S.S. 1969. "Significant features in the perception of (Hindi) consonants". *Journal of the Acoustical Society of America,* Vol. 45, pp. 758-63.

Allen, W.S. 1953. *Phonetics in Ancient India.* London: Oxford University Press.

Arun, V.B. 1961. *A Comparative Phonology of Hindi and Punjabi.* Ludhiana: Punjabi Sahitya Academy.

Balasubramanian, T. 1980. "Nasalization of Vowels in Tamil". *Journal of Phonetics,* Vol. 8, pp. 361-73.

——. 1981a. "Lip and jaw movements during the articulation of the vowels in Tamil". *Journal of Phonetics,* Vol. 9, pp. 121-27.

——. 1981b. "Duration of vowels in Tamil". *Journal of Phonetics,* Vol. 9, pp. 151-61.

Beames, J. 1872-79/reprint 1966. *A Comparative Grammar of the Modern Indo-Aryan Languages of India.* Delhi: Munshiram Manoharlal.

Belasco, S. 1953. "The influece of force of articulation of cosonants on vowel duration". *Journal of the Acoustical Society of America,* Vol. 25, pp. 1015-16.

Bell, M. 1867. *Visible Speech: The Science of Universal Alphabetics.* London: Simpkin, Marshall and Co.

Benguerel, A.P., and Lafargue, A. 1981. "Perception of vowel nasalization in French". *Journal of Phonetics,* Vol. 9, pp. 309-21.

Bhatia, T.K. 1976. "On the predictive role of the recent theories of aspiration". *Phonetica,* Vol. 33, pp. 62-74.

Bhatia, T.K., and Kenstowicz, M.J. 1972. "Nasalization in Hindi: a reconsideration". *Papers in Linguistics,* Vol. 5, pp. 202-15.

Burrow, T. 1955. *The Sanskrit Language.* London: Faber and Faber.

Cairns, C.E. 1969. "Markedness, neutralization, and universal redundancy rules". *Language,* Vol. 45, pp. 863-85.

Cagliari, L.C. 1977. *An Experimental Study of Nasality with Particular Reference to Brazilian Portuguese.* Unpublished Ph.D. thesis, University of Edinburgh.

Catford, J.C. 1977. *Fundamental Problems in Phonetics*. Edinburgh: Edinburgh University Press.

——. 1981. "Observations on the recent history of vowel classification". In Asher, R.E. and Henderson, E.J.A. (eds.), *Towards a History of Phonetics*. Edinburgh: Edinburgh University Press, 1981, pp.19-32.

Chatterji, S.K. 1926/1970. *The origin and Development of the Bengali Language*. London: George Allen and Unwin (2 Vols).

——. 1960. *Indo-Aryan and Hindi*. 2nd Ed. Ahmedabad: Gujarat Vernacular Society.

Chatterji, S.K., and Mishra, B. (eds.) 1940. *Varnaratnākar*, Bibliotheca Indica: 262. Calcutta: Royal Asiatic Society of Bengal.

Chaudhary, R. 1976. *A Survey of Maithili Literature*. Deoghar: Shanti Devi, Shanti Niwas.

Chen, M. 1970. "Vowel length variation as a function of voicing of the consonant environment". *Phonetica,* Vol. 22, pp. 129-59.

——. 1973. "On the formal expression of natural rules in phonology". *Journal of Linguistics,* Vol. 9, pp. 223-49.

Chomsky, N., and Halle, M. 1968. *The Sound Pattern of English.* New York: Harper and Row.

Dakin, J. 1968. "Language and education in India". In Dakin, J., Tiffen, B., and Widdowson, H.G. (eds.), *Language in Education: The Problem in Commonwealth Africa and the Indo-Pakistan Sub-continent*. London: Oxford University Press, 1968, pp. 3-61.

Dave, R. 1977. *Studies in Gujarati Phonology and Phonetics*. Unpublished Ph.D. thesis, Cornell University.

Davis, A. 1973. "Maithili sentences". In Hale, A. (ed.), *Clause, Sentence and Discourse Patterns in Selected Languages of Nepal*, Vol. 1. Kathmandu: Summer Institute of Linguistics, 1973, pp. 259-319.

Delattre, P. 1962. "Some factors of vowel duration and their cross-linguistic validity". *Journal of the Acoustical Society of America*, Vol. 34, pp. 1141-43.

——. 1969. "Explaining the chronology of nasal vowels by acoustic and radiographic analysis". In *The General Phonetic Characteristics of Languages*. U.S. Department of Health, Education and Welfare, Office of Education, Institute of International Studies, pp. 101-19.

——. 1971. "Consonant gemination in four languages: an acoustic, perceptual and radiographic study, Part I". *International Review of Applied Linguistics,* Vol. 9, pp. 31-52; Part II. *International Review of Applied Linguistics,* Vol. 9, pp. 97-113.

Elert, C-C. 1965. *Phonologic Studies of Quantity in Swedish.*Uppasala: Almqvist and Wiksell.

Fairbanks, G. 1969a. "Language split". *Glossa*, Vol. 3, pp. 49-66.

——. 1969b. "Comparative Indo-Aryan". In Sebeok, T.A. (ed.), *Current Trends in Linguistics: Linguistics in South Asia,* Vol. 5. The Hague: Mouton and Co., 1969, pp. 36-45.

Fant, G. 1960. *Acoustic Theory of Speech Production.* The Hague: Mouton and Co.

Ferguson, C.A. 1974. "Universals of nasality". *Stanford University Working Papers on Language Universals,* Vol. 14, pp. 1-16.

Fischer-JØrgensen, E. 1964. "Sound duration and the place of articulation". *Zeitschrift fur Phonetik Sprachwissenschaft und Kommunikationsforchung,*Vol. 17, pp. 175-207.

——. 1975. *Trends in Phonological Theory.* Copenhagen: Akademisk Forlag.

Foley, J. 1970. "Phonological distinctive features". *Folia Linguistica,* Vol. 4, pp. 87-92.

——. 1977. *Foundations of Theoretical Phonology.* Cambridge: Cambridge University Press.

Fry, D.B. 1955. "Duration and intensity as physical correlates of linguistic stress". *Journal of the Acoustical Society of America,* Vol. 27, pp. 765-68.

——. 1958. "Experiments in the perception of stress". *Language and Speech,* Vol. 1, pp. 126-52.

Gay, T. 1968. "Effect of speaking rate on diphthong formant movements". *Journal of the Acoustical Society of America,* Vol. 44, pp. 1570-73.

Gerber, S.E. 1972. "Perception of segmented diphthongs". In Rigault, A., and Charbonneau, R. (eds), *Proceedings of the Seventh International Congress of Phonetic Sciences.* The Hague: Muton and Co., 1972, pp. 480-92.

Gimson, A.C. 1970. *An Introduction to the Pronunciation of English.* 2nd. Ed. London: Edward Arnold.

Gleason, H. A. 1955. *An Introduction to Descriptive Linguistics.* New York: Henry Holt and Co.

Goswami, G.C. 1966. *An Introduction to Assamese Phonology.* Poona: Deccan College.

Gregoire, A. 1911. "Influences des consonnes occlusives sur in dures des syllabes precedentes". *Revue de Phonetique,* Vol. 1, pp. 260-92.

Grierson, G.A. 1881. *An Introduction to the Maithili Language of North Bihar,* Part I 'Grammar'. Calcutta: Asiatic Society of Bengal.

——. 1882. *An Introduction to the Maithili Language of North Bihar,* Part 2 'Chrestomathy and Vocabulary'. Calcutta: Asiatic Society of Bengal.

——. 1883a. *Seven Grammars of the Dialects and Subdialects of the Bihari Language,* Part I, 'Introductory'. Calcutta: Bengal Secretariat Press.

——. 1883b. *Seven Grammars of the Dialects and Subdialects of the Bihari Language,* Part III, 'Magadhi Dialect of South Patna and Gaya'. Calcutta: Bengal Secretariat Press.

——. 1883c. "Essays on Bihari Declension and conjugation". *Journal of the Asiatic Society of Bengal,* Vol. 52, pp. 119-59.

——. 1884a. *Seven Grammars of the Dialects and Subdialects of the Bihari Language,* Part II, 'Bhojpuri Dialect'. Calcutta: Bengal Secretariat Press.

——. 1884b. *Seven Grammars of the Dialects and Subdialects of the Bihari Language,* Part IV, 'Maithili-Bhojpuri Dialect'. Calcutta: Bengal Secretariat Press.

——. 1885. *Seven Grammars of the Dialects and Subdialects of the Bihari Language,* Part V, 'South Maithili Dialect'. Calcutta: Bengal Secretariat Press.

——. 1886. *Seven Grammars of the Dialects and Subdialects of the Bihari Language,* Part VI, 'South Maithili-Magadhi Dialect'. Calcutta: Bengal Secretariat Press.

——. 1887a. *Seven Grammars of the Dialects and Subdialects of the Bihari Language,* Part VII, 'South Maithili-Bengali Dialect of South Bhagalpur'. Calcutta: Bengal Secretariat Press.

——. 1887b. *Seven Grammars of the Dialects and Subdialects of the Bihari Language,* Part VIII, 'Maithili-Bengali Dialect'. Calcutta: Bengal Secretariat Press.

——. 1903/reprint 1967. *Linguistic Survey of India* 5:2. Delhi: Motilal Banarsidass.

——. 1909/reprint 1968. *Linguistic Survey of India* 3:1. Delhi: Motilal Banarsidass.

Grierson, G.A. 1918 "Indo-Aryan vernaculars". *Bulletin of the School of Oriental Studies,* Vol. 1:2, pp. 47-81.

——. 1919. "Indo-Aryan vernaculars". *Bulletin of the School of Oriental Studies,* Vol. 1:3, pp. 51-85.

——. 1927/reprint 1967. *Linguistic Survey of India* 1:1. India: Motilal Banarsidass.

Gumperz, J.J. 1957/reprint 1962. "Language problems in the rural development of North India". In Rice. F.A. (ed.), *Study of the Role of Second Languages in Asia, Africa and Latin America.* Washington: Center for Applied Linguistics of the Modern Language Association of America, 1962, pp. 79-90.

Halle, M., and Stevens, K.N. 1967. "On the mechanism of glottal vibration for vowels and consonants". *Quarterly Progress Report,* No. 85. Cambridge, Mass.: The MIT Press, pp. 267-70.

——. 1971. "A note on laryngeal features". *Quarterly Progress Report,* No. 101. Cambridge, Mass.: Research Laboratory Electronics, MIT, pp. 198-213.

Hardcastle, W.J. 1976. *The Physiology of Speech Production.* New York: Academic Press.

Hayes, B. 1986. "Inalterability in C-V phonology". *Language,* Vol. 62, pp. 321-51.

Hegedüs, L. 1959. "Beitrag zur Frage der Geminaten". *Zeitschrift für Phonetik,* Vol. 12, pp. 68-106.

Henderson, M.M.T. 1976. "Redundancy, markedness, and simultaneous constraints in phonology". *Language,* Vol. 52, pp. 314-325.

Hibbitt, G.W. 1948. *Diphthongs in American Speech.* New York: (privately published).

His Majesty's Government of Nepal. 1972. *The National Census Report* (1952/54, 1961, 1971). Kathmandu: Central Bureau of Statistics.

——. 1982. *The National Census Report of 1981.* Kathmandu: Central Bureau of Statistics.

——. 1992. *The National Census Report of 1991.* Kathmandu: Central Bureau of Statistics.

Hoard, J.E., and Sloat, C. 1973. "Variation in English stress placement". In Bailey, C-J. N., and Shuy, R.W. (eds.), *New Ways of Analysing Variation in English.* Washington, D.C.: Georgetown University Press. 1973, pp. 265-75.

Hoenigswald, H. 1960. *Language Change and Linguistic Reconstruction.* Chicago: The University of Chicago Press.

——. 1964. "Graduality, sporadicity, and the minor sound change processes". *Phonetica,* Vol. 11, pp. 202-15.

——. 1966. "Criteria for sub-grouping languages". In Birnbaum, H., and Puhvel, J. (eds.), *Ancient Indo-European Dialects.* Los Angeles: University of California Press, 1966, pp. 1-12.

Hoernle, A.F.R. 1880. *A Comparative Grammar of the Gaudian Languages.* London: Trübner and Company.

Hoernle, A.F.R., and Grierson, G.A. 1885. *A Comparative Dictionary of the Bihari Language,* Part I. Calcutta: Bengal Secretariat Press.

——. 1889. *A Comparative Dictionary of the Bihari Language,* Part II. Calcutta: Bengal Secretariat Press.

Hollien, H. 1974. "On vocal registers". *Journal of Phonetics,* Vol. 2, pp. 125-43.

House, A.S. 1961. "On vowel duration in English". *Journal of the Acoustical Society of America,* Vol. 33, pp. 1174-77.

House, A.S., and Fairbanks, G. 1953. "The influence of consonant environment upon the secondary acoustical characteristics of vowels". *Journal of the Acoustical Society of America,* Vol. 25, pp. 105-13.

House, A.S., and Stevens, K.N. 1956. "Analog studies of the nasalization of vowels". *Journal of Speech and Hearing Disorders,* Vol. 21, pp. 218-32.

Hyman, L. 1975. *Phonology: Theory and Analysis.* New York: Holt, Rinehart and Winston.

Ingemann, F., and Yadav, R. 1978. "Voiced aspirated consonants". In Lance, D.M., and Gulstad, D.E. (eds.), *Papers from the 1977 Mid-American Linguistics Conference.* Columbia, Missouri: University of Missouri, pp. 337-44.

Jakobson, R. 1962. *Roman Jakobson: Selected Writings.* The Hague: Mouton and Co.

Jakobson, R., Fant, C.G.M., and Halle, M. 1952. *Preliminaries to Speech Analysis.* 5th printing 1963. Cambridge, Mass.: The MIT Press.

Jakobson, R. and Halle, M. 1956. *Fundamentals of Language.* The Hague: Mouton and Co.

Jeffers, R.J. 1976. "The position of the Bihārī dialects in Indo-Aryan." *Indo-Iranian Journal,* Vol. 18, pp. 215-25.

Jha, B.K. 1984. *A Descriptive Study of Maithili Language of Nepal.* Unpublished Ph.D. thesis, Poona University.

Jha, D. 1952 (B.S. 2008). *Mithilā Bhāsā Kos* (Maithili Dictionary). Patna: Shree Rambhajan Press (in Maithili).

Jha, D.K. 1979. *Maithilī Sāhitya ka Alochanātmaka Itihāsa* (A Critical History of Maithili Literature). Patna: Maithili Academy (in Maithili).

Jha, G. 1958. "Verb conjugation in Maithili". *Journal of the Bihar Research Society*, Vol. 44, pp. 169-76.

——. 1974 *Maithilī Bhāsā kā Vikāsa* (The Development of the Maithili Language). Patna: Bihar Hindi Granth Academy (in Hindi).

——. 1979. *Ũccatara Maithilī Vyākarana* (A Higher Maithili Grammar). Patna: Maithili Academy (in Maithili).

Jha, R. 1971. *Origin and Development of the Maihili Script.* Patna: Kalika Press (in Maithili).

Jha, S. 1941. "Maithili phonetics". *Indian Linguistics,* Vol. 8 (1940-1944), pp. 39-70.

——. 1958. *The Formation of the Maithili Language.* London: Louzac and Co.

Jha, Sh. 1957. "A bird's eye view of the Maithili language". *Journal of the Bihar Research Society,* Vol. 43, pp. 67-73.

Jha, S.K., 1984. *A Study of Some Phonetics and Phonological Aspects of Maithili.* Unpublished Ph. D. thesis, Essex University.

——. 1985. "Acoustic analysis of the Maithili diphthongs". *Journal of Phonetics,* Vol. 13, pp. 1-9.

——. 1986. "The nasal vowels in Maithili: an acoustic study". *Journal of Phonetics,* Vol. 14, pp. 223-30.

——. 1990. "The influence of aspiration on vowel duration". *CIEFL Bulletin: New Series,* Vol. 2, pp. 42-54.

——. 1991a. "The morphophonology of the Maithili verbs: a study on the elision of the stops in Maithili". *Nepalese Linguistics,* Vol. 5-8, pp. 26-57.

——. 1991b. "The Maithili Vowels". *Contributions to Nepalese Studies,* Vol. 18, pp. 107-22.

——. 1992. "Gemination of consonants in Maithili". Paper presented at the Annual Conference of the Linguistic Society of Nepal, Kirtipur, Kathmandu.

——. 1993. "The Maithili consonants". *Contributions to Nepalese Studies,* Vol. 20, pp. 91-103.

——. 1994. "Vowel duration in Maithili: an electroglottographic study". Paper presented at the Annual Conference of the Linguistic Society of Nepal, Kirtipur, Kathmandu.

——. 1999. "The inclusion of aspiration in distinctive feature theory." In Yadav, Y.P., and Glover, W.W. (eds.), *Jopics in Nepalese Linguistics*. Kathmandu: Royal Nepal Academy, 1999, pp. 78-89).

Jha, V. 1977. *Maithilī o Santhālī: Samparka ā Sāmipya* (Maithili and Santhali: Acquaintance and Attachment). Patna: Maithili Academy (in Maithili).

Jones, D. 1948. "Chronemes and tonemes". *Acta Linguistica,* Vol. 1, pp. 1-10.

——. 1956a. *An Outline of English Phonetics.* 8th Ed. Cambridge: Heffer.

——. 1956b. *The Pronunciation of English.* 4th Ed. Cambridge: Cambridge University Press.

Jones, L.G. 1959. "The contextual variants of the Russian vowels". In Halle, M. (ed.), *The Sound Pattern of Russian.* The Hague: Mouton and Co., 1959, pp. 157-67.

Joos, M. 1948. *Acoustic Phonetics.* Baltimore: Linguistic Society of America, Waverly Press.

Junghare, I. Y. 1972. "The perfect aspect in Marathi, Bhojpuri and Maithili". *Indian Linguistics,* Vol. 33, pp. 128-34.

Kagaya, R. 1974. "A fiberoptic and acoustic study of the Korean stops, affricates and fricatives". *Journal of Phonetics,* Vol. 2, pp. 161-80.

Kagaya, R., and Hirose, H. 1975. "Fiberoptic, electromyographic and acoustic analyses of Hindi stop consonants". *Annual Bulletin,* Research Institute of Logopedics and Phoniatrics (Tokyo), Vol. 9, pp. 27-46.

Kellogg, S.H. 1876/2nd Ed. 1893. *A Grammar of the Hindi Language.* London: Routledge and Kegan Paul.

Kenstowicz, M., and Pyle, C. 1973. "On the phonological integrity of geminate clusters". In Kenstowicz, M., and Kisseberth, C. (eds.), *Issues in Phonological Theory.* The Hague: Mouton and Co., 1973.

Kim, C-W. 1965. "On the autonomy of the tensity feature in stop classification". *Word,* Vol. 21, pp. 339-359.

——. 1970. "A theory of aspiration". *Phonetica,* Vol. 21, pp. 107-116.

Kongsdal, J.O. 1967. "Features of the acoustical and physiological structure of the French nasal vowels". *Annual Report of the Institute of Phonetics* (University of Copenhagen), Vol. 1, pp. 59-66.

Kostic, D., and Das, R.S. 1972. *A Short Outline of Bengali Phonetics.* Calcutta: Statistical Publishing Society.

Kozhevnikov, V.A., and Chistovich, L.A. 1965. *Speech: Articulation and Perception.* Moscow-Leningrad Translated by Joint Publications Research Service. Washington, D.C. No. JPRS 30, 543.

Labov, W., Yaeger, M., and Steiner, R. 1972. *A Quantitative Study of Sound Change in Progress.* Philadelphia: U.S. Regional Survey.

Ladefoged, P. 1964. *A Phonetic Study of West African Languages.* Cambridge: Cambridge University Press.

——. 1967. *Three Areas of Experimental Phonetics.* London: Oxford University Press.

——. 1971. *Preliminaries to Linguistic Phonetics.* Chicago: The Universiy of Chicago Press.

——. 1975/2nd Ed. 1982. *A Course in Phonetics.* New York: Harcourt Brace Jovanovich, Inc.

——. 1976. "The stops of Owerri Igbo". *Studies in African Linguistics,* Supplement 6, pp. 147-63.

——. 1980. "What are linguistic sounds made of?". *Language,* Vol. 56, pp. 485-502.

Lashley, K.S. 1951. "The problem of serial order in behaviour". In Jeffress, L.A. (ed.), *Cerebral Mechanisms in Behaviour.* New York: John Wiley and Sons, 1951, pp. 112-36.

Lass, R. 1976. *English Phonology and Phonological Theory: Synchronic and Diachronic Studies.* Cambridge: Cambridge University Press.

Laver, J. 1980. *The Phonetic Description of Voice Quality.* Cambridge: Cambridge University Press.

Lehiste, I. 1970a. *Suprasegmentals.* Cambridge, Mass.: The MIT Press.

——. 1970b. "Temporal organization of spoken language". *Working Papers in Linguistics* (Ohio State University), Vol. 4, pp. 96-114.

Lehiste, I., and Peterson, G.E. 1961. "Transitions, glides and diphthongs". *Journal of the Acoustical Society of America,* Vol. 33, pp. 268-77.

Lehiste, I., Morton, K., and Tatham, M.A.A. 1973. "An instrumental study of consonant gemination". *Journal of Phonetics,* Vol. 1, pp. 131-48.

Lieberman, P. 1960. "Some acoustic correlates of word stress in American English". *Journal of the Acoustical Society of America,* Vol. 32, pp. 451-54.

Lightner, T.M. 1970. "Why and how does vowel nasalization take place?". *Papers in Linguistics,* Vol. 2, pp. 179-226.

Lindau, M. 1978. "Vowel features". *Language,* Vol 54, pp. 541-63.

Lindblom, B. 1963. "Spectrographic study of vowel reduction". *Journal of the Acoustical Society of America,* Vol. 35, pp. 1773-81.

Lisker, L., and Abramson, A. 1964. "A cross-language study of voicing in initial stops: acoustical measurements". *Word,* Vol. 20, pp. 384-422.

Lyons, J. 1968. *Introduction to Theoretical Linguistics.* Cambridge: Cambridge University Press.

MacCarthy, J.J. 1986. "OCP effects: gemination and antigemination". *Linguistic Inquiry,* Vol. 17, pp. 207-63.

Maddieson, I, 1976. "Further studies on vowel length before aspirated consonants". Paper presented at the 91st meeting of the Acoustical Society of America, Washington, D.C.

Maddieson, I., and Gandour, J. 1977. "Vowel length before aspirated consonants". *Indian Linguistics,* Vol. 38, pp. 6-11.

Malmberg, B. 1963. *Structural Linguistics and Human Communication.* Berlin: Springer-Verlag.

Manrique, A.M.B. 1979. "Acoustic analysis of the Spanish diphthongs". *Phonetica,* Vol. 36, pp. 194-206.

Mehrotra, R.C. 1980. *Hindi Phonology: A Synchronic Description of the Contemporary Standard.* Bhasika Prakashan.

Metz, C. 1914. "Ein experimentall-phonetischer Beitrag zur Untersuchung der italienischen Konsonanten-gemination". *Vox*, Vol. 23, pp. 201-70.

Meyer, E.A. 1904. "Zur Vocaldauer im Deutschen". *Nordiska Studier tillegnade A. Noreen,* pp. 347-56.

Miller, P. 1972. "Some context-free processes affecting vowels". *Ohio State University Working Papers in Linguistics,* Vol. 11, pp. 136-67.

——. 1973. "Bleaching and coloring". In Corum, C. *et al.* (eds.), *Papers from the Ninth Regional Meeting of the Chicago Linguistic Society.* Chicago: Chicago Linguistic Society, 1973, pp. 386-97.

Mishra, J. 1969. "The case of Maithili". *Language and Society in India: Transactions of Indian Institute of Advanced Study* (Simla, India), Vol. 8, pp. 266-75.

——. 1976. *History of Maithili Literature.* New Delhi: Sahitya Akademi.

Mittal, L.N., and Gupta, J.P. 1971. "A preliminary study on the formant frequencies of Hindi vowels". *Gavesana* Vol. 17, pp. 129-30.

Mohr, B. 1971. "Intrinsic variations in the speech signal". *Phonetica,* Vol. 23, pp. 65-93.

Morton, K., and Tatham, M.A.A. 1980. "Devoicing, aspiration and nasality: cases of universal misunderstanding". In Tatham, M.A.A. (ed.), *Occasional Papers,* Vol. 23. Department of Language and Linguistics, University of Essex, 1980, pp. 91-103.

Narang, G.C., and Becker, D.A. 1971. "Aspiration and nasalization in the generative phonology of Hindi-Urdu". *Language,* Vol. 47, pp. 646-67.

Nihalani, P. 1974a. "An aerodynamic study of stops in Sindhi". *Phonetica,* Vol. 29, pp. 193-224.

——. 1974b. "Lingual articulation of stops in Sindhi". *Phonetica,* Vol. 30, pp. 197-212.

——. 1975a. "Air flow rate in the production of stops in Sindhi". *Phonetica,* Vol. 31, pp. 198-205.

——. 1975b. "Velopharyngeal opening in the formation of voiced stops in Sindhi". *Phonetica*, Vol. 32, pp. 89-102

Ohala, M. 1983. *Aspects of Hindi Phonology*. Delhi: Motilal Banarsidass.

Ohala, M., and Ohala, J. 1972. "The problem of aspiration in Hindi phonetics". *Project of Linguistic Analysis,* Series 2: 16. University of California, pp. 63-70.

Palmer, F.R. 1971. *Grammar.* Penguin.

Pathak. R.S. 1976. "Nasalization in Bagheli: an electrokymographic study". *Indian Linguistics,* Vol. 37, pp. 312-15.

Pattanayak, D.P. 1966. *A Controlled Historical Reconstruction of Oriya, Assamese, Bengali and Hindi*. The Hague: Mouton and Co.

Peterson, G.E., and Lehiste, I, 1960. "Duration of syllable nuclei in English". *Journal of the Acoustical Society of America,* Vol. 32, pp. 693-703.

Peterson, G.E., and Shoup, J.E. 1966. "A physiological theory of phonetics". *Journal of Speech and Hearing Research,* Vol. 9, pp. 5-67.

Prasad, B.N. 1950. *A Phonetic and Phonological Study of Bhojpuri.* Unpublished Ph.D. thesis, University of London.

Pray, B.R. 1969. *Agreement in Hindi-Urdu and Its Phonological Implications.* Unpublished Ph.D. thesis, University of Michigan.

Quirk, R., Greenbaum, S., Leech, G., and Svartvik, J. 1972. *A Grammar of Contemporary English.* London: Longman.

Robins, R.H. 1971. *General Linguistics: An Introductory Survey.* 2nd Ed. London: Longman.

Ross, J.R. 1973. "A reanalysis of English word stress (part 1)". In Brame, M.K. (ed.), *Contributions to Generative Phonology.* Austin: University of Texas Press. pp. 229-323.

Rousselot, J. 1891. *Les modifications phonétiques du langage etudiées dans le patois d'une famille de Cellefrouin.* Paris.

Royal Nepal Academy. 1973-74. *Paryāyavāchī Shavda-Kos* (Dictionary of Synonyms). Kathmandu: Royal Nepal Academy (in Nepali).

Ruhlen, M. 1973. "Nasal vowels". *Stanford University Working Papers on Language Universals,* Vol. 12 pp. 1-36.

Russell, G.O. 1928. *The Vowel: Some X-ray and Photo Laringoperiskopic Evidence.* Columbus: Ohio State University Press.

——. 1936. "Synchronised x-ray ocillograph, sound and movie experiments showing the fallacy of vowel triangle and open-closed theories". In Jones, D., and Fry, D.B. (eds.), *Proceedings of the Second International Congress of Phonetic Sciences.* London, 1935. Cambridge: Cambridge University Press, 1936, pp. 198-205.

Schachter, P. 1969. "Natural assimilation rules in Akan". *International Journal of American Linguistics,* Vol. 35, pp. 342-55.

Schane, S.A. 1972. "Natural rules in phonology". In Stockwell, R.P., and Macaulay, R.K.S. (eds.), *Linguistic Change and Generative Theory.* Bloomington: Indiana University Press, 1972, pp. 199-229.

——. 1973. *Generative Phonology.* New Jersey: Prentice-Hall, Inc.

Schein, B., and Sleriade, D. 1986. "On geminates". *Linguistic Inquiry,* Vol. 17, pp. 691-744.

Sharma, R.P. 1979. *Mithilā kā Itihāsa* (History of Mithila). Darbhanga: Kameshwar Singh Darbhanga Sanskrit-University (in Hindi).

Sievers, E. 1876. *Grundzüge der Lautphysiologie.* Leipzig.

Singh, U.N. 1979a. *Some Aspects of Maithili Syntax: A Transformational-Generative Approach.* Unpublished Ph.D. thesis, Delhi University.

——. 1979b. "Agreement rule, language universals and Maithili". *South Asian Language Analysis,* Vol. 1, pp. 107-14.

——. 1980. "Relative clause formation in Maithili". *Nepalese Linguistics,* Vol. 1, pp. 27-39.

Singh, U.N., and Bandyopadhyay, S.K. 1978. "Some aspects of interrogation in Bengali, Assamese and Maithili". *Papers in Linguistic Analysis,* Vol. 2, pp. 19-34.

Skousen, R. 1972. "On capturing regularities". In Peranteau, P.M., Levi, J.N., and Phares, G.C. (eds.), *Papers from the Eighth Regional Meeting of the Chicago Linguistic Society.* Chicago: Chicago Linguistic Society, 1972, pp. 567-77.

Slis, I.H. 1968. "Experiments on consonant duration related to the time structure of isolated words". *IPO Annual Progress Report,* Vol. 3, Institute for Perception Research (Eindhoven), pp. 71-80.

Slis, I.H., and Cohen, A. 1969. "On the complex regulating the voiced-voiceless distinction 1". *Language and Speech,* Vol. 12, pp. 80-102.

Sloat, C. 1974. "Stress in English". *Glossa*, Vol. 8, pp. 121-39.

Sloat, C., Taylor, S.H., and Hoard, J.E. 1978. *Introduction to Phonology.* New Jersey: Prentice-Hall, Inc.

Smith, S. 1951. "Vocalization and added nasal resonance". *Folia Phoniatrica,* Vol. 3, pp. 65-69.

Sommerstein, A.H. 1977. *Modern Phonology.* London: Edward Arnold.

Southworth, F.C. 1961. "Review of *The Formation of the Maithili Language,* by S. Jha, 1958". *Language*, Vol. 37, pp. 168-73.

Stampe, D. 1972. "On the natural history of diphthongs". In Peranteau, P.M., Levi, J.N., and Phares, G.E. (eds.) *Papers from the Eighth Regional Meeting of the Chicago Linguistic Society.* Chicago: Chicago Linguistic Society, 1972, pp. 578-90.

Stanley, R. 1967. "Redundancy rules in phonology". *Language,* Vol. 43, pp. 393-436.

Stetson, R.H. 1951. *Motor Phonetics.* 2nd Ed. Amsterdam: North Holland Publishing Co.

Stevens, K.N. 1972. "Segments, features, and analysis by synthesis". In Kavanagh, J.F., and Mattingly, I.G. (eds.), *Language by Ear and by Eye.* Cambridge, Mass.: The MIT Press, 1972, pp. 47-52.

Sweet, H. 1877. *A Handbook of Phonetics.* Excerpted in Henderson, E.J.A., *The Indispensable Fountain.* London: Oxford University Press, 1971.

Tomas, N. 1916. "Cantidad de las vocales acentuadas". *Revista Filologia Espanola,* Vol. 3, pp. 387-408.

Trager, G.L. and Smith, H.L. 1951. *An Outline of English Structure.* Norman, Oklahoma: Battenburg Press.

Trail, R.L. 1973a. *Word Lists.* Kathmndu: Summer Institute of Linguistics, Tribhuvan University.

——. 1973b. (ed.). *Patterns in Clause, Sentence and Discourse in Selected Languages of India and Nepal:* Vol. 2. Kathmandu: Summer Institute of Linguistics, Tribhuvan University.

Trubetzkoy, N. 1939/1969. *Principles of Phonology.* Originally published in German (Grundzüge der Phonologie) as *Travaux du Cercle Linguistique de Prague 7.* Translated by Christiane A.M. Baltaxe. Berkeley and Los Angeles: University of California Press.

Varma, S. 1929/reprint 1961. *Critical Studies in the Phonetic Observations of Indian Grmmarians.* London: Royal Asiatic Society.

Vennemann, T. 1971. "Natural generative phonology". Paper read at annaul meeting of the Linguistic Society of America, St. Louis, Missouri.

Wang, W. S-Y. 1972. "The many uses of Fo". In Valdman, A. (ed.) *Papers in Linguistics and Phonetics to the Memory of Pierre Delattre.* The Hague: Mouton and Co., 1972, pp. 487-503.

Williams, J. 1973. "Clause patterns in Maithili". In Trail, R.L. (ed.), *Patterns in Clause, Sentence and Discourse in Selected Languages of India and Nepal*, Vol. 2. Kathmandu: Summer Institute of Linguistics, Tribhuvan University, 1973, pp. 345-453.

Wood, S. 1975. "The weakness of the tongue-arching model of vowel articulation". *Working Papers No. 11.* Lund: Phonetics Laboratory, Lund University, pp. 55-107.

——. 1977. "A radiographic analysis of constriction locations for vowels". *Working Papers No. 15.* Lund; Phonetics Laboratory, Lund University, pp. 101-31.

Yadav, R. 1976. "Generative phonology and the aspirated cosonants of colloquial Maithili". *Contributions to Nepalese Studies,* Vol. 4, pp. 77-91.

——. 1979a. *Maithili Phonetics and Phonology.* Unpublished Ph.D. thesis, University of Kansas.

——. 1979b. "A fiberoptic study of stop production in Maithili". *Kansas Working Papers in Linguistics,* Vol. 4, pp. 55-69.

——. 1979c. "The influence of aspiration on vowel duration in Maithili". *South Asian Languages Analysis,* Vol. 1, pp. 157-65.

——. 1980a. "Acoustic correlates of word stress in Maithili". *Nepalese Linguistics,* Vol. 1, pp. 1-7.

——. 1980b. "Some stress placement rules in Maithili". *Contributions to Nepalese Studies,* Vol. 8, pp. 181-88.

——. 1981. "Maithili language and linguistics: some background notes". *Kailash: A Journal of Himalayan Studies,* Vol. 8, pp. 71-87.

——. 1982. "Acoustic characteristics of vowel nasalization in Maithili". *Indian Linguistics,* Vol, 43, pp. 1-11.

——. 1984. *Maithili Phonetics and Phonology.* Mainz: Selden and Tamm.

——. 1991. "Clitic versus affix: Maithili E and O". *Contributions to Nepalese Studies,* Vol. 18, pp. 123-32.

Yadav, Y.P. 1981. "Question movement in Maithili and binding conditions". *Indian Linguistics,* Vol. 42, pp. 1-9.

——. 1982a. "Aspect in Maithili: a formal analysis". In Kansakar, T.R. (ed.), *Occasional Papers in Nepalese Linguistics.* Kathmandu: Linguistic Society of Nepal, Publication No. 1, 1982, pp. 74-85.

——. 1982b. "Maithili sentence: a transformational analysis". *Indian Linguistics,* Vol. 43, pp. 7-28.

——. 1983. *Movement Rules in Maithili and English: Their Implications for the Theory of Government and Binding.* Unpublished Ph.D. thesis, CIEFL Hyderabad.

——. 1984. "The word order phenomenon in Maithili simple sentences: a TG approach". *Contributions to Nepalese Studies,* Vol. 12, pp. 1-13.

Zimmerman, S.A., and Sapon, S.M. 1958. "Note on vowel duration seen cross-linguistically". *Journal of the Acoustical Society of America,* Vol. 30, pp. 152-53.

INDEX